The Political Economy of the Interior Gold Coast

The Political Economy of the Interior Gold Coast

The Asante and the Era of Legitimate Trading, 1807–1875

Jarvis L. Hargrove

LEXINGTON BOOKS
Lanham • Boulder • New York • London

Published by Lexington Books
An imprint of The Rowman & Littlefield Publishing Group, Inc.
4501 Forbes Boulevard, Suite 200, Lanham, Maryland 20706
www.rowman.com

Unit A, Whitacre Mews, 26-34 Stannary Street, London SE11 4AB

British Library Cataloguing in Publication Information Available

Library of Congress Cataloging-in-Publication Data
Hargrove, Jarvis L., author.
The political economy of the interior Gold Coast : the Asante and the era of legitimate trading, 1807–1875 / Jarvis L. Hargrove.
pages cm
Includes bibliographical references and index.
ISBN 978-0-7391-8785-2 (cloth : alk. paper) — ISBN 978-0-7391-8786-9 (electronic) 1. Ashanti (African people)—Commerce—History—19th century. 2. Slave trade—Ghana—History. 3. Ghana—Economic conditions—19th century. 4. Ghana—Relations—Europe. I. Title.
DT507.H36 2015
966.7004963385—dc23 2015033436

∞™ The paper used in this publication meets the minimum requirements of American National Standard for Information Sciences—Permanence of Paper for Printed Library Materials, ANSI/NISO Z39.48-1992.

Printed in the United States of America

To My Family and Friends
Thank You For Your Support

Contents

List of Figures

List of Tables

Preface

The Trans-Atlantic Slave Trade beginning in the fifteenth century has forever been surrounded by controversy. The 200th Anniversary of the Abolition of the Slave Trade celebrated only a few years ago continues to add to this debate as Britain and the United States held several events, small and large, celebrating their roles in abolishing the trade throughout 2007 and 2008. In highlighting this monumental moment, the continent of Africa and its people were recognized in events conducted by the United Nations (UN) but were entirely overlooked in celebrations.

Ghana, one of many West African territories which engaged in slave trading, chose to put more of its attention on the nations' independence from British colonialism. Formerly known as the Gold Coast, the region experienced a substantial transition during the development of this medium of exchange from gold, which continued in the trade's final days back to legitimate goods. The Gold Coast and the Asante people hold critical answers to the role in which West Africa played in the trade's final days, well into the post-abolition period, also referred to as the era of legitimate trade or period of illegal slave trading. An analysis of the people and the region during the closure of the trade will show the economic changes the state experienced were indeed influenced by the political alterations within the ruling elite. Therefore, political and economic changes which occurred across the region and the interior state were indeed connected to one another. Moreover, it is these changes which have a substantial impact on trading throughout the nineteenth century which commonly fluctuated up and down during the period. Studying these changes will prove the region and state were adjusting to trading legitimate goods without the interference from outside forces.

On January 1, 1803, Denmark officially became the first nation to close the slave trade to its citizens[1] only to see it reopen; four years later Britain followed, closing its trade on March 25, 1807. Although not the first to repress the slave trade, suppression laws passed by Britain, the largest slave trading nation of the period, officially began the post-abolition period and the start of the era of illegal slave trading.[2] Once passing its own abolition laws, the British crown began to pressure other nations to follow suit, which included: the United States in 1808 and again later the creation of the Africa Squadron in 1842 to patrol West African waters, Sweden and Norway in 1813, Netherlands in 1814, Portugal north of the equator in 1815 and officially in 1836, Spain north of the equator in 1811 and officially in 1818, and finally France in 1818. Two hundred years after the passage of its own laws abolishing the slave trade, Britain began celebratory events highlighting its role in closing the trade in captive Africans from West Africa focusing on British citizens, namely Thomas Clarkson and William Wilberforce. These ceremonies, lasting throughout the year, were highlighted by events held in Britain's major cities: Liverpool, Hull and London; their former Caribbean territories: Jamaica, St. Lucia and Trinidad and Tobago; and Ghana which celebrated the overthrow of British colonialism.

Prior to the opening of British ceremonies, in 2006, then British Prime Minister Tony Blair in a statement to the *New Nation Newspaper*, said:

> Slavery's impact upon Africa, the Caribbean, the Americas and Europe was profound. . . . As we approach the commemoration for the 200th anniversary of that abolition, it is only right we also recognize the active role Britain played until then in the slave trade. British industry . . . were intimately intertwined in it. Britain's rise to global pre-eminence was partially dependent on a system of . . . slave labor and, as we recall its abolition, we should also recall our place in its practice.[3]

In his statement, then Prime Minister Tony Blair acknowledged the role of Britain in the slave trade as well as its benefit from the trade. Made only a month before the large scale abolition ceremonies began in Britain, this served as one of the many official statements from the Prime Minister's office regarding the abolition events over the course of the year.

In British port cities of Bristol, Liverpool, London and Hull, events were organized by voluntary groups and the government. This collaborative effort between the two sides culminated in several museum and exhibit openings with the most notable being: The Wilberforce House Museum, the International Slavery Museum as well as exhibits such as "London, Slavery and Sugar" and "Breaking the Chains," all of which gained international attention. These museums and exhibits across Britain remained open well after the year-long celebrations ended, showing a commitment of the British government to preserve this point in history. Celebrations held in both the Caribbean and Africa gained a similar audience attention, even though many were not on the grand scale that those across Britain reached.

In 2008, Britain furthered its commitment to the commemoration of the abolition events. By partnering together with United Nations Educational, Scientific and Cultural Organization (UNESCO), Britain established the 23rd day of August as UNESCO International Day for the Remembrance of the Slave Trade and its Abolition, with its Resolution 29/C40.[4] This was done in response to the growing interest in the UNESCO Slave Route Project, established in 1994. In conjunction with UNESCO, and the British observance of abolition laws, the Caribbean territories of Jamaica, St. Lucia and Trinidad and Tobago all held events commemorating the 200th Anniversary of the Abolition of the Trans-Atlantic Slave Trade. In St. Lucia the Honorable Rufus Bousquet, Minister of External Affairs, in the opening ceremonies commemorating the end of the slave trade stated:

> We gather here today in a mood of reflection, of remembrance, but also of celebration. Reflection on the dehumanizing nature of the slave trade and all its ramifications, remembrance of the struggles which our ancestors had to endure and celebration, that in spite of all this, the children of the slave trade have survived, have excelled and have prospered.[5]

Similar comments were made in Jamaica and in Trinidad and Tobago as the Caribbean celebrated the suppression of the slave trade.

In the United States, very few events occurred to commemorate the 200th Anniversary of the Abolition Slave Trade. Unlike the events which occurred in the United States to celebrate the closure of the slave trade beginning in 1809 and lasting through the 1830s, which were well-known events in cities such as Boston, New York and Philadelphia, for their songs, poems, pamphlets and speeches, those surrounding the 200th Anniversary were limited in their influence. Throughout the earlier half of the nineteenth century, sermons in the various cities over the years were delivered by Absalom Jones, Peter Williams, Jr., Henry Sipkins, Jedidiah Morse, Jeremiah Gloucester, George Lawrence, William Miller and Russell Parrott. Two hundred years later in the United States, the slave trade's closure received very little attention, only to be highlighted by those who study the topic and period the most.[6]

Those events held in the United States, not reaching the magnitude of British celebrations, instead highlighted the global study of the slave trade, Africans in the Diaspora, and the contemporary effects of the abolition. In conjunction with the National Archives, the Bicentennial Committee for the Abolition of the Slave Trade held a one day symposium to commemorate this event. This one-day event featured some of the countries' leading scholars from history, music, science, economics and psychology.[7] This event served as one of the only events to commemorate the abolition of the slave trade within the United States.

On December 18, 2007, just days before the Bicentennial of the 200th Anniversary of the United States passing its law officially abolishing the Trans-Atlantic Slave Trade, Congress held a number of sessions to discuss issues closely relating to the slave trade. In several of these sessions, officials discussed the effects of this trade on the descendants of those who were transported across the Atlantic Ocean some five hundred years earlier.[8] Like similar discussions held by the United States Congress, this also turned into a debate about reparations and not about the history of the Trans-Atlantic Slave Trade.

The support of reparations for descendants of Africans in the United States is a continually discussed topic, a charge which is led by Harvard University Law Professor Charles Ogletree. Speaking before the Judiciary Committee of the House of Representatives, Professor Ogletree stated, "I support the call for reparations for the descendants of the millions who toiled in this country for decades, and who were never compensated for their labor."[9] In his testimony before the Judiciary Committee, Professor Ogletree, does not mention the 200th Anniversary of the Abolition of the Trans-Atlantic Slave Trade.

The former Gold Coast territory, now Ghana, conducted a number of events celebrating its independence from colonial rule and the suppression of the slave trade. The Joseph Project was established by the Ghanaian government in 2007 to celebrate both the 50th Anniversary of Ghana's Independence and the 200th Anniversary of the Abolition of the Trans-Atlantic Slave Trade.[10] During these events, the former President Joseph A. Kufuor of Ghana, sparked controversy by declaring Africans should not receive reparations. Then President Joseph A. Kufuor, believed the best way to move forward with the commemoration of this international event was for those nations who benefitted from the slave trade to show remorse and grant the descendants of those victims full human rights.[11] This event, along with those held in the various parts of the Caribbean and Africa, shows the importance of the slave trade's final closure to those descendants of Africans living within the African Diaspora.

By 1957, following the lead of the Gold Coast, known as Ghana thereafter, other African nations embarked on a similar path toward gaining their independence. This move marked a turning point in the history of Africa, as well as a new approach to the study of African History worldwide. In this new alternative approach to the study of African History, the continent, its peoples and cultures were reclaimed by new independent governments and people throughout the African Diaspora. The reclamation of a past stripped away by years of the slave trade, colonial and imperial rule, re-wrote centuries of Euro-centric history.[12] In this new analysis were the histories of African empires, the influence of religion and trade, the significance of geographical features and finally the impact of Africa on the world.

The arrival of Portuguese on the coast of West Africa marks a watershed in history, as it eventually sets the stage for European exploration of both Africa and later the "New World." West Africa in particular, served as the starting point for European exploration and the Gold Coast became more important in the latter part of the fifteenth century to Europeans searching for gold. The Gold Coast, lies between regions referred to as the Slave Coast, encompassing modern day Togo, Benin, Western Nigeria and the Ivory Coast (Cote d'Ivoire). This region contained three of the most sought after commodities of the sixteenth century: ivory, captive Africans and gold. Portuguese explorers were the first to capitalize on these commodities trading with Africans as well as other European nations. As more Europeans began to expand their trading grounds and reach into West Africa, with both merchants and a growing navy presence, they all began to capitalize on African commodities, and the Gold Coast saw this first hand.

Although colonial rule in Africa did not start until 1885, seventy-eight years after the slave trade was formally abolished by written laws, the British began making their presence permanent by creating protected territories commonly known as protectorates.[13] The Gold Coast and its people saw their trading shift to other commodities away from the New World plantations, as the growth of British exploration expanded into the interior of the region. This influence led several groups in the Gold Coast to participate with and against the British in its war campaign in the region. By the start of colonial rule in 1884–1885, the British had been overseers of the region for ten years, a rule that lasted until independence eighty-three years later.[14]

Today, more than two hundred years since the slave trade officially closed, there are still debates as to how and why it finally came to a close. While this debate has continued on, scholars and non-scholars alike have looked to numerous places for answers: Britain, the Caribbean, South America and the United States. Many studies, analyze the impact of abolition on the regions which acquired captives and the roles of European nations and the United States in abolishing the trade. These same studies omit the role in which African people played in abolition. The Asante people of West Africa's Gold Coast especially had an important impact on the slave trade finally being abolished by both the British and the Americans from the region as treaties signed between nations needed to be carried out first within the interior to insure captives were no longer the preferred item of exchange.

Several questions regarding the Trans-Atlantic Slave Trade have gone unanswered for numerous reasons. In order to answer the questions about African groups which supplied slaves during the abolition and illegal slave trading era, we first have to analyze societies and the role of slavery prior to European arrival. Secondly, we have to answer, how were African societies involved in the slave trade? A third question which must be answered was the involvement of African societies politically or economically motivated?

The Asante people and the Gold Coast, one of the largest dealers in captive Africans, and an area that supplied numerous captives, is one of many groups and regions in Africa that will answer questions which have been overlooked. While the Gold Coast region supplied captives to several European nations, its involvement in the Trans-Atlantic Slave Trade continually changed, in times of war and peace, as the value of other items increased and again as the slave trade expanded in other regions. Although the reasons for the closure of the trade have been interpreted and re-interpreted over the years (i.e. moral and economic reasons) it is now time to discuss the African involvement in suppressing the trade after 1807.

A reanalysis of the history of the Asante people and the Gold Coast will give us a better understanding of what role the Gold Coast played during the suppression era and how this group was involved in the closing of the slave trade and establishing what became known as legitimate commerce. Understanding the involvement of this group and others which are similar will also force us to review the roles of both Britain and the United States in the closure of this illegal era of slave trading. We must now challenge the belief that all African societies pushed for a continuation and development of this trade well into the latter part of the nineteenth century.

Ghana formerly the Gold Coast has been a key region in several historical studies regarding the slave trade since the country gained its independence in 1957. Relying on many of the same archival collections as traditionalist and later revisionist scholars in the United States,[15] Britain[16] and Ghana,[17] it will be essential to obtain ample material from each location to support my research. The suppression of the slave trade is a topic which has garnered substantial attention, but many of the questions in regards to my thesis have gone unanswered by previous works.

NOTES

1. In 1792 Denmark became the first European nation to regulate its citizens' involvement in the Trans-Atlantic Slave Trade. After hundred and fifty years of buying captives off the West African coast, Fredrick VI, in a royal edict declared in 1802 that the slave trade by the citizens of Denmark was an illegal act. On January 1, 1803, the slave trade officially became illegal.

2. Robin Law refers to the period of illegal slave trading as years 1815–1839. See: Robin Law, *Ouidah: The Social History of a West African Slaving Port, 1727–1892* (Athens, OH: Ohio University Press, 2004), p. 155.

3. *New Nation Newspaper*, British Prime Minister Tony Blair's Article (November 27, 2006). For full article see: http://www.number10.gov.uk/Page10487

4. For an outline of the purpose of UNESCO International Day for the Remembrance of the Slave Trade and its Abolition see: http://www.direct.gov.uk/dr_consum_dg/groups/dg_digitalassets/@dg/@en/documents/digitalasset/dg_170814.pdf (Accessed October 4, 2009).

5. Remarks by Honorable Rufus Bousquet Minister for External Affairs, International Financial Services, Information and Broadcasting at the Ceremony in Observance of the 200th Anniversary of the Abolition of the Slave Trade at Derek Walcott Square, Sunday March 25, 2007. For entire speech see: http://www.stlucia.gov.lc/addresses_and_speeches/rufus_bousquet/remarks_by_hon_rufus_bousquet_at_the_ceremony_in_observance_of_the_200th_ann_of_the_abolition_of_the_slave_trade.htm (Accessed November 18, 2009).

6. Several of these sermons are listed in the works: Richard Newman, Patrick Neal and Phillip Lapsansky, eds., *Pamphlets of Protest: An Anthology of Early African American Protest Literature, 1790–1860* and Peter C. Hogg, *The African Slave Trade and its Suppression: A Classified and Annotated Bibliography of Books, Pamphlets and Periodical Articles.*

7. The National Archives and the Bicentennial Committee for the Abolition of the Slave Trade (Committee Members: Joseph E. Harris, Howard Dodson, John W. Franklin and James Early) commemorated the passage of United States suppression laws with a daylong symposium. This symposium was titled: Abolition and the Road to Freedom: National Archives Symposium 200th Anniversary of the Slave Trade Act of 1808. Participants of this symposium included: Allen Weinstein, Lonnie Bunch, David Levering Lewis, Joseph Inikori, Ira Berlin, Sylviane Diouf, Marika Sherwood, Lisa Crooms, Selwyn H. H. Carrington, Gwendolyn Midlo Hall, Michael Gomez, Michael Turner, Bernice Reagon, Ali A. Mazrui, Georgia Dunston, George Dalley and Clarence Lausane. This event was held on January 10, 2008, at the National Archives building.

8. The sessions which investigated the call for reparations were titled: Judiciary Committee of the House of Representatives 110th Congress, Sub-Committee on the Constitution, Civil Rights and Civil Liberties: Oversight Hearing on the Legacy of the Trans-Atlantic Slave Trade. This session was held on Tuesday December 18, 2008.

9. Testimony to Judiciary Committee of the House of Representatives 110th Congress, Sub-Committee on the Constitution, Civil Rights and Civil Liberties: Oversight Hearing on the Legacy of the Trans-Atlantic Slave Trade, December 18, 2007, by Charles J. Ogletree, Jr., Executive Director of the Charles Hamilton Houston Institute for Race and Justice, Harvard Law School (Washington: DC, U.S. Government Printing Office, 2008), p. 14. Accessible at: http://juidiciary.house.gov.

10. The Joseph Project was established by the Ghanaian Ministry of Tourism to further the relationship between Africa and the Diaspora. Hoping to build on a legacy Pan-Africanism in the country, Ghana wanted to encourage tourism to Africa among its descendants in the Diaspora. The Joseph Project included a number of events including tours of the country as well as cultural events. The events culminated in celebratory events regarding the 50th Anniversary of Ghana's Independence and Britain's 200th Anniversary of the Abolition of the Slave Trade.

11. President Joseph A. Kufuor discusses Ghana's Independence and the 200th Anniversary of the Abolition of the Trans-Atlantic Slave Trade in Joe Okyere and Nehemiah Owusu Achiaw, "Ghana Marks 200 Years of Abolition of Slave Trade," *National Commission on Culture* (March 27, 2007). For entire article see: http://www.ghanaculture.gov.gh/index1.php?linkid=65&adate=27/03/2007&archiveid=1045&page=1 (Accessed January 12, 2009).

12. Several slave traders documented their travels and experiences with the people whom they came into contact with the African coast. Often the accounts of slave traders were entitled, *A New and Accurate Description of Africa* or *A New and More Accurate Description of Africa.* Two works to include this in their title are works by William Bosman and William Snelgrave. These early accounts were used by scholars during the twentieth century when describing Africa and its peoples.

13. After the British abolished slavery in its empire and territories, they began signing treaties with several different groups in Asia as well as Africa. See: C. W. Newbury, *British Policy Towards West Africa: Select Documents, 1786–1874* (Oxford: Clarendon Press, 1965).

14. The Ashanti Expedition and the burning of Kumasi in 1874, served as the start to British Colonial rule on the Gold Coast. See: Robert B. Edgerton, *The Fall of the Asante Empire: The Hundred-Year War for Africa's Gold Coast* (New York: The Free Press, 1995).

15. In the United States the National Archives and its regional affiliates hold numerous sources regarding the role of the US in the slave trade. Invaluable sources they hold include: Presidential responses and Congressional debates as well as records regarding the suppression of the slave trade.

16. The British National Archives holds records regarding its major slave territories in the Caribbean as well as the role of the government in the slave trade. Other valuable sources include Parliament debates regarding the suppression of the slave trade.

17. The National and Regional Archives of Ghana hold records regarding the Asante as well the economy of the country.

Acknowledgments

This work continues upon my graduate studies which began at Howard University in Washington, DC. During these formative years, the idea first developed for me to research the Trans-Atlantic Slave Trade and its eventual closure from the region of known as the Gold Coast, today the modern day country of Ghana. The earliest stages of this research began as a graduate assistant while at Howard University in the South African Research and Archival Project, directed by Dr. Joseph E. Harris and Dr. Charles D. Johnson, to whom I am greatly indebted. As a graduate student working as a research assistant in the South African Research and Archival Project, I was asked to investigate the end of the slave trade.

This initial research was conducted under the direction of Dr. Harris who was preparing for the 200th Anniversary of the United States Abolition of the Trans-Atlantic Slave Trade Symposium. This symposium was given at the National Archives in Washington, DC, in 2008 and brought together some of the nations' most recognized historians, archivists, genealogists and scientists. Ultimately, this served as one of the only events held in the United States to commemorate the final closure of the Trans-Atlantic Slave Trade.

I am also grateful to several other people who helped this project reach its completion beginning in the dissertation stage and now as a completed book. I want to begin by thanking Ms. Vivian Childs of Durham, NC, who helped me plan and outline my trip to Ghana in the summer of 2010. Without her support in the early stages, a trip to Ghana may not have been possible. Mr. Sammy Asirifi-Addo and his parents Mr. Samuel Asirifi-Addo and Mrs. Vida Asirifi-Addo who aided me day-to-day during my stay in Ghana. Others I want to thank include, Ms. Irene Amakye and Mrs. Herty Bainson with whom I resided while in Cape Coast, Ghana, as well as Prophet Sampson Amoateng and Mr. Stephen Kpabitey with whom I resided with during my stay in Accra, Ghana. I also want to acknowledge Professor James Kwesi Anquandah of the University of Ghana who provided support and advice for my research during my stay in the country. Each of these individuals was crucial to my time in Ghana and without them there would have been great difficulty in ultimately completing this work.

Furthermore, my research in Accra, and Cape Coast, Ghana; London, England; and Washington, DC, was also greatly enhanced by the archivists at each location. The Public Records and Archival Administration in Accra, Ghana, the Moorland-Spingarn Research Center at Howard University along with the National Archives in Washington, DC, and the British National Archives located at Kew Gardens in London, England, were instrumental sources of information. The staffs of each institution were extremely helpful while I was doing research. I want to also thank the staff of Roman & Littlefield Publishers for their efforts in seeing this project through to its completion.

The history department of North Carolina Central University has also been extremely supportive seeing this work through its final completion. Each one of the faculty members has been supportive in a number of ways beyond discussing history. I would also like to acknowledge Dr. Aziz Batran, my former graduate advisor, who was very helpful and supportive toward the completion of the dissertation before his untimely death. Also I want to acknowledge Dr. Jean-Michel Mabeko-Tali, Dr. Selwynn H. H. Carrington, Dr. Emory Tolbert all from Howard University and Dr. Jim Harper from North Carolina Central University, who all served as members of my dissertation committee. Through there tireless efforts and support in the early stages, this work has now transitioned from a dissertation to a completed book. Finally, I want to thank each member of my family who have all encouraged me through the completion of this work.

Introduction

In the first half of the sixteenth century as Western European countries began to grow and expand their reach across the Atlantic Ocean, the need for cheap and inexpensive labor doubled. This need for labor began to intensify with each passing year, leading to an expanded trade in captives from West Africa or the start of Trans-Atlantic Slave Trade. Connecting several continents, countries and lasting more than 300 years, the Trans-Atlantic Slave Trade has been one of the most analyzed topics across numerous historical fields with several arguments regarding the subject. Furthermore, this discussion has only continued to develop since the turn of the twenty-first century or after Britain and the United States began to celebrate the 200th Anniversary of the Abolition of the Trans-Atlantic Slave Trade which occurred in 2007 and 2008, respectively. Additionally, this event, the 200th anniversary, has only increased the necessity for more localized studies of West African states in the trade's infancy, in its years of expansion, during its eventual closure and the transition experienced in the declining years after 1807–1808.

Since the inception of the Trans-Atlantic Slave Trade in the sixteenth century, beginning first with slave traders, missionaries, and explorers of West Africa and ultimately the victims themselves, there have been many individuals who have offered comments on the role of the trade. Several of the earliest works, written by outsiders, often presented the people, religion and cultures of Africa along with the value of the slave trade and slavery to the world in a very biased perspective. As numerous European states desired to extend into new territories, these countries often justified the expansion to new lands and any destruction this caused. Eventually, later scholars used these early works along with numerous studies written by victims to devote a substantial amount of time and effort to a reinterpretation of Trans-Atlantic Slave Trade and its continued study.

Although much has been analyzed about the causes and effects of the slave trade, there is still a substantial amount of work to be done, all of which will shape the study and direction of future historical works on this topic. The 200th Anniversary of the Abolition of the Trans-Atlantic Slave Trade presents us with an opportunity to bring forward new evidence which discusses the closure of the trade and the period of illegal slave trading. Albeit, as this occurs, just prior to the push by European nations to acquire an African territory and the eventual start of colonial rule, 1874–1884, this is an extremely important era in the economic history of West Africa. Along the Gold Coast and into its interior region, there were substantial economic changes which occurred during this era. This illegal period or era of legitimate commerce, as it is also referred, is one which begins in the aftermath of the British and American decision to pass legislation closing the slave trade, 1807–1808, and the expeditions by Europeans into the interior of Africa in the middle of the century through the earliest half of the 1870s.

Therefore, a study should be conducted which focuses on a West African state involved in the start slave trade, its eventual expansion and one also impacted by its final closure. Moreover, the state should also have been influenced by the transition to legitimate commerce and expeditions into the interior region between 1807 and 1875. The Asante state, one of the largest interior groups within the Gold Coast, serves as a state which was involved first in the exchange of gold and later contributed to the growth of the slave trade between the seventeenth and nineteenth centuries from the region. Furthermore, prior to its closure the state supplied captives to a number of European nations along its Southern coastline through middlemen; which included the British, Dutch, Portuguese and Spanish, from the interior. The Asante state was also impacted by the interior expeditions beginning in the middle of the nineteenth century and the extension of a sphere of influence by the British lasting through the middle of the 1870s; this all occurred prior to the eventual start of colonial rule in the region.

This work is a study of the Gold Coast and the Asante people and their interactions with the British, Dutch and Fante, during the post-abolition period of the slave trade from 1807 through the era of expeditions and extension of protectorates in the region in the mid-1870s. Moreover, a study of this period encompasses both the era of legitimate commerce or illegal slave trading, interior explorations by Europeans and the formation of new trade partnerships.

Albeit, this also reveals the multiple modifications which the interior Asante state and Gold Coast region experienced during the nineteenth century. Previous works completed on this same time period while studying the economic conditions overlook the political ramifications from within the Asante state. This study in particular considers the impact of the political changes within the state as well as the region on the economic conditions along with the fluctuations in trade experienced by the people and area in the nineteenth century.

Moreover, this study encompasses the period from 1807 to 1874, which encompasses both the start of legitimate trade and the extension of British claims on the Gold Coast. In analyzing these years, this work will also look into three important facets of the Asante state in the years after abolition. In particular, the development of international trade partnerships with the Dutch and British, the changing status of elite and its connection to individual wealth within the state and the creation of new settlements to handle the agricultural expansion of the nineteenth century. Diplomacy was a point emphasized by each Asantehene and often reinforced through numerous international agreements throughout the eighteenth and nineteenth centuries.[1] Each will provide critical evidence regarding the transition of the state in the nineteenth and its ability to adapt to the needs and desires of a changing world-wide market for Gold Coast goods.

Over this span of sixty-seven years, the size and scope of the Asante state began to change just as the leadership itself changed. These numerous changes which the Asante experienced both politically and economically, between the states creation in latter half of the seventeenth through the middle stage of the nineteenth century impacted those who traded within the region during the era as well as those who called the state home. Although there is much debate as to why the slave trade closed (i.e. moral and economic reasons), there seems to be little discussion about the role of individual African regions and states during this era, which is a major emphasis of this study. New questions are being asked and evidence is being presented which will only advance the study of this period in African and World History.

By focusing on one of the largest groups along the Gold Coast and West Africa, the Asante, there are numerous sources which are essential to the completion of the study on the group and its effects on the slave trade. Regional archives at Accra, Kumasi, Tamale and Cape Coast contain valuable information about slave castles and slave markets within the region. An analysis of the Asante oral records, Basel Missionary Records and British documents on treaties in the region, uncover information concerning the opening and closure of the slave trade. The accounts of slave traders, although controversial, contain detailed information about the interactions with the various African groups they came into contact with as well as maps of the areas regions they reached. Moreover, accounts of traders do reveal evidence about how active individuals were in trading along the coast at the various markets.

Furthermore, between the abolition of slave trade and the earliest years of expeditions into the interior region, several works were published on the history of West Africa and the Gold Coast itself. Many of these works by slave traders and Europeans residing throughout the various forts built along the coastline of Africa attracted a specific audience, who viewed the continent and its people as objects of curiosity. On the Gold Coast, a number of Europeans were among those able to travel between the two dominant states of the region, the Fante and the Asante, trading goods and chronicling their travels. Nevertheless, of these works written on the Gold Coast several were published by Joseph Dupuis,[2] J. Beecham,[3] Henry Meredith,[4] Thomas E. Bowdich,[5] Brodie Cruickshank,[6] A. B. Ellis[7] and William Ernest Frank Ward.[8]

Each of these travelers chronicled their visits throughout the Gold Coast and to the two largest states in the region. Visiting the coastal Fante and interior Asante, travelers gave very similar interpretations during the nineteenth and early years of the twentieth centuries. Furthermore, each of these works, published prior to the independence of Ghana, between 1812 and 1939 shaped the direction of traditionalist scholarship as well as views of the country and its people. Henry Meredith in 1812 wrote:

> The intention of the following lines is . . . to introduce into public favour . . . the Nation with a portion of gold and ivory, collected along its coast . . . during a residence of some years on the Gold-coast . . . the following has been . . . compiled . . . the Gold-coast is almost neglected by the British merchants. . . . I trust some favourable change will take place . . . to increase trade, and to attract the attention of the public at large. . . . The Gold-coast . . . is capable of affording incalculable advantages, if the inhabitants can be excited to industry.[9]

These works are much more about the arrival of Europeans along the Gold Coast, criticisms of one another, their interior explorations and the plan for the advancement of trading, and not the history of the people or the various states of the region. This is a point emphasized in the introduction of Meredith's 1812 work, as he became one of the earliest British traders to enter the interior of the region.

In the opening line of his work, Joseph Dupuis in 1820 writes:

> The British trade with the Gold Coast of Africa was placed by charter, in the reign of Charles II under the controul of the Royal African Company, whose governor-general . . . had the direction of matters on the African shore . . . under instructions sent from England by a body . . . called the African Committee . . . for the trade was only nominally free—in fact it was monopolized by the governor . . . and so much of the public grant . . . served only to keep the public out of the African market . . .[10]

This continues to build upon earlier statements made by Meredith in his work published in 1812.

The work of C. C. Reindorf[11] a minister with the Basel Missionary Society titled, *History of the Gold Coast and Asante: Based on Traditions and*

Historical Facts, Comprising a Period of More Than Three Centuries from about 1500 to 1860, served as one of the first challenges to what became traditionalist scholarship. Basel Missionary Minister Reindorf, in the introduction of his work writes:

> A history of the Gold Coast written by a foreigner would most probably not be correct in its statements, he not having the means of acquiring the different traditions in the country and of comparing them with those which he may have gathered from a single individual. Unless a foreigner writes what he witnesses personally, his statements will comparatively worthless, as it is the case with several accounts of the Gold Coast already published.[12]

Such a statement, points directly to his attitude regarding the earlier works published about the Asante and the Gold Coast in the nineteenth and first half of the twentieth centuries. Ultimately, such a statement can also point to discrepancies in literature on the Gold Coast in the years after, including the start of colonial rule through the birth of the independence movement in the country.

Albeit, between the abolition of the slave trade and the extension of the protected territory, the British were able to make several changes to its policies across the Gold Coast in the nineteenth century. Along with establishing itself as the dominant group in the region, the British also abolished slavery, established a police presence, created a court system as well as instituted policies which excluded Africans from having access to education, medical facilities or systems of administration. By 1911, J. E. Casely Hayford, a journalist and lawyer along with the National Congress of British West Africa, began challenging the British occupation of the Gold Coast, based on constitutional law.[13]

Among those residing in the Gold Coast after the start of colonial rule, J. E. Casely Hayford served as one of the many Africans to contest British imperialism through his writings. J. E. Casely Hayford[14] encouraged Africans across the Gold Coast to call for the British to immediately grant their independence. This call was heard and pushed forward by a young Kwame Nkrumah who by the middle of the century helped the country gain its independence in 1957, before the citizens of the country soon elected him president of the newly independent nation. With his Pan-African background, Kwame Nkrumah began pushing the rest of Africa to fight for their independence, as he never saw Africa as Ghana, but instead Ghana as one piece of Africa.[15]

Nevertheless, a theoretical shift in 1965 resulted in many of publications taking a vastly different approach from their predecessors to the history of indigenous people and Africa. This paradigm shift, occurring following the achievement of independence by many nations, brought about many changes as works began to highlight African culture, religion, political movements and economic development of the continent and its people, previously dismissed.

The African independence movement created a surge of scholars around the world publishing works using primary sources to rewrite the history of Africa, a move highlighted by revisionist scholarship. By 1965, in Ghana, this paradigm shift was led by a number of scholars from the country as well as those in the Caribbean, Britain and the United States. Initial works focused on the region of West Africa and in the coming years more studies became localized concentrating on people and those within the borders created by colonial rule. Many of these initial works published between 1966 and 1983 all represented a new theoretical framework to the study of African History.

In light of the 200th Anniversary of the Abolition of the Trans-Atlantic Slave Trade, a reanalysis of this topic from the perspective of the African continent, and in particular, the political economy of the Gold Coast which was in the midst of experiencing changes should be studied. Political economy has come to be defined as the management of the economic affairs of the state.[16] A second definition from John Neville Keynes states, "Political economy, is regarded as a positive science of the phenomena of wealth . . . political economy may be defined as the science which treats the phenomena arising out of the economic activities of mankind in society."[17] An analysis of the term political economy has left many with the conclusion that economy is unavoidably political.[18] This is especially the case for a region brought squarely into a world economy transitioning to capitalism in the nineteenth century. Immanuel Wallerstein in his work writes, ". . . a capitalist system requires a very special relationship between economic producers and the holders of political power."[19] The Asante state in the nineteenth century sought to maintain their economic and political freedom during this transition period after 1807.

Therefore, such a study should consider the political changes and their impact economically on both the coastline and within the interior among the Asante people in the nineteenth century. Connecting the political and economic environment of the state during the era will show the interior Asante states' reaction to capitalism varied from that of the coast and moreover depended upon several factors which included: state institutions, captive labor, resources, trade and the ruling elite.[20] Furthermore, the interactions which the Fante experienced with the entering British officials along the coast were consequently different than those experienced among the Asante within the interior.

Moreover, this study challenges the idea that the Gold Coast and the Asante state in the nineteenth century: (1) were politically and economically not capable of joining the emerging world economy without being under the control of the British protectorate or a member of their growing colonial regime; (2) struggled to join the world economy in the years after the slave trade was closed due to the constant turmoil among the numerous states; (3) experienced trading opportunities for the Asante were very limited due to internal political institutions; (4) the Asante were not open to a trading relationship with the British or any European nation; (5) the Asante decision to expand its borders could only be tempered by the British push to establish a protectorate over the coastal Fante; and (6) the extension of a British Protectorate stretching from the coastline across the interior region was needed to bring about a modern capitalist economy into the Gold Coast in the nineteenth century.

In Ghana, there have been a number of works that have analyzed the Asante in past years, but many questions still remain unanswered. Using the identified collections in the United States, Britain and Ghana, this work attempts to answer the following key questions: (1) How did the final closure Trans-Atlantic Slave Trade impact the Gold Coast and the Asante in the nineteenth century, (2) how economically valuable was the illegal slave trade to the Gold Coast and the Asante, (3) how was the Asante economy affected by the changing world economy by the late nineteenth century, (4) what were the effects of legitimate commerce along the coastline and within the interior, (5) how did the changing structure of the Asante family unit affect the slavery within the state, (6) finally, what impact did the political leadership of the Asante state in the nineteenth century have on changing Gold Coast economy of the same period?

As the independence of African nations approached in the mid-twentieth century, several works were published on the history of West African regions. Nevertheless, as Ghana gained its independence, many of the earliest works came from British and Ghanaian scholars J. D. Fage[21] and A. Adu Boahen.[22] Both historians studied West Africa and Ghana both prior to colonial rule and after it officially came to an end in the territory. The numerous studies on West Africa and Ghana continued to grow after the 1960s as individual works on the history of the many indigenous groups were being published.

The Asante, one of the largest groups in West Africa, became the subject of several studies after this paradigm shift. In 1966, Ivor Wilks published an article entitled, "Aspects of Bureaucratization in Ashanti in the Nineteenth Century" examining the history and leadership of Asante people. This article along with several other later works from Ivor Wilks served as instrumental studies on the Asante people, referring to the state as a complex society with an advanced social structure. K. A. Busia also published a work on the Asante soon after Ghanaian independence titled, *The Position of the Chief in the Modern Political System of Ashanti*. This work discusses in greater detail the role of the Asante chief, religious practices of the state, succession in Asante and the rights of the leadership and people within the group. Both of these works were some of the first to consider the Asante as a complex society that consists of several functioning and moving parts.

Kwame Arhin soon followed Wilks and Busia with his articles, "The Financing of Ashanti Expansion, 1700–1820" and "The Structure of Greater Ashanti, 1700–1824" both published in 1967. In these two articles, Arhin focuses the structure and role of Greater Asante to the central region of the Gold Coast and later the expansion of the state toward the coast. This expansion eventually impacted the political well-being and economy of the state and its people, as well as affected the Fante people who resided along the coast. Also important to Arhin's discussion is the development of Greater of Asante and Kumasi, and their impact on trading, which developed both before and after the closure of the slave trade.

By the 1970s works became much more centralized on the Asante as publications began to analyze the history of the state, its interactions with neighboring groups as well as their dealings with Europeans settling in the region, challenging earlier works from Wilks. Two works to do so were the 1971 publication of J. K. Fynn, *Asante and Its Neighbors, 1700–1807* and the 1972 publishing of T. C. McCaskie's "Innovational Eclecticism: The Asante Empire and Europe in the Nineteenth Century." Fynn's work concentrates on the interactions among Asante and its neighbors, its establishment, expansion and army prior to the closing of the slave trade. Moreover, McCaskie chooses to focus on the effects of European expansion on the Asante. Numerous works published afterward continued to highlight the social, cultural and economic interactions which occurred between the Asante, its neighbors and Europeans.

Poly Hill's timeless work on the migrant labor in Ghana by the end of the nineteenth focuses on the cocoa, one of the regions' most well-known commodities, and those that farm this crop in the region. Although much of her work focuses on the region after 1892, as she argues these farmers hoped to expand their business and should be viewed as capitalist in a changing state, much information can be derived from her study. While, as she suggests their involvement in the world economy could not have occurred within a twenty-year span.[23] Instead one should look at this economic transition beginning much earlier than previous works suggest. Edward Reynolds in his work ultimately argues a subsistence economy was beginning to develop prior to the extension of the Gold Coast Protectorate, paving the way for region to enter into the world economy at the start of the nineteenth century.[24]

Furthermore, both works suggest the Gold Coast relied upon the start of British colonial rule to enter the world economy. This is an argument that should be challenged with evidence regarding the reasoning for the British spread into the interior and hopes of the Asantehene to establish trade partnerships. Thomas J. Lewin analyzes the Asante state prior to the arrival of British within the region in the latter half of the nineteenth century. Although his work analyzes the late years of the century, he gives a detailed history of the state prior to the British arrival and the Asante political scene and the changeover of the economy.[25] Adu A. Boahen similarly discusses Ghana in the nineteenth and twentieth centuries but admittedly realizes the limit reach of his work in the years after the slave trade was closed in comparison to those after the turn of the century at the time of publication.[26]

Although there are works written prior to 1975 on the Gold Coast and the Asante, the publication of David Kimble's *A Political History of Ghana: The Rise of Gold Coast Nationalism, 1850–1928*, Ivor Wilks, *Asante in the Nineteenth Century* and Joseph K. Adyaye's *Diplomacy and Diplomats in the Nineteenth Century Asante* continued to challenge previous works and set the foundation for later publications that followed. While each work is essential to the study of the Gold Coast and the Asante, each also sparked much debate among scholars. Much of the debate and criticism from scholars regarding the Wilks study comes from statements made in his preface about the overall purpose of his work. In this preface, Wilks states, ". . . throughout this study I have been concerned less with those aspects of Asante society which are unique to it, and more with those aspects which it has in common with other complex societies whether on the African continent or elsewhere."[27] This comment sparked debate and outrage from scholars of African History and those which study the Asante, especially from T. C. McCaskie, a former student of Ivor Wilks. Although each has a different purpose, their works has generated a great amount of debate in the field both in the form of negative and positive responses.

Nevertheless, Mary McCarthy's 1983 work, *Social Change and the Growth of British Power in the Gold Coast: The Fante States, 1807–1874*, is instrumental as her work analyzes another Akan group, the Fante. McCarthy insists it was internal factors which brought about the start of colonialism across the Gold Coast.[28] Many of these earlier works, each instrumental, do not account for the changes within the ruling elite in positions of leadership, namely the Asantehene or his relationship with the numerous British governors and explorers or the queen herself.

Twenty-three years later in 1993, after debate generated by his work on the Asante, Wilks again published another work on the Asante. This work was a collection of essays entitled: *Forests of Gold: Essays on the Akan and the Kingdom of Asante*. Many of these essays, written in response to criticism about his first book, make their focus point on the establishment of Akan society, the Asante culture, religious influences and finally its civil administration. While this work adds to his previous work on the Asante, like his first study, this second book also sparked controversy. In response to Wilks, a number of scholars have presented their interpretation of the complexities of the Asante society. These critiques came from historians Kwame Arhin, T. C. McCaskie and Akosua Perbi to name a few.[29]

Ghanaian historian, Akosua Perbi, in her work *A History of Indigenous Slavery in Ghana: From the fifteenth to the nineteeth Century*, argues that many of the previous areas covered by earlier works only analyzed the coastal regions. As a result of this, an entire history of slavery and its impact on the outside world is dismissed or considered irrelevant until the coming of British colonial rule.[30] Perbi's work focuses on the indigenous slavery which occurred in the interior of the Gold Coast and analyzes its long-term effects on the local population and the Europeans living in the region. Although considered a localized scholarship, Perbi's study applies to a vast region in and outside of the Gold Coast.

As more historical studies are published to analyze African groups in terms of gender, ethnicity, culture, religion, economy and other social aspects, a number of individuals have studied the Asante from these perspectives. Gwendolyn Mikell, Sandra Greene, Gareth Austin and more recently Bayo Holsey have all written works that further the study of the Asante people and the Gold Coast. Although these works use some aspects from the previously published studies, they place a greater emphasis on understanding the day-to-day workings of the society, the matrilineal lineages, economy, and roles of individuals including slaves and the effects of indigenous slavery and the Trans-Atlantic Slave Trade.

Gwendolyn Mikell's work, *Cocoa and Chaos in Ghana*, analyzes the importance of cocoa to the development of the Gold Coast and later Ghana, in period much earlier than Poly Hill's classic work. Her work focuses on the economic well-being of Ghana beginning in 1850 and lasting through the post-colonial era of the country. In doing so, she discusses its growth, impact on slavery and the place of the family in this economy which were well established before cocoa becomes an important crop as Mikell explains in her work. She writes, ". . . the increasing bureaucratization of the interior as Ashanti responded to the economic and political challenges of Western penetration . . ."[31] Traditional societal aspects are put to use as the economy transitions to exporting this cash crop and Mikell uses cocoa and its impact on gender, family, kinship rights and commerce to explain its effect on the country.

Following Gwendolyn Mikell's study, Sandra Greene in a similar approach focused solely on the aspects of gender and ethnicity in this region. Greene's work *Gender, Ethnicity, and Social Change on the Upper Slave Coast: A History of the Anlo-Ewe* serves as one of the important works written on the Gold Coast. Although a cultural study, Green's work highlights the role of men, women and children in society as well as the family structure which dictates an individuals' role in that arrangement. Like Mikell, Greene also discusses the importance of the family and its structure on the commerce of the country an aspect which was overlooked in many of the earliest works published in the 1960s and 1970s.

Two of the more recent studies regarding the effects of slavery in Ghana are the publications of Gareth Austin, *Labour, Land and Capital in Ghana: From Slavery to Free Labour in Asante, 1807–1956* and Bayo Holsey's *Routes of Remembrance: Refashioning the Slave Trade in Ghana*. Each has played a role in shaping the future direction of the study of the Asante, the slave trade and slavery in Ghana. Gareth Austin focuses on the Asante and the Gold Coast from 1807 to 1956 and, unlike many of the previous studies, analyzes the resources used in production and the development of the export economy. This occurs with what he suggests is a limited rural population before becoming a commercial agricultural center.[32] Moreover, Holsey studies the effects of the slave trade and slavery on the country today, proving there is still much to be researched about the region. As scholarship on the history of Ghana and the Asante continues to present new information and spark debate among scholars, this also has carried over into the publications on the Trans-Atlantic Slave Trade.

The earliest published accounts on the Trans-Atlantic Slave Trade come from those who traded captive labor across the Atlantic Ocean and whose works were viewed by many as both exhilarating accounts of world travels and historical works on the continent of Africa. Transporting Africans across the Atlantic Ocean, slave traders, came from all European nations: Britain, France, Portugal, Spain and Denmark and later from the New World territories of South America, the Caribbean and the United States. In their journeys between the start and end of the slave trade, numerous works were published about their experiences on land and on ship as well as their contact with the various African groups.

These writings at their publication provided many with their first and only look into the continent of Africa. Also, these initial publications ingrained specific thoughts into the minds of their readers about Africa and its people.[33] These accounts, famous at the time of publication, have recently been scrutinized by today's contemporary scholars, who believe these works were written for alternative reasons. Since these works were published, our knowledge about the Trans-Atlantic Slave Trade has doubled and continues as we gain more understanding about the effects of the trade on society, culture and the economy.

Furthermore, the slave traders' accounts were published during both the legal and illegal slave trades; the most famous of these accounts include William Bosman's *A New and Accurate Description of the Coast of Guinea: Divided into the Gold, the Slave and the Ivory Coasts* (1721), William Snelgrave's *A New Account of Some Parts of Guinea and the Slave Trade* (1734), Alexander Falconridge's *An Account of the Slave Trade on the Coasts of Africa* (1788), Archibald Dalzel's *The History Dahomey: An Inland Kingdom of Africa* (1793) and Brantz Mayer's *Captain Canot: Twenty Years of an*

African Slaver Being an Account of His Career and Adventures on the Coast, In the Interior, On Shipboard, and in the West Indies (1854) all of which would greatly affect the writings of later traditionalists scholars.

Several of today's scholars have been very critical of many of these accounts in recent years. Scholarly critiques on slave traders have come from Loren K. Waldman and I. A. Akinjogbin who assess critically Archibald Dalzel[34] and more recently Robin Law in his assessment of William Snelgrave. Law's critique focuses on unpublished sections of Snelgrave's account that have been recently discovered, stating in his work, "The discovery of a . . . earlier manuscript version of Snelgrave's account is of more than bibliographical interest, since it differs in many particulars from the published version."[35] This leaves one to ask the question, why were these accounts written, who were they written for, what were there affects and why have they been altered so much? According to Patrick Manning one of the main effects of these writings in particular that of Archibald Dalzel, ". . . a *History of Dahomey* which described the . . . cruelties . . . attributed them to the inherent nature of African society rather than the slave trade."[36] Using Manning's assessment of Dalzel, his work placed the blame on the Africans themselves and argue they were there to help them transition into civilization.

Although under intense scrutiny, many of these accounts were considered factual evidence and riveting stories at their publication. Similar to Archibald Dalzel, Captain Canot in the reinterpretation of his life as a slave trader wrote in his account:

> As a national institution, it seems to have existed always. Africans have been bondsmen everywhere: and the oldest monuments bear . . . images linked with . . . servitude. . . . I have no hesitation in saying, that three fourths of the slaves sent abroad from Africa are the fruit of native wars, fomented by the avarice and temptation of our own race. . . . We stimulated the negro's passions by the introduction of wants . . . never dreamed of by the simple native. . . . But what was once a luxury has now ripened into an absolute necessity; so that man, in truth, has become the coin of Africa, and the legal tenders of a brutal trade.[37]

Both Canot and Dalzel place blame on African chiefs for enslavement of people in both Africa and the "New World" they overlook the role of Europeans. In doing so, they omit the willingness, desire, need and opportunity of Europeans to enslave the African for his own economic benefit.

Nevertheless, before and after Britain and the United States passed laws to suppress the traffic of captive Africans in 1807 and 1808, respectively, a number of works were written establishing the moral reasons to end this horrific traffic of Africans. The moral reasons for the abolition of the trade were shaped by the works of British abolitionists William Wilberforce, *A Letter on the Abolition of the Slave Trade*, and Thomas Clarkson's *The History of the Rise, Progress, and Accomplishment of the Abolition of the African Slave-Trade*. Both eventually gained far greater followers with the publication of Olaudah Equiano's *Interesting Narrative of the Life of Olaudah Equiano*, who spoke of his horrible experiences.

Albeit, at the time of their publication and even today, these works and others like them are considered masterpieces. For many, throughout Europe and in Britain, these works spoke of the horrors of slavery and the slave trade in ways the accounts of slave traders previously had not. As Wilberforce, Clarkson, Equiano and abolition societies in the United States began to gain support, the moral obligation suggested by abolitionists was challenged by the shifting belief that economic conditions no longer made slavery and the slave trade economically valuable. One of the first economic challenges came directly from Adam Smith's *The Wealth of Nations*.[38] Smith points to factors such as cheap land, the inability to maintain authority over traders and distance from mother country as reasons for the growth in slave trading.[39] All published in the same time period, offered their readers a different interpretation of the trade's closure, moral and economic factors.

The beginnings of the Trans-Atlantic Slave Trade like the reasons for its eventual abolition were not humanitarian, but instead the economic conditions which were shaped by the current circumstances in "New World" during the era. Continuing in the tradition of Adam Smith, Karl Marx and Friedrich Engels, the 1944 publication of Eric Williams' *Capitalism and Slavery* analyzed the reasons for the slave trade's closure from the perspective of the Caribbean islands marked a turning point in the study of slave trade and its closure.[40]

With the change in world economic policies from mercantilist to a capitalist system in the latter half of the eighteenth century, the value of Africans changed considerably to land owners, businesses and governments, all of who were hoping to maximize their potential profits in territories. Eric Williams best discusses the transition to a capitalist economy and its affects both on West Indian slavery and British capitalism. There have been several theories in the reasons for the start of the shipment of Africans to the New World, and Eric Williams insists, "The reason was economic, not racial; it had to do not with the color of the laborer, but the cheapness of the labor. As compared with Indian and white labor, Negro slavery was eminently superior."[41]

There have been several others to follow Williams' thesis, notably Walter Rodney, John Henrik Clarke and Selwynn H. H. Carrington. In 1982, Walter Rodney's *How Europe Underdeveloped Africa* takes Williams' thesis to the next stage by discussing the effects of European capitalism on Africa. His work discusses the effects of the slave trade, capitalism and the move toward colonialism, which damaged and destroyed the African systems of development to the benefit of European expansion. This was further backed again with the writings of John Henrik Clarke. Clarke's 1993 work, *Christopher Columbus and the Afrikan Holocaust: Slavery and the Rise of European Capitalism*, painted a similar picture to that of both Williams and Rodney analyzing the role of the slave trade and the development of European capitalism. Selwynn H. H. Carrington work, *The Sugar Industry and the Abolition of the Slave Trade, 1775–1810*, takes Williams thesis and applies it to the British Caribbean, the largest sugar-producing area and importer of captives, explaining its economic decline beginning after the start of the American Revolution. Immanuel Wallerstein as previously mention has also contributed greatly to this debate on the rise of world economic systems.[42]

This discussion of slave trading and the economic and moral factors which brought about its final closure continued in later works. Several of these works continued by analyzing the reasons for the enslavement of Africans, the numbers of victims shipped to the New World and the impact of slave trading on West Africa. Moreover, several of these notable works to analyze these aspects include: Philip Curtin, *Atlantic Slave Trade: A Census*, Basil Davidson, *Black Mother: The Years of the African Slave Trade*; Joseph E. Inikori, *Forced Migration: The Impact of the Export Slave Trade on African Societies*; Walter Rodney, *West Africa and the Atlantic Slave Trade*; David Brion Davis, *In the Image of God: Religion, Moral Values, and Our Heritage of Slavery;* and Patrick Manning, *Slavery and African Life: Occidental, Oriental and African Slave Trades.*

Peter C. Hogg has compiled a bibliography of speeches made in the eighteenth and nineteenth centuries calling for the suppression of the slave trade titled, *The African Slave Trade and Its Suppression: A Classified and Annotated Bibliography of Books, Pamphlets and Periodical Articles.* This bibliography lists a number of speeches and pamphlets from around the world regarding the closure of slave trade. In analyzing the closure of the trade, the most important work and possibly one of the most groundbreaking pieces to analyze any aspect of the trade is W. E. B. DuBois' *The Suppression of the African Slave-Trade to the United States of America, 1638–1870.* This research, done during DuBois' time as a graduate student at Harvard University, has been re-published in a number of editions. Since its publication there have been a number of works attempting to regionalize DuBois' work. The latest being, Ernest Obadele-Starks' *Freebooters and Smugglers: The Foreign Slave trade in the United States after 1808.*

Albeit, Africans also brought along with them to the region knowledge of crops planted in their homeland that eventually resulted in economic growth for individuals, groups and countries that actively traded in captive labor, which is emphasized in the work written by Judith Ann Carney and Richard Nicholas Rosomoff titled *In the Shadow of Slavery: Africa's Botanical Legacy in the Atlantic World.* In this instance we see the reason for the enslavement of Africans is directly related to the cost of the labor relative to other labor sources available to Europeans. Captives from the Gold Coast being transported to New World territories steadily increased between the eighteenth and nineteenth centuries leading to a growth in the prices for these captives. According to Daniel P. Mannix and Malcolm Cowley, "Slaves from the Gold Coast were highly regarded by the English and usually sold at a higher price than those from other regions."[43] This point is well documented by Joseph John Williams in his work *Psychic Phenomena of Jamaica*.[44]

As of today, now over one hundred years later, there still remains considerable debate as to whether the final closure of the trade was due to moral and religious factors or the economic conditions which affected the world, namely the transition to capitalism. A host of past and present works have contributed to this debate and as the world commemorated this event in 2007 and in 2008, more scholars have published new works, and new editions to past works have been released. A review of these works shows, while scholars have contributed greatly to the study of this event, there is still a considerable amount of research to be done on this era of history.

While this period of "self-congratulatory" events surrounding the laws passed to suppress the traffic of Africans flowing across the Atlantic brought about new discussions, it has also forced scholars to review many of the past thoughts. The past debates, first put forth by world-renowned historians, in recent years because of new archival evidence and technological advances, which were previously unknown, have recently given way to new and different interpretations of the trade in Africans. Recent work done by scholars has either debunked or reinterpreted all together past works about the events surrounding the trade in Africans which were to be sold and enslaved on plantations in the New World. These recently published works have called attention to specific industries, banks and families.

The recent celebrations sponsored by various countries, states and organizations have sparked a new-found interest in reasons for the abolition of the slave trade. This has also led scholars to analyze the effects of Africans on both the world economies, especially that of the United States and Britain following the trades' final suppression during the nineteenth century. This becomes a crucial element often overlooked during the Industrial Revolution, which began in England. While there are several works to analyze the Industrial Revolution, the most notable of these, which takes into account the role of Africans is Joseph E. Inikori's *Africans in the Industrial Revolution: A Study in International Trade and Economic Development*.

Robin Blackburn offers a different interpretation as to the role of the slave trade writing, "The racial character of New World slavery was invented by European slave traders and settlers. . . . The Early Spanish and Portuguese authorities justified slavery as a means to the conversion of Africans.

European traders and colonists of the early modern period . . . rarely displayed any eagerness to convert them."[45] David Brion Davis like Blackburn argues against the idea, slavery in the New World is an extension of Islamic attitudes about race in the Iberian Peninsula calling it "ethnocentric ignorance."[46] A previous study of Davis', entitled, *The Problem of Slavery in the Age of Revolution, 1770–1823*, examines the moral argument against the enslavement of Africans in the culture of white slave owners. The idea Africans were fit to be enslaved also found grounds in science.

Although the trade in Africans by Britain and the United States was officially abolished in 1807 and 1808, both countries and its subjects continued to be direct benefactors of the trade long after abolition laws were put into effect. Scholars have analyzed the roles of the countries, but the recent publication of Marika Sherwood's work *After Abolition: Britain and the Slave Trade Since 1807* seeks to establish connections between these governments and those to benefit from the trade after suppression laws were passed.

Furthermore, the study of African slavery will also provide substantial evidence as to why the trade was suppressed. A number of studies over the years have been conducted by scholars, the most notable of which include: Claude Meillassoux, *The Anthropology of Slavery: The Womb of Iron and Gold*. Meillassoux work published in 1991 can be linked directly to later works which it influenced. The edited publication of a work by Sylviane A Diouf titled, *Fighting the Slave Trade: West African Strategies,* looks at the role Africa played in the slave trade as well as the fight of individuals and groups not to become victims.

The slave trade has been and will continue to be one of the most studied subjects in history. As previously stated, we are now in a period of "self-congratulations" for the abolition of the slave trade, but this has also sparked a new found interest in the subject. The next question becomes, where does the study of the slave trade turn to next? Past studies have focused on the numbers of Africans shipped across the Atlantic, the Middle Passage and life after arrival on the other side of the Atlantic. New studies with the use of information gained from abolition studies to further the information regarding the slave trade. One topic that has recently gained attention is the economic conditions of the African economy and the world economy transitioning from a market dictated by captives to one dictated by other goods. While the foundations for these works have been laid by previous works, scholars will seek to take these works to the next level and leave their marks on the study of the slave trade.

Recent scholarship trends regarding the study of the slave trade have chosen to analyze and re-analyze both old and new evidences. This event, referred to by a few as a holocaust and genocide,[47] culminated in the growth of legitimate trade or commerce from Africa. Although both revisionist and traditionalist scholarship disagree on the reasons for the start and end of the trade, each gives Europeans credit for ending the trade by establishing "legitimate" trade and commerce.

This work will examine the political economy of the Gold Coast during the era of illegal slave trading (i.e. post-1807 era) through the start of colonial rule. Examining the final eradication of the Trans-Atlantic Slave Trade from West Africa and the trading patterns of the Asante will serve as key points of emphasis as I seek to prove that African states were key to the closure of the slave trade. An analysis of this point will prove not all Africans were complicit in this trade and among the Asante; this could vary with the leadership of each Asantehene. I intend to show the Asante went through economic changes which affected slave trading and while these changes were substantial they did not do major harm to the Asante economy which continued trading to both the north and the south. Scholars in recent decades have referred to the period following the passage of laws abolishing the trade in Africans as the start of the trade in products in the category of legitimate commerce. In emphasizing this point, they do not define "legitimate commerce" in a manner which fits all parties. This in turn is a convoluted term beneficial only to the European consciousness.

Emphasis will also be placed on the roles of the British and American efforts or lack thereof to suppress the trade in Africans. This economic suppression will be highlighted from the perspective of the African continent while still stressing the transformation from exporting slave labor to making use of this labor for the purposes of expansion. This economic suppression of the slave trade supersedes any humanitarian effort that scholars have overemphasized in recent years (i.e. 200th Anniversary of the Trans-Atlantic Slave Trade). I will also argue protecting and establishing commercial enterprises and not suppressing the slave trade became the top priority for the French, British and American naval squadrons and explorers.

As worldwide celebrations commenced in 2007 by individual countries celebrating their roles in closing the slave trade, I believe this work will become an asset to studies about the trade. It will not only add an important piece in the history of Ghana but it could also lead to similar studies in other African nations. The African role in the final closure of the Trans-Atlantic Slave Trade in its illegal stages has been and continues to be overlooked. In reinterpreting the trades' closure, this work will provide substantial research benefits to those who not only study the history of Africa but to those in the African Diaspora.

Ghana is home to a host of ethnic groups, one of the largest being the Akan. Within the Akan there are five distinct groups: the Fante, Akuapim, Akyem, Kwahu and the Asante, who all speak the common language, Twi, but with distinct dialects that distinguish each group from one another. They all have a long history that pre-dates the arrival of Europeans in the region and in many instances provide accounts of interactions with one another. This study will focus on the Asante, one of the largest of the Akan groups in Central Ghana and active participants in selling captive Africans and the closure of the Trans-Atlantic Slave Trade from the Gold Coast of Africa.

NOTES

1. Joseph K. Adjaye, *Diplomacy and Diplomats in Nineteenth Century Asante* (New York: Lanham Books, 1984), p. 2.
2. Joseph Dupuis, *Journal of a Residence in Ashantee* (London: 1820).
3. J. Beecham, *Asantee and the Gold Coast* (London: 1841).
4. Henry Meredith, *An Account of the Gold Coast of Africa: With a Brief History of the African Company* (London: Longman, Hurst, Rees, Orme, and Brown, Paternoster Row, 1812).
5. T. E. Bowdich, *Mission From Cape Coast Castle to Ashantee, with a Descriptive Account of that Kingdom* (London: Griffith & Farran, 1817).
6. Brodie Cruickshank, *The Gold Coast of Africa: Including an Account of the Native Tribes, and Their Intercourse with Europeans* (London: Hurst and Blackett, Publishers, 1853).
7. A. B. Ellis, *A History of the Gold Coast of West Africa* (London: Chapman and Hall, 1893).
8. William Ernest Frank Ward, *A Short History of the Gold Coast* (Berkley, CA: University of California Press, 1939).
9. Meredith, *An Account of the Gold Coast*, i–viii.
10. Dupuis, *Journal of a Residence in Ashantee*, i.
11. C. C. Reindorf, *History of the Gold Coast and Asante: Based on Traditions and Historical Facts, Comprising A Period of More Than Three Centuries from about 1500 to 1860* (Christianborg, Gold Coast: Basel Mission Book Depot, 1895).
12. Ibid, III–IV.
13. Robert William July, *The Origins of Modern African Thought: Its Development in West Africa During the Nineteenth and Twentieth Centuries* (Trenton, NJ: Africa World Press, Inc., 2004), p. 329.
14. J. E. Casely Hayford published numerous works including *Ethiopia Unbound, The Truth About the West African Land Question, Gold Coast Native Institutions* and *Gold Coast: Land Tenure and Forest Bill.*
15. Interview with Kwame Ture, May 6, 1998, Ida Lewis, ed., "Kwame Ture on Kwame Nkrumah," *The New Crisis Magazine*, July 1998.
16. James A. Caporaso and David P Levine, *Theories of Political Economy* (New York: Cambridge University Press, 1992), p. 1.
17. John Neville Keynes, *The Scope and Method of Political Economy*, 3rd ed. (London: Macmillan and Co., 1904), pp. 100–101.
18. Caporaso and Levine, *Theories of Political Economy*, 3.

19. Immanuel Wallerstein, *World-Systems Analysis: An Introduction*, 2nd ed. (Durham, NC: Duke University Press, 2005), p. 24.

20. Peter C. W. Gutkind and Immanuel Wallerstein, eds. *The Political Economy of Contemporary Africa* (Beverly Hills, CA: Sage Publications, 1976), p. 9.

21. J. D. Fage published several works on Africa after Ghana's independence. Although Fage is from the University of London where many of his colleagues shared the thoughts of Trevor Roper and A. P. Newton and many of its publications concluded the same thought, He directly challenged this sentiment after Ghana's independence. His work include: J. D. Fage, *An Introduction to the History of West Africa* (London: Cambridge University Press, 1955); J. D. Fage, *Africa Discovers Her Past* (London: Oxford University Press, 1970); J. D. Fage and William Tordoff, *A History of Africa* (London: Hutchinson and Company, 1978). Fage also published an introductory work on Ghana. See: J. D. Fage, *Ghana: A Historical Interpretation* (Madison, WI: University of Wisconsin Press, 1959).

22. A. Adu Boahen published several works on Africa and Ghana following the country's independence. His works include: A. Adu Boahen, *Britain, the Sahara, and the Western Sudan, 1788–1861* (Oxford: Clarendon Press, 1964); A. Adu Boahen and James B. Webster, *The Revolutionary Years: West Africa Since 1800* (London: Longmans, 1967). He has published several works on Ghana, the first being: A. Adu Boahen, *Ghana: Evolution and Change in the Nineteenth and Twentieth Centuries* (London: Longmans, 1975).

23. Polly Hill, *Migrant Cocoa Farmers of Southern Ghana: A Study of Rural Capitalism* (London: Cambridge University Press, 1970), pp. 2–11.

24. Edward Reynolds, *Trade and Economic Change on the Gold Coast, 1807–1874* (New York: Longman Group, 1974), pp. 2–3.

25. Thomas J. Lewin, *Asante Before the British: The Prempean Years, 1875–1900* (Lawrence, KS: The Regents of Kansas Press, 1984), pp. 9–12.

26. A. Adu Boahen, *Ghana: Evolution and Change in the Nineteenth and Twentieth Centuries*, 2nd ed. (Accra, Ghana: Sankofa Educational Publishers, 2000), p. xi.

27. Ivor Wilks, *Asante in the Nineteenth Century: The Structure and Evolution of a Political Order* (New York: Cambridge University Press, 1975), p. xiv.

28. Mary McCarthy, *Social Change and the Growth of British Power in the Gold Coast: The Fante State, 1807–1874* (Lanham, MD: University Press of America, 1983), p. x.

29. T. C. McCaskie, a former student of Wilks, was highly critical of his work *Asante in the Nineteenth Century*. In his preface to *Forests of Gold: Essays on the Akan and the Kingdom of Asante*, Wilks discusses the harsh criticism from his former student. McCaskie who insists *Asante in the Nineteenth Century* should not have been written and is theoretically wrong. Wilks also comments on a late colleague who argued he makes guesses about his research. For a full synopsis and response regarding these comments see: Ivor Wilks, *Forests of Gold: Essays on the Akan and the Kingdom of Asante* (Athens, OH: Ohio University Press, 1993), pp. xiii–xvi.

30. As British influence on the Gold Coast grew during the 1850s, this directly affected both the economy and the society. With this growing influence on the Gold Coast and the local population, indigenous slavery came under attack from British

settlers. The burning of Kumasi in 1874, a direct attack by the British on the Asante, was followed by the passing of an abolition of slavery law in Gold Coast.

31. Gwendolyn Mikell, *Cocoa and Chaos in Ghana* (New York: Paragon House, 1989), p. 23.

32. Gareth Austin, *Labour, Land and Capital in Ghana: From Slavery to Free Labour in Asante, 1807–1956* (Rochester, NY: University of Rochester Press, 2005), p. 1.

33. The accounts of slave traders, combined with the story of Noah and the *Curse of Ham* only added to the belief Africans were inferior and made to serve as slaves. See works by Lester B. Scherer, *Slavery and the Churches in Early America, 1619*–1819 (Grand Rapids, MI: William B. Eerdmans Publishing Co., 1975) and Edith R. Sanders, "The Hamitic Hypothesis: Its Origins and Functions in Time Perspective," *Journal of African History*, Vol. 10, No. 4 (1969), pp. 521–532.

34. Both Loren K. Waldman, "An Unnoticed Aspect of Archibald Dalzel's the History of Dahomey," *The Journal of African History*, Vol. 6, No. 2 (1965), pp. 185–192 and I. A. Akinjogbin, "Archibald Dalzel: Slave Trader and Historian of Dahomey," *The Journal of African History*, Vol. 7, No. 1 (1966), pp. 67–68, question the purpose of Dalzel writing his account of Dahomey.

35. Robin Law, "The Original Manuscript Version of William Snelgrave's New Account of Some Parts of Guinea," *History in Africa*, Vol. 17 (1990), p. 367.

36. Patrick Manning, *Slavery and African Life: Occidental, Oriental, and African Slave Trades* (New York: Cambridge University Press, 1990), p. 15.

37. Brantz Mayer, *Captain Canot; Twenty Years of an African Slaver Being an Account of His Career and Adventures on the Coast, in the Interior, on Shipboard, and in The West Indies* (New York: D. Appleton and Company, 1854), pp. 126–127.

38. Adam Smith in his classical work *The Wealth of Nations* argued the work done by wage laborers comes cheaper than the work performed by slaves. See: Adam Smith, *The Wealth of Nations*, 5th ed. (New York: Bantam Books, 2003), p. 113.

39. Ibid., 318.

40. Eric Williams himself receives a considerable amount of credit for developing and advancing a thesis first introduced by Lowell J. Ragatz in 1928 and again 1932 who discussed the fall of the planter class in the British Caribbean. In 1928 Lowell J. Ragatz published *The Fall of the Planter Class in the British Caribbean, 1763–1833* (New York: Century Company, 1928). This was followed by his work *A Guide for the Study of British Caribbean History, Including the Abolition and Emancipation Movements 1763–1834* (Washington, DC: U.S. Government Printing Office, 1932).

41. Eric Williams, *Capitalism and Slavery*, 2nd ed. (Chapel Hill, NC: University of North Carolina Press, 1994).

42. Immanuel Wallerstein has several works which emphasize the changing economic conditions and the establishment and growth of capitalism. These works include: *The Capitalist World Economy* and his three volume series *The Modern World System: Capitalist Agriculture and the Origins of the European World Economy, Mercantalism and the Consolidation of the European World Economy, 1600–1750* and *The Second Era of Great Expansion of the Capitalist World-Economy, 1730s–1840s*.

43. Daniel P. Mannix and Michael Cowley, *A History of the Atlantic Slave Trade: Black Cargoes* (New York: Viking Compass Book, 1962), p. 17.

44. Chapter 1 of Joseph J. Williams work *Psychic Phenomena of Jamaica* discusses the cultural influence of Ashanti Jamaica. See: Joseph J. Williams, *Psychic Phenomena of Jamaica* (New York: The Dial Press, 1934), pp. 23–50. Also see: Joseph J. Williams, *Hebrewisms of West Africa: From Nile to Niger With Jews* (Chicago, IL: Research Associates School Times Publications & Frontline Distribution International Inc., 2010).

45. Robin Blackburn, *The Making of New World Slavery: From the Baroque to the Modern, 1492–1800* (London: Verso Books, 1998), p. 12.

46 David Brion Davis, *In the Image of God: Religion, Moral Values, and Our Heritage of Slavery* (New Haven, CT: Yale University Press, 2001), p. 138.

47. There are several scholars of African History who refer to the Trans-Atlantic Slave Trade as a Holocaust of African people. John Henrik Clarke's *Christopher Columbus and the Afrikan Holocaust: Slavery and the Rise of European Capitalism* refers to this event as a Holocaust. A former pupil of Clarke's Marimba Ani, *Let the Circle be Unbroken: The Implications of Afrikans Spirituality in the Diaspora,* uses the term "Maafa" which in Ki-Swahili means "disaster." Asa G. Hilliard, III, also uses the term "genocide" when explaining the circumstances African people and their descendants faced. See Asa G. Hilliard, III, *SBA: The Reawakening of the African Mind.*

Chapter 1

European Arrival in West Africa and the Gold Coast

Portuguese, Dutch, and British, 1440–1680

In the fifteenth century, European explorers set out in search for routes to the areas they believed to be producing gold in vast quantities. Hopeful to gain access to the West African gold deposits in the richest areas, they sought to do so without any outside or Muslim interference. The Portuguese in the fifteenth century became the first Europeans to explore the region, bringing along with them numerous commodities for exchange including brass, copper and cloth. Their arrival along the coast of West Africa occurring nearly 200 years before the emergence of the Akan and Asante State resulted in several European nations and explorers setting out for the coastline of West Africa between the fifteenth and sixteenth centuries. The earliest of this wave of European nations and explorers searching for gold first arrived in the region of Senegambia, then the islands of Principe and Sao Tome and ultimately Benin. Furthermore, these numerous travels throughout the century continued along the coastline of West Africa and eventually around the Southern tip of the continent. Only a few years after these travels began, this route included a stop in the region which became known as the Gold Coast.

As travels to West Africa and the Gold Coast increased between the fifteenth and nineteenth centuries, several European nations began to maintain large scale forts along the coastline of the African continent. The purpose and need for these forts developed in part due to the increased trade opportunities Europeans began to experience starting in the fifteenth century throughout West Africa. Albeit, this ultimately led to European nations constructing forts in numerous locations throughout West Africa, as trading between European and African states near the coastline steadily increased. Moreover, as trading increased, so too did the size and scope of the surrounding settlements, consisting largely of individuals hoping to take advantage of trading along the coastline. Forts served as the centerpieces of these consistently growing communities linking these settlements to four different areas of trading opportunities: the interior of Africa, the coastline of Africa, Europe and the emerging Atlantic economy. Built throughout West African territories, these settlements along with the forts which accompanied them enabled European nations to preserve their standing as political and economic powers well into the nineteenth century.

Furthermore, these numerous forts and settlements allowed European nations to stretch their individual influence beyond the borders of Europe, the Caribbean Islands and the Americas well before the start of colonialism in the latter half of the nineteenth century. Stretching the coastline of the Gold Coast region, numerous European nations also constructed forts and established settlements to take advantage of the growing West Africa trading opportunities which presented themselves. Moreover, the role of each European nation by the start of the seventeenth century was especially prevalent in the region as trading expanded to include gold, manufactured items, agricultural goods and captives, and by the nineteenth century more legitimately traded items.

As trading in the Gold Coast began to flourish first between the fifteenth and sixteenth centuries, the region became a prime location for the exchange of the most sought after goods, namely gold, as each European nation hoped to gain a stake in this emerging West African economy. The West African economy, most notably along the Gold Coast region, proved so valuable that numerous nations constructed forts along the coastline, openly working with closest African states to their location. Along this region, those opportunities began in the fifteenth century with the arrival of the first Portuguese ships. Among the earliest European nations to arrive and make a permanent presence in the Gold Coast for several centuries include: Portugal, France, Netherlands and Britain. The arrival of these European nations and the construction of forts and settlements also coincided with the increase in trading to and from the Americas and the Caribbean Islands.

The Gold Coast, with the development and expansion of slave trading in the sixteenth and seventeenth centuries, also brought with it the emergence of a separate system exchange centered on both manufactured and agricultural goods. Nonetheless, the development of this large scale system of both slave trading and exchange of legitimate goods in the region relied heavily on the development and maintenance of interior routes across all of West Africa. These paths of exchange stretching across the Gold Coast connected the interior to the coastline and overseas markets. Nonetheless, with the arrival of more European traders, the need of these routes increased; by the middle of the nineteenth century explorers used these paths to enter the interior as they established their own connections to the region without the need for middlemen.

Additionally, by the middle of nineteenth century these routes were highly sought after by several interior and coastal nations throughout the Gold Coast as they proved to be just as valuable as the commodities being transported along them. These numerous routes, stretching from the coastline to the hinterland, proved critical to the economic prosperity and viability of each coastal and interior state. Not only did these numerous routes crisscross the entire region in all directions linking the various states and peoples to one another but also connected them to the European forts and settlements waiting for goods on the coastline. The importance of the Gold Coast region coupled with the rise of trading to Europe and the Americas over several centuries was significant, as this area came to supply numerous high-value items to both regions.

The Portuguese became the first Europeans to reach West Africa, in the middle of the fifteenth century searching for the source of gold crossing the Sahara Desert north into Europe between the seventh and fourteenth centuries. Their first ships made landfall at the mouth of the Senegal River in 1441 and explored the area through 1445 before ultimately later moving to the island chain of Cape Verde in 1456, an area afterward used for slave trading. Through these early landings, the Portuguese still had not found the region they believed to be the source of gold reaching the Iberian Peninsula, while they lived under Islamic control. The arrival of the Portuguese and the opening of a commercial exchange to the West and across the Atlantic Ocean served as the first rival to the still expanding Trans-Saharan Trade in the fifteenth century.[1]

Nevertheless, Portuguese investment in West Africa began first with their decision to explore the region, ultimately cutting out the Muslim middlemen who operated along the trade routes crossing the Sahara Desert. Paul Lovejoy writes, “Structurally, therefore, both the Portuguese and the Muslim trader filled the same functions: they connected. . . . Africa with the Mediterranean world and . . . the regional commerce of West Africa.”[2] The arrival of the Europeans along the coastline of West Africa created a significant shift in trading, as prior to their arrival the Mediterranean region of Europe was connected to Africa through Muslim traders; thereafter, the Portuguese were able to circumvent their power by limiting their involvement in the European markets. With the construction of their own ships and an increased desire to explore, the Portuguese were able to remove any outside factors. Moreover, in the coming years, the Portuguese and later arriving Europeans connected Africa with the Mediterranean and the world across the Atlantic Ocean. This economic advantage presented to Europeans brought about the construction of newer and faster ships which also caused a change to trading patterns across interior West African states from north and northwest to the south and southwest, respectively.

Although the trade in captives did not begin immediately with the arrival of the first Portuguese ships, several were taken back to the country by the earliest travelers as objects of curiosity. Moreover, this resulted in several returning to Africa to take part in trade after learning the Portuguese language serving as translators aiding in negotiations along with working as both domestics and semi-skilled artisans.[3] Several Africans, among the first to return were converted to Christianity at the insistence of Prince Henry the Navigator, who hoped their changeover could open doors for Portuguese traders previously locked out by Muslims and a language barrier. Similarly, this he also hoped it would impact trade routes crisscrossing West African states away from the Sahara Desert to the coastline, linking them directly to Portugal.[4]

Albeit, Prince Henry died prior to seeing this come true, but his early push for exploration of unknown locations began the process of European exploration into Africa for all nations which followed. Moreover, this early exploration ultimately developed into numbers of Africans being brought into Portugal in the fifteenth century, working in several different capacities as chattel slaves, agricultural serfs and household domestics.[5] Nevertheless, by 1448, the number of Africans carried back to Portugal or the Portuguese Islands of Azores and Madeira to work as domestics, reached nearly one thousand in total; procured largely by privately financed expeditions to West Africa.[6]

Nonetheless, between 1471 and 1472, nearly thirty years after reaching West Africa, two Portuguese explorers, Martim Fernandes and Alvaro Esteves, reached three central regions of trade in West Africa. Regions, which later became valuable to the trade of gold, sugar and, in due course, captive Africans, all presented explorers and traders with new opportunities for riches and wealth. These areas and commodities included: the island of São Tomé and Príncipe, sugar; the Bight of Benin, captives; and the area they believed to be the source of the gold crossing the Sahara Desert into Europe, Cabo des Tres Pontas or Cape Three Points, a coastal point on the region they later called the Gold Coast.[7] This region referred to as the Gold Coast lied between Cape Three Points and River Volta, with a coastline which ran east-northeast.[8]

Reaching the region they believed to be the source of gold and exploring further, they finally settled in the vicinity of Cabo des Tres Pontas or Cape Three Points, an area they christened *A Mina Do Ouro*, today commonly referenced by its most distinguishable fort El Mina. Soon after making landfall at Cabo des Tres Pontas and establishing a linkage with the indigenous population, they immediately began trading for the region's main commodity, gold. People along the West African coastline were already connected to one another prior to the landing of Portuguese and their arrival in West Africa only further expanded these connections. These connections continued to expand along already established routes of the Gold Coast after the arrival of the Portuguese. Furthermore, newly established connections between the Portuguese and African nations near Cape Three Points helped strengthen growing bonds between the Gold Coast region, Europe and in the coming years the New World.[9]

When reaching the coast of West Africa, the Portuguese witnessed a people which already mastered the use of canoes to travel and trade. Further, along the numerous waterways stretching throughout the Gold Coast, in particular, people used canoes to trade along the interior waterways and bring items to the coastline.[10] The use of canoes along waterways and the construction of routes connected the interior and the coastline in two different ways increasing the opportunities for trade and exchange of ideas and culture. This coupled with the Portuguese landing on the Gold Coast and the construction of European trading centers, connected Europe to Africa, and also linked people and areas hundreds of miles apart from one another to their landing area at Cape Three Points and the interior of this vital region. Upon their arrival, at Cape Three Points, the Portuguese immediately came into contact with an indigenous people consisting of several different groups with a common history with one another but divided individual characteristics. Among the earliest leaders of the local indigenous state include: Nana Kobina Amankwaa (1320–1355), Nana Kweigy Ansah (1355–1390), Nana Ampon Kuma (1390–1426), Nana Ebo I (1426–1450), Nana Amankwaa II (1450–1475) and Nana Kwamena Keigya Ansah I (1475–1510) who was king at the arrival of the Portuguese.[11]

Nevertheless, in the coming years after their arrival along the Gold Coast, the Portuguese were able to create a sphere of trade which included states and people from as far away as Dahomey, Ouidah/Whydah, Cape Verde, São Tomé and Príncipe, the Senegambia, the Bight of Benin and ultimately the Angola and the Congo. Furthermore, this growing network of West African trade not only connected each of these regions and numerous states to one another, but also linked them to Europe and later the Americas. Although, the trade network was established connecting the regions to one another, each area was impacted in varying degrees by the system of commercial exchange. With their numerous trading ships in the fifteenth century, the Portuguese were the only European nation at that time, in Africa and began quickly carving out its niche into the numerous local economies.

During its early years in the region, to gain access to gold for export back to Europe, Portuguese traders imported items into the Gold Coast from the previously named locations. Cloths, blankets and linen from Morocco; brass, iron kettles and bars from Northern Europe; and captives were imported from several areas of Africa.[12] Within only a few short years of hearing news of gold being transported back to Portugal by traders, several European nations soon set out to take advantage of this new trading opportunity. With a vested economic interest not only in the Gold Coast but all of West Africa, Europeans, by the start of the sixteenth century, were a daily visible presence along the coastline.

The expansion of the Portuguese and later all European nations into West Africa and the Gold Coast occurred at the height of overseas commercial expansion into the Americas. Acquired gold was used to finance numerous treks across the Atlantic Ocean between the fifteenth and seventeenth centuries and was so abundantly and readily available to Portuguese traders upon their arrival, the trade in captives was not seen as a vital component to the regions participation in Afro-European commercial network. While the case along the Gold Coast region, this was not the circumstance of such places as Benin and Angola, where the trade in captives was critical to their connection to the trade network as the Portuguese arrived in the same time period.[13] Although well behind Europe as an importer of captives during the period, the Gold Coast still saw a steady influx of captives brought into the region, as all European nations soon began to bring in captives to trade for gold. Spanish traders, in 1479, stopped along the Windward Coast, where the, traded their goods for captives which they ultimately sold on the Gold Coast for gold only miles away from the Portuguese traders.[14]

Portuguese traders early on were able to establish themselves as the key Europeans on the Gold Coast playing a critical role in the trade of captives and gold. Obtaining captives from Dahomey, Ouidah, Benin and Congo for example, the Portuguese used these captives to gain gold, later helping finance the Portuguese expansion into the New World and their development as the major European economy of the day. Discussing the Portuguese trade in gold and captives in West Africa and on the Gold Coast, Saidiya Hartman states:

> The Afro-European trade in slaves did not begin in Ghana as it did elsewhere with Africans selling slaves and Europeans buying them. It began with Europeans selling slaves and Africans buying them. The Portuguese started out as middlemen in the internal slave trade. They kidnapped and purchased slaves from Kongo and Benin and sold them on the Gold Coast. For each slave sold to African merchants and royals, the Portuguese received three to six ounces of gold. Slaves fetched better prices on the Gold Coast than they did in Lisbon. The gold transported from El Mina spurred the traffic in slaves and rewarded the Portuguese with the premier place in the Atlantic Slave Trade for its first two centuries.[15]

This exchange of commodities along the coast of West Africa in the coming centuries created a system in which all Europeans nations quickly sought to join. The increasing desire of Europeans to enter the Gold Coast grew immediately as this news of the Akan gold fields began to spread. This caused a great stir as other nations followed the Portuguese and soon began buying

Africans from other locations along West Africa to transport into the Gold Coast in exchange for gold. With the growing interest of European nations in West Africa the value of gold and the need for captives increased once again.

In 1482, the trade for gold reached new heights, expanding for a second time in only a matter of years when the Portuguese began construction of São Jorge da Mina in the same area they reached nearly ten years earlier, *A Mina Do Ouro*. Choosing to construct a trading castle between Benya Lagoon and Edina, thereafter named Elmina, Portuguese ship captain Don Diego d'Azambuja, first gained the permission to begin from King Kwamena Ansa. Albeit, once completed São Jorge da Mina also referred to as "The Mine," today commonly referred to as Elmina Castle, provided a permanent residence for Portuguese traders wanting to settle on the African coast to acquire gold.[16] The Portuguese imported both materials and labor for its construction, which according to its original plan was not fully completed until 1486, although it was operational prior to this date.[17] Once completed, São Jorge da Mina became the first European style building constructed in West Africa.[18] This also enabled the Portuguese to construct permanent homes just outside the fort walls.

With the construction of Sao Jorge da Mina, the Portuguese further authority by granting the newly completed construction all rights and immunities of any city and thereafter established the Guinea Company. The construction of the castle, immunities granted and the establishment of the trading company gave the Portuguese a monopoly overall trade to and from West Africa.[19] Initially, built as a trading center for the buying and selling of gold as well as other highly sought after items found on the Gold Coast, the castle later became known for slave trading castle in the sixteenth century. With its construction, the Portuguese officially established a permanent presence in the area resulting in their population expanding shortly thereafter.[20] This monopoly held by the Portuguese over West Africa and Gold Coast trading remained in place until the Reformation, resulting in the British, Dutch and French to soon make their way to West Africa.[21]

For well over one hundred years after their arrival, the Portuguese continued to import captives into the Gold Coast, for the purpose of acquiring gold deposits. Akan gold became the most sought after commodity on the Gold Coast by the Portuguese and the coming European nations between the fifteenth and sixteenth centuries. Beginning with their arrival through the middle of fifteenth century, Portuguese traders were able to carry away £100,000 of gold per year. This was later cut with arrival of the French and English in the middle of the sixteenth century, who carried away £50,000 and the Royal African Company £25,000 a year over the two centuries.[22] In the coming centuries, as the Portuguese trading went into decline in the region they were replaced by the Dutch West India Company who between 1621 and 1634 matched the output of their predecessor transporting £99,584 per year.[23] Upon the arrival of traders, many witnessed the great abundance of gold as stated by A. B. Ellis who wrote, ". . . women, are, as it were, laden with collars, bracelets, hoops and chains . . . of gold, copper or ivory. . . . Some . . . wear . . . beaten gold on their fingers rings of gold wire, with a knot or wreath . . ."[24] Although this system of trade was largely determined by gold, other commodities, such as textiles, were just as valuable to the trade.

Ultimately, the arrival of both Portuguese explorers and traders, coupled with the eventual coming of several other European groups in the sixteenth century, began a new era in the history of West Africa and the Gold Coast. Thereafter, each European nation began to specifically refer to the area which they settled as their own Gold Coast region.[25] In these early years of European arrival along the Gold Coast, the region continued to prove to be central to the development and expansion of each foreign nation's economy into other areas of West Africa and later their interaction with the emerging economy of the Americas. Through each nation's arrival, the Gold Coast areas continued to be a large importer of captive Africans well into the sixteenth century, while surrounding regions to the north, the Senegambia, to the east Dahomey and Ouidah, and as far south as Angola all became exporters of captives.

As the Atlantic Commercial Economy of the fifteenth and sixteenth centuries continued to expand, this growing system of exchange found along the Gold Coast continued to impact trading throughout West Africa and the Americas. Furthermore, it was this early exchange of gold which between the two centuries laid the foundation for the expansion of slave trading to and from the Gold Coast. James K. Anquandah states:

> It appears then that in the 15th and 16th centuries, the Portuguese established the practice of purchasing slaves from West and Central African societies outside the Gold Coast and exchanging them for gold, ivory and other inanimate products at Elmina castle. This "slave for gold" enterprise supplied a labour force for working in local gold mines and for head loading vast quantities of Portuguese imported textiles, metal ware, rum etc. into the Gold Coast hinterland. In this way, it is estimated that some 10,000 West African slaves were imported into the Gold Coast between 1490 and 1630.[26]

Though a relatively small number compared to those arriving in Europe and eventually in the Americas, those captives transported into the Gold Coast were put to work. Each played a crucial role in an emerging economy that was developing between Europe and West Africa as they worked in the numerous gold mines and transported supplies between interior and coastline. This transportation of captives from one area of Africa to another within a few years of making contact with West Africa decreased due to the need for labor in the Americas.

Ahead of the Trans-Atlantic Slave Trade beginning, most West African nations were already experienced in trading captives across its own land, taking part this internal African trade. Portuguese traders entering the continent created the occidental trade in captives to the north and eventually the New World.[27] Just as the trade in gold reached its height after the construction of São Jorge da Mina, Christopher Columbus's landing in the New World increased the value of captives, once second to gold to a top priority. The value of Africans increased after European traders realized the possible profits from New World territories.[28] The need for labor in the New World was critical to the trade in Africans across the Atlantic Ocean as the enterprise began boom in the coming years after Columbus' landing. Between 1471 and 1518, not only did the role of Africa, Europe and the New World change, but the role of the Gold Coast in particular shifted from being an exporter of gold and an importer of captives to mainly an exporter of captives. This change was due in part to the increase in value and creation of labor intensive sugar plantations being developed in the recently discovered "New World" territories.

This relationship was highly dependent first on the construction of forts, both fortified and unfortified, which were particularly useful to the gold trade. The emergence of a plantation system between the sixteenth and seventeenth centuries created even more competition for West Africa and, in particular, the Gold Coast as the region was brought into the exportation of captives business. This brought a number of Europeans nations to the area; the Portuguese were followed by the Danes, French, Swedes, Dutch and, later, the English. As a result of this high competition for the area, a total of forty-six forts were built along the coastline through the seventeenth century.[29] In due course, these forts constructed along the Gold Coast coastline, first used to trade gold later shifted to other necessities, namely captives, as the plantation economy expanded; the region thereafter was directly seen as an exporter or supplier of captives.

The need for captives only expanded with Christopher Columbus, sailing across the Atlantic Ocean into the New World territory in 1492 landing in what today encompasses Haiti and the Dominican Republic. This initial landing, coupled with the construction of São Jorge da Mina in 1482, expanded the global trade network across the Atlantic Ocean. This also set the stage for a global trading network that in the coming centuries linked four continents and numerous groups throughout each location to one another. Commodities, which European traders coming to the Gold Coast, once only shipped between the coastal territory and Europe in the sixteenth century, were then being transported across the Atlantic Ocean.

Not only did the arrival of Christopher Columbus in the Americas create an expanded global trading network, it also brought about a conflict between two nations, Spain and Portugal. This international conflict put both Africa and the Americas at the forefront of an economic dispute between the two nations. As the world's only two naval powers, both viewed the new territory and Africa as vital to the economic prowess and survival of their country into the next century. The Catholic Church headed by Pope Alexander VI issued a Papal Bull,[30] referred to as the Treaty of Tordesillas in 1494, dividing the world between the two nations. In order for Spain to claim this New World territory, the Pope stated, "To secure the benefits of discovering they must be possessed, that is occupied."[31] This treaty ultimately settled disputes between the two countries over the region, but left other European nations out of the discussion. Although the true extent of the landmass encompassing the New World was still unknown during these disputes over the territory, Pope Alexander VI handed Spain both North America and parts of South America and the Portuguese claims to Africa, and the area of New World that later became known as Brazil.[32]

Immediately after landing in the New World, the Spanish crown began to take advantage of the indigenous population of the territory, using them in a number of capacities including agriculture and mining. Furthermore, the population was reduced by the harsh impact of war and labor as well as the introduction of European diseases such as influenza, typhus, yellow fever, measles and syphilis, in which all impacted the local population but more fell victim to small pox than any other. Although the overall drop in numbers of the indigenous population continues to be debated among historians of European, Latin and Caribbean History, the number most recently suggested lay between 200,000 and 1,200,000, and as result of these outside factors this number was reduced to a mere 62,000.[33]

Twenty years after the arrival of Columbus in Hispaniola and issuing of the Treaty of Tordesillas by Pope Alexander VI, Father Bartholomew Las Casas, also a member of the Catholic Church called for the introduction of African labor into the region. The introduction of African labor came after the indigenous population had been decimated by both diseases and overwork due to the demands of the Europeans for the various goods of the area. The first group of Africans arrived in 1518 immediately setting in course a chain reaction. The reaction to the landing of the first groups of Africans set in motion the transportation and distribution of African captives throughout vast regions of the "New World," eventually comprising of areas from as far North as the New England states of America to the southern tip of South America. The landing of Columbus and the years immediately following his arrival served as a starting point for the foundation and emergence of a global system of trade regulated by mercantilism which transitioned into capitalism, and finally European colonial domination of Africa.[34]

Between 1471 and 1518, relying heavily on forts along the West African coast once used for gold trading, the global trade network linked Europe, Africa and the emerging territories of the Americas. Initially traveling to the West African coast in search of gold, ivory, spices and other goods, almost thirty years after Columbus' landing, African captives became the chief commodity sought after by Europeans, thus signaling the transition to labor being the main and most lucrative commodity leaving Africa. The period of trade and exploration forever changed the course of history for several continents and people.

Portuguese expansion, first into West Africa and later following the Spanish into the New World, in particular to the modern day continent of South America, brought about monumental changes, especially in the need for African labor. These epic changes influenced Europe, West Africa and, eventually, both South and North America as well. The start of Africans being shipped across the Atlantic Ocean helped shift the center of the economic world from the Muslim stronghold of West Africa, to Europe and its new territories in the New World. These changes affecting the entire world occurred over eighty years, beginning first with the Portuguese decision to search West Africa for gold. Changes continued to occur worldwide after the landing of Columbus and once again after the introduction of Africans into the New World territories, especially those of the Caribbean.[35]

The Gold Coast became critical to the labor supply being shipped to the New World. Ray A. Kea discussed the importation of captives in the Gold Coast by writing:

> From the beginning, slavery and slave trading played crucial roles in the Afro-European commerce that developed in the Gold Coast. Indeed, from 1475 to 1540, more than 12,000 people passed through its coastal ports as human commodities. These, however, were not slave exports from the region. Rather, people were among the goods that African merchants wanted to buy from their new Portuguese trading partners.[36]

As the Gold Coast transitioned to being an exporter of captives to the New World territories, Ray A. Kea continues by saying, "After . . . slave imports declined . . . forts such as Elmina and Axim continued to be major slave markets for slaves brought into the Gold Coast. During the seventeenth century between forty thousand and eight thousand slaves entered the region via the coastal ports."[37] Although the region became an exporter of captives, it still was not the largest exporter of captives.

Just as the demand for African captives increased so too did the export of coffee, indigo, sugar, tobacco and cotton from the Americas to Europe. The development of this overseas commercial empire across the Atlantic

Ocean became largely dependent on the continuing cycle of labor imported commodities exported.[38] This global phenomenon escalated even further, especially after the French, Dutch and British following the Spanish and Portuguese expanded into the Americas in the 1600s.

Over the first two hundred years from 1450s through the 1650s, West Africa's commerce was largely determined by products such as gold, ivory, wood, with only a small number of captives being taken outside the continent.[39] During this early era of trading, Spanish and Portuguese were the only nations trading between Africa and the New World, with the latter holding a monopoly over the supply of captives transported from Africa. By 1543, with the introduction of the asiento system, the Spanish were able to make contracts with Portuguese traders to deliver a specified number of Africans into the Spanish New World territories, often times 500 with one third being sold for the benefit of the crown.[40]

Furthermore, between 1630 and 1645, several conflicts over the fort, São Jorge da Mina or Elmina Castle constructed in 1486, occurred between traders and settlers of Portuguese and Dutch descent. The Dutch captured portions of Brazil from the Portuguese in 1630 which began their early participation in the transporting of Africans into the Americas. Eventually, the Dutch were also able to acquire the Portuguese stronghold, São Jorge da Mina, which became the first of many fort exchanges on the Gold Coast between European nations. This acquisition of prime coastal trading real estate during the sixteenth century became a key feature to the Dutch expansion of trading into West Africa for the next two hundred years. Moreover, by 1650, the new Atlantic Economic Order emerged, and people of African descent were instrumental in the export of commodities from the various West African regions to areas of the Americas and back to the Europe.[41]

In describing the growth of the Dutch trade during the period, William H. Worger, Nancy L. Clark and Edward A. Alpers write:

> During the seventeenth century, Dutch traders expanded aggressively into the international seaborne trade, driving the Portuguese from many of their bases in West and East Africa, the Indian subcontinent, and Southeast Asia. They wrested much of Brazil from Portuguese control in 1630 (though they were driven out in 1654) and established their own sugar plantations in the Caribbean. In search of slaves for their plantations and making considerable profits as suppliers of slaves to other European settlers, the Dutch had their main base at Elmina (in present day Ghana), which they had seized from the Portuguese in 1637.[42]

This decision to go after the Portuguese fort of Elmina was coupled with the expanding presence of Dutch traders in the Americas who began the era of their dominance over international trading. With the growing population of

Europeans in Africa and the Americas, an Atlantic economy was developing, which finally overshadowed the Trans-Saharan Trade routes, and the Dutch were at the forefront of this development.

During the height of the Dutch slave trade from the Gold Coast, slave trader William Bosman worked as head of Dutch trading from Elmina.[43] William Bosman in his work *A New and Accurate Description of the Coast of Guinea Divided into the Gold, the Slave, and the Ivory Coasts* describes the Dutch involvement in the region of Elmina. In his description of the region he writes:

> Famous throughout the World: its takes its Name from the Town, but why the Portuguese who were its Baptizers, gave it this Name, I cannot determine; for no Gold Mines are found for several Miles . . . but if I may guess . . . it was because here they found a great affluence of Gold from all Parts . . . might probably induce them to give it this Name. . . . I cannot pretend to inform you exactly when they began to build the Castle, but can only tell you that we took it from them in 1638 . . .[44]

Furthermore, he continues by describing the outlay of both the castles and the town of the Elmina. (See Figure 1.1.) He refers to the outlay of the castle as one of beauty and strength with very high walls, four batteries, a place to store water for use and room for 200 or so men. Albeit, he also describes the homes surrounding the castle as being built of both clay and wood, and although small pox killed so many the town was still populous.[45] Today, Elmina still stands, just as Bosman described it some 400 years later, high walls, solid stone and European style homes still surrounding the castle.

Capturing Elmina in 1638, only five days after the fighting began, the Dutch were able to formally take over the castle and began making immediate changes which resulted in captives being bought for labor on their plantations in Brazil.[46] Only miles down the coast, at Cape Coast Castle, the Dutch were also able increase their influence. Similar to happenings at Elmina, the Dutch also managed to gain control of Cape Coast Castle in 1663, from the Swedes in hopes of keeping both Portuguese and English traders out of the region. In a matter of thirty years, the Dutch were able to become the most dominant European nation along the Gold Coast, taking the place of the Portuguese. John Barbot gives a description of Cape Coast based upon his observations during his travels to the region. (See Figure 1.2.) His description suggests that Cape Coast itself was smaller than Elmina, but still contained some 500 houses and its population was only reduced as a result of the earlier Komenda Wars.[47]

Although both traded goods on a large scale, they were overshadowed in terms of trade by the Dutch port of Mouri and Fort Nassau. The settlement

Figure 1.1 William Bosman Map of Elmina. *Source*: William Bosman, *A New and Accurate Description of the Coast of Guinea, Divided into the Gold, the Slave, and the Ivory Coasts*, Letter III (London: James Knapton, 1705), p. 41.

was smaller than both Elmina and Cape Coast in terms of population but trade was much more prosperous according to Bosman. This left the Dutch in control of Fort St. Sebastian, Fort St. Anthony, Elmina, Fort Nassau and Cape Coast Castle to name a few of the locations.[48] Prior to capturing Elmina many Dutch who were living along the coastline, calling this region home, were employed as fishermen leaving their residences each morning to work, paying tolls to the Dutch governor along the way.[49]

Figure 1.2 Jean Barbot Map of Elmina. *Source*: Jean Barbot, *A Description of the Coasts of North and South Guinea* (London: Henry Lintot and John Osborn, 1746) in James Kwesi Anquandah, *Castles and Forts of Ghana* (Ghana Museums and Monuments Board: Atalante, Paris, 1999), p. 59.

Apart from joining the overseas commercial exchange, the dutch were also involved, the creation of the Dutch West India Company. Between 1629 and 1674, the Dutch West Indian Company transported goods to Dutch settlers in Africa and the American territories. Even after losing their portions of Brazil, the Dutch West India Company continued to trade in captives long after, as the need for labor in their Caribbean territories still remained and the Gold Coast and West Africa provided a steady supply of labor. In 1662, the company gained an asiento from the Spanish crown, supplying captives to all Spanish territories in the Americas before eventually going bankrupt in 1674. In the aftermath of wars fought between the Dutch, the French and the English, a second West India Company was created, which held a monopoly until it surrendered all its territories except the Gold Coast in the 1730s, where the Dutch remained productive until the middle of the nineteenth century.[50]

In hopes of extending its presence and influence along the Gold Coast after acquiring Portuguese forts and territories, both the first and second Dutch West India Companies each set forth plans for its colonists to grow and export their own crops. This included crops such as: sugar, tobacco, indigo and cotton. Just as the Asante were emerging within the interior of the Gold Coast, the Dutch were able to plant and export cotton at a successful rate.

The Dutch began to force many other Europeans out, namely Danish traders in the region of the Gold Coast. Although trying to push all other Europeans out, the Dutch, viewed the Danish as the weakest of all groups and when they were ready, the Danish were easier to remove. For some time this strategy proved effective until King Fetu's army attacked the Dutch fort at Carolusburg. The Swedish and the Swedish Africa Company quickly moved in and purchased the fort and began trading. Upset about its loss, the Dutch paid local Africans to attack the fort in 1663 setting the stage for a bidding war between the Dutch and English.[51]

Between 1664 and 1665 as both the British and the Dutch increased their New World possessions, their competition also increased on the Gold Coast as well. In two years, Koromantin, an English trading center fell, and they gained control of Cape Coast Castle. To challenge English growth on the Gold Coast, the Dutch acquired Koromantin, changing its name to Fort Amsterdam, as well as built Fort Coenraadsburg. By 1672, the Dutch were engaged in naval wars with both the French and the English setting the stage for financial difficulties.[52]

Even through these difficulties, the Dutch remained competitive on the Gold Coast, building Fort Orange and Sekondi in the 1670s, the Komenda Wars ultimately allowed the Dutch and British to make headway among the local population. This influence was the greatest among the Akan, allowing Europeans ultimately to play a role in shaping the politics and people of the region immensely.[53]

Nevertheless, the British also carved out its niche both on the Gold Coast and in the Caribbean territory. Queen Elizabeth, in 1565, gave John Hawkins permission to make the first British voyage to the New World and in four years he made three voyages. These voyages expanded the British sphere of influence and increased the labor intensification plantations in the Caribbean and in the North American territories. British traders coming to the New World were largely funded by joint stock companies, whose founders were involved in the political and economic well-being of Britain.[54] As the population of the British colonies increased, the plantation system also grew placing a demand on West African captives. The British further developed their growing interest in the emerging world market by expanding its reach in the Americas, Caribbean and, on the Gold Coast. Furthermore, the escalation of sugar production in the Caribbean islands also greatly impacted the role of Africans in the growing European economic system. This again was altered after the American war for independence, also known as the American Revolution.[55]

British colonies, in its early years were largely supplied with goods and captives by the Company of Royal Adventures. With the growth of the British population, merchants, traders and planters pushed to break up the companies' monopoly on trade.[56] The growth of the British plantation system in the Caribbean and the expansion as well as the establishment of British colonies in North America put increased pressure on the Gold Coast to supply labor. The acquisition of African labor on the Gold Coast was aided by a number of British merchants who set up permanent residences and trading post in the region. In its early stages, one of the most influential British merchants in the Gold Coast was Nicholas Crispe and his family. Between 1625 and 1666, Crispe, financed much of the British trading on the Gold Coast, first using the area of Kromantin as a headquarters before ultimately changing to Cape Coast Castle in 1665.[57]

Even though very few African states and its people were involved in the growing Atlantic economy, even fewer actually benefited from this trade in goods.[58] Forts built to trade in gold became much more important to the trade in captives by the start of the seventeenth and eighteenth centuries. Although forts and castles built along the West African coastline played a role in global trading, those erected along the Gold Coast were critical in the start of the gold trade, and later in the development of the Trans-Atlantic Slave Trade. Early traders coming into the Gold Coast often carried captives north first into European countries and eventually west into the New World. While the Trans-Atlantic Slave Trade spans four hundred years (1511–1888), the construction of forts along the Gold Coast began prior to the start of the trade itself. Construction of these castles covers the first three hundred years (1482–1768), and encompasses the entire coastline of the region from its furthest Western point, Appollonia, to the furthest Eastern point, Crepe Aquamoo and Adampee.

Several European nations following the lead of the Portuguese took a meticulous interest in the Gold Coast by building forts for trade along the West African coastline. Over a three-hundred-year span, stretching the coastline of the Gold Coast, forts were built by the Danish, French, British, Dutch, Portuguese and Swedes. (See Figure 1.3.) Many of these forts, initially built to discover a sea route to the East or for the trade in gold and other items found on the Gold Coast, afterward became centers of trade for European nations seeking to expand their influence in Africa.[59] These forts are linked

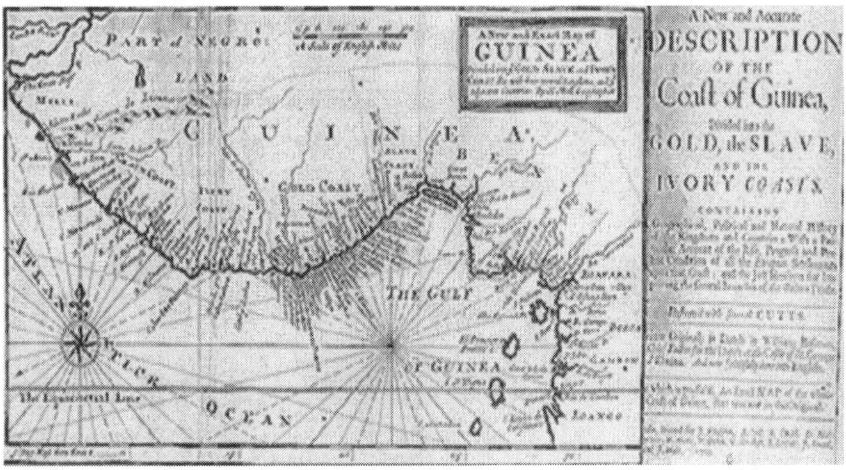

Figure 1.3 William Bosman Map of Guinia Coast. *Source*: William Bosman, *A New and Accurate Description of the Coast of Guinea, Divided into the Gold, the Slave, and the Ivory Coasts* (London: James Knapton 1705).

directly to expansion of the European sphere of influence, the growth of a worldwide economy and eventually the transportation of Africans across the Atlantic Ocean. The Gold Coast proved especially valuable as the coastline had numerous locations where ports where easily accessible by ship. Over a three-hundred year period some eighty different types of fortifications were built along the Gold Coast beginning with the Portuguese.[60]

Among the forts built on the Gold Coast, several of those key locations included: São Jorge da Mina or Elmina Castle (1482; See Figure 1.4), Fort St. Anthony-Axim (1515), Fort St. Sebastian-Shama (1520s), Fort Amsterdam-Cormantin (1638), Cape Coast Castle (1653; see Figure 1.5), Fort Batenstein (1656), Christanborg Castle (1661), Fort St. Jago Coenraadsburg-Elmina (1660s), Fort Orange-Sekondi (1670s), Friedrichsburg (1683), Fort Metal

Figure 1.4 São Jorge da Mina or Elmina Castle. Photo provided by author.

Figure 1.5 Inside Cape Coast Castle. Photo provided by author.

Cross-Dixicove (1692), Fort Patience (1697), Fort Good Hope (1705), Fort William (1753) and Fort Apollonia (1768).[61] Each of these forts changed hands among European nations several times between the years 1482–1872. The construction and maintenance of these forts over several centuries becomes all the more important with the growth of international trade between the three continents of Africa, Europe and the Americas.

During the 1600s, the earliest years of the growing Atlantic commercial system, the Gold Coast, watched as European nations fought over prime locations in the region and forts already built. As the Trans-Atlantic Slave expanded due to the growing plantation system in North and South America as well as the Caribbean territories, the Gold Coast saw a rise in the exportation of captives leaving the area (see Table 1.1). During the seventeenth-century scramble for the coastline of Africa, on the Gold Coast, the Dutch, Danes and English divided parts of the region between themselves. Three castles, Cape Coast Castle (British), Elmina (Dutch) and Christiansborg (Danish) served as their headquarters of trade, with several forts in between maintained by these nations.[62]

Although, The Dutch and other European nations remained on the Gold Coast; the British quickly became the chief traders in the region, through its contacts with the local population as well as the African who returned to the Gold Coast after attending schools in London. With the emergence of the Ashanti (Asante) in 1701, the relationship with Europeans in the region, over trading and political rights to land was tested like never before, resulting in the highest numbers of captives being transported from the Gold Coast than any of the previous centuries of the Trans-Atlantic Slave Trade from the region.

Long before the arrival of European nations, West Africa had been for centuries involved in long-distance trading connecting a number of people and regions of the world together, both over land and across water. Several kingdoms nations sent traders to the region first to obtain gold and ultimately captives, both of which were seemingly limitless in its supply. This network stretching across the continent of Africa both east and north developed into the Trans-Saharan Trade, establishing commercial centers and towns along its routes, as well as bringing the Arabic language and Islam into the region. The Trans-Saharan Trade created routes stretching from Northern Africa into West Africa and Iberian Peninsula, that for over seven centuries people used to obtain commodities. This link tied the region and its largest kingdoms, Ghana, Mali and Songhay as well as its smaller developing states to their Southern border, with the world that was beginning to take notice of the wealth West Africa possessed.

Just as the influence and dominance of large West African empires began to decline, and the states closer to the coastline began to emerge as the key

Table 1.1 Seventeenth-Century Captive Exportation from the Gold Coast

	Europe		*Mainland North America*		*British Caribbean*		*French Caribbean*		*Dutch Americas*	
	Embarked	*Disembarked*	*Embarked*	*Disembarked*	*Embarked*	*Disembarked*	*Embarked*	*Disembarked*	*Embarked*	*Disembarked*
1619–1620	0	0	0	0	0	0	0	0	0	0
1641–1650	0	0	0	0	1674	1398	0	0	0	0
1651–1660	0	0	0	0	0	0	0	0	0	0
1661–1670	682	576	0	0	15082	11923	376	323	1836	1576
1671–1680	0	0	726	568	18252	14241	1829	1524	7690	6509
1681–1690	0	0	0	0	9682	6991	0	0	4574	3839
1691–1700	0	0	0	0	25139	19750	1287	856	2916	2437
Total	**682**	**576**	**726**	**568**	**69828**	**54304**	**3492**	**2703**	**17016**	**14361**

	Danish West Indies		*Spanish Americas*		*Brazil*		*Total*	
	Embarked	*Disembarked*	*Embarked*	*Disembarked*	*Embarked*	*Disembarked*	*Embarked*	*Disembarked*
1619–1620	0	0	68	48	0	0	**68**	**48**
1641–1650	0	0	0	0	755	642	**2429**	**2040**
1651–1660	0	0	364	316	376	323	**740**	**639**
1661–1670	0	0	0	0	1217	1067	**19193**	**15465**
1671–1680	0	0	338	291	0	0	**28835**	**23133**
1681–1690	0	0	351	268	1667	1434	**16274**	**12532**
1691–1700	2707	2140	930	643	7465	6784	**40443**	**32609**
Total	**2707**	**2140**	**2052**	**1565**	**11480**	**10250**	**107982**	**86467**

Source: David Eltis et al., *TheTrans-Atlantic Slave Trade Voyages Database*, http://slavevoyages.org/tast/assessment/estimates.faces?yearFrom=1619&yearTo=1700&embarkation=4 (Accessed November 25, 2010.

providers of commodities, Portuguese traders made landfall in Western Africa. In only a matter of years after their reaching West Africa, the Gold Coast became a crucial location to the expansion of the Portuguese sphere of influence and its expansion in Africa. As other European countries entered Africa before finally crossing the Atlantic Ocean into the New World, they too saw the Gold Coast as a key link to the growth of their economies into a growing international market. The arrival of the Portuguese explorers and traders in West Africa and the region they referred to as the Gold Coast serves as a turning point in history. This marks a transition in long standing trading partnerships which crossed the Sahara Desert and sets the stage for the emergence of an ever-expanding and growing Atlantic commercial system at the turn of the century.

NOTES

1. Paul E. Lovejoy, *Transformations in Slavery: A History of Slavery in Africa*, 2nd ed. (New York: Cambridge University Press, 2000), p. 36.
2. Ibid.
3. M. Malowist, "The Struggle for International Trade and its Implications for Africa." In Bethwell A. Ogot, ed., *General History of Africa: Africa from the Sixteen to the Eighteenth Century*, Vol. V (Berkley, CA: United Nations Educational, Scientific and Cultural Organization, 1992), p. 7.
4. J. D. Fage, *An Introduction to the History of West Africa* (Cambridge: Cambridge University Press, 1959), pp. 44–45.
5. Basil Davidson, *Black Mother: The Years of the African Slave Trade* (Boston, MA: Little Publishers, 1961), pp. 35–40.
6. Hugh Thomas, *The Slave Trade: The Story of the Atlantics Slave Trade: 1440–1870* (New York: Simon and Schuster Paperbacks, 1997), p. 59
7. Cape Three Points is located just to the east of Elmina and stretches to Cape Palamas. See: Thomas, 345.
8. Ibid., 346.
9. Ibid., 345–347.
10. Robert Smith, "The Canoe in West African History," *The Journal of African History*, Vol. 11, No. 4 (1970), pp. 515–517.
11. Ato Ashun, *Elmina, The Castle and the Slave Trade* (Cape Coast, Ghana: Nyakod Printing Works, 2004), p. 6.
12. James Kwesi Anquandah, *Castles and Forts of Ghana* (Ghana Museums and Monuments Board: Atalante, Paris, 1999), p. 52.
13. Walter Rodney, "Gold and Slaves on the Gold Coast," *Transactions of the Historical Society of Ghana*, Vol. 10 (1969), pp. 13–14.
14. Stephanie E. Smallwood, *Saltwater Slavery: A Middle Passage from Africa to American Diaspora* (Cambridge, MA: Harvard University Press, 2007), p. 15.

15. Saidiya Hartman, *Lose Your Mother: A Journey Along the Atlantic Slave Route* (New York: Farrar, Straus and Giroux, 2007), p. 51.

16. Bayo Holsey, *Routes of Remembrance: Refashioning the Slave Trade in Ghana* (Chicago, IL: University of Chicago Press, 2008), p. 29.

17. Anquandah, 52.

18. Holsey, 29.

19. Alfred Burdon Ellis, *A History of the Gold Coast of West Africa* (London: Chapman and Hall, LD, 1893), pp. 25–26.

20. Anquandah, 53.

21. Ellis, 26.

22. Richard Bean, "A Note on the Relative Importance of Slave and Gold in West African Exports," *The Journal of African History*, Vol. 15, No. 3 (1974), pp. 351–352.

23. Ibid., 352.

24. Ellis, 27.

25. Each European nation arriving on the Gold Coast claimed specific points along the coastline as their own. These areas included the Dutch Gold Coast, the British Gold Coast, the Danish Gold Coast and Portuguese Gold Coast.

26. James K. Anquandah, "Researching the Historic Slave Trade in Ghana-An Overview." In *The Trans-Atlantic Slave Trade: Landmarks, Legacies, Expectations, Proceedings of the International Conference on Historic Slave Route Held at Accra, Ghana on 30 August-2 September, 2004*, ed. James K. Anquandah (Legon, Accra, Ghana: Sub-Saharan Publishers, 2007), p. 27.

27. Patrick Manning, *Slavery and African Life: Occidental, Oriental and African Slave Trades* (New York: Cambridge University Press, 1990), p. 12.

28. Ibid., 32.

29. Magnus Huber, *Ghanaian Pidgin English in its West African Context: A Socio-historical and Structural Analysis* (Philadelphia, PA: John Benjamins Publishing, 1999), p. 9.

30. Arthur Davis, "Columbus Divides the World," *The Geographical Journal*, Vol. 133, No. 3 (September, 1967), p. 3.

31. Ibid.

32. Ibid.

33. Peter Bakewell, *A History of Latin America to 1825*, 3rd ed. (United Kingdom: Wiley-Blackwell, 2010), pp. 110–111.

34. John Henrik Clarke, *Christopher Columbus and the Afrikan Holocaust: Slavery and the Rise of European Capitalism*, 3rd ed. (Brooklyn, NY: A & B Publishers Group, 1998), p. 15.

35. Eric Williams, *Capitalism and Slavery*, 2nd ed. (Chapel Hill, NC: University of North Carolina Press, 1994), p. 9.

36. Ray A. Kea, *Settlements, Trade, and Polities in the Seventeenth-Century Gold Coast* (Baltimore, MD: John Hopkins University Press, 1982), 197 in Stephanie E. Smallwood, *Saltwater Slavery: A Middle Passage from Africa to the American Diaspora* (Cambridge, MA: Harvard University Press, 2007), p. 15.

37. Ray A. Kea, *Settlements, Trade and Polities in the Seventeenth-Century Gold Coast* (Baltimore, MD: John Hopkins University Press, 1982), pp. 197–201 in Robert

Harms, *The Diligent: A Voyage Through the Worlds of the Slave Trade* (New York: Basic Books, 2002), p. 135.

38. James A. Rawley and Stephen D. Behrendt, *The Trans-Atlantic Slave Trade: A History*, Revised Edition (Lincoln, NE: University of Nebraska, 2005), p. 3.

39. Joseph Inikori, "Changing Commodity Composition of Imports into West Africa, 1650–1850." In *The Trans-Atlantic Slave Trade: Landmarks, Legacies, Expectations, Proceedings of the International Conference on Historic Slave Route Held at Accra, Ghana on 30 August–2 September, 2004*, ed. James K. Anquandah (Legon, Accra, Ghana: Sub-Saharan Publishers, 2007), p. 59.

40. Linda A. Newson and Susie Minchin, *From Capture to Sale: The Portuguese Slave Trade to Spanish South America in the Early Seventeenth Century* (Netherlands: Hotei Publishing, 2007), p. 20.

41. Joseph Inikori, "Slavery and Atlantic Commerce, 1650–1800," *The American Economic Review*, Vol. 82, No. 2 (May, 1992), pp. 151–152.

42. William H. Worger, Nancy L. Clark and Edward A. Alpers, *African and the West: A Documentary History, Vol. 1 From The Slave Trade to Conquest, 1441–1905*, 2nd ed. (New York: Oxford University Press, 2010), p. 49.

43. William L. Bosman is one of the most analyzed slave traders of the period. Since 1974, his book, William L. Bosman, *A New and Accurate Description of the Coast of Guinea*, has been challenged by a number of scholars in history including Albert van Dantzig and Ivor Wilks, claiming he had an alternate agenda and his description of the African coast is not accurate.

44. William Bosman, *A New and Accurate Description of the Coast of Guinea, Divided into the Gold, the Slave, and the Ivory Coasts*, Letter III (London: James Knapton, 1705), pp. 41–42.

45. Ibid., 42–43.

46. Robin Blackburn, *The Making of New World Slavery: From the Baroque to the Modern, 1492–1800* (New York,: Verso Books, 1997), p. 195. Under Portuguese control the fort maintained religious sanctuary above the captive pens. Under Dutch control this religious practices were conducted in the center of the fort.

47. John Barbot, *A Description of the Coasts of North and South Guinea*, Letter IV (London, 1746) in Kwamina B. Dickinson, *A Historical Geography of Ghana* (New York: Cambridge University Press, 1969), p. 67.

48. Albert van Dantzig, *Forts and Castles of Ghana* (Accra, Ghana: Sedco Publishing, 1999), p. 18.

49. William Bosman, *A New and Accurate Description of the Coast of Guinea, Divided into the Gold, the Slave, and the Ivory Coasts*, Letter IV (London: James Knapton, 1705), pp. 55–56.

50. Johannes Postma, "The Dimension of the Dutch Slave Trade from Western Africa," *The Journal of African History*, Vol. 13, No. 2 (1972), pp. 238–246.

51. George Norregard, *Danish Settlements in West Africa, 1658–1850* (Boston, MA: Boston University Press, 1966), pp. 19–20.

52. Van Dantzig, 35–36.

53. Kwasi Kondadu, *The Akan Diaspora in the Americas* (New York: Oxford University Press, 2010), p. 70.

54. Ronald Pollitt, "John Hawkins Troublesome Voyages: Merchants, Bureaucrats, and the Origin of the Slave Trade," *Journal of British Studies*, Vol. 12, No. 2 (May, 1973), pp. 26–40.

55. Selwyn H. H. Carrington, "The American Revolution and the British West Indies' Economy," *Journal of Interdisciplinary History*, Vol. 17, No. 4 (Spring, 1987), p. 824.

56. Williams, 30–31.

57. R. Porter, "The Crispe Family and the African Trade in the Seventeenth Century," *The Journal of African History*, Vol. 9, No. 1 (1968), pp. 61–65.

58. Africans lack of benefit from early trading with Europeans and its impact during the colonial years is discussed in detail by Walter Rodney's book, *How Europe Underdeveloped Africa* (Washington, DC: Howard University Press, 1982).

59. Harvey M. Feinberg, *Africans and Europeans in West Africa: Elminans and Dutchmen on the Gold Coast During the Eighteenth Century* (Philadelphia, PA: The American Philosophical Society, 1989), p. 2.

60. James Kwesi Anquandah, *Castles and Forts of Ghana* (Ghana Museums and Monuments Board: Atalante, Paris, 1999), p. 20.

61. James Anquandah's work is a short history of several prominent castles located in Ghana today. See: James Kwesi Anquandah, *Castles and Forts of Ghana* (Ghana Museums and Monuments Board: Atalante, Paris, 1999), pp. 24–96.

62. William St. Clair, *The Door of No Return: The History of Cape Coast Castle and the Atlantic Slave Trade* (New York: Bluebridge Press, 2007), p. 34.

Chapter 2

The Akan and the Formation of the Asante State

The reorganization of several Akan interior and coastal peoples and eventual formation of the Asante state caused a restructuring of trading across the region and ultimately throughout the entirety of the Gold Coast. This restructuring of indigenous peoples and states in the interior forest zone territory in both the seventeenth and eighteenth centuries impacted trade with European countries for several years after this process got underway. Furthermore, the most noticeable impact witnessed during this restructuring was on the Trans-Atlantic Slave Trade which was well under way from the Gold Coast when the Akan and Asante were experiencing their reorganization in the latter half of the seventeenth century. An analysis of the Akan and the eventual formation of the Asante people will show their role first in the history of the Gold Coast, second their impact on the other states in the region and finally their influence on the emerging global economy of the seventeenth and eighteenth centuries. Albeit, the region's impact stretched across West Africa to include areas of Europe and the developing colonies of the Caribbean, South America and North America. Therefore, the Asante state in the seventeenth, eighteenth and later the nineteenth centuries, after their formation, had a significant impact on trading partnerships established in the region, and should be viewed as a highly advanced state with strong political and economic ties.

With the continued arrival of each European nation and the constant construction of forts, the coastline experienced its own economic changeover during the centuries. Moreover, the changeover which impacted the coastline was a separate experience from that of the interior forest zone, which occurred in phases over two separate transitions; first during the early migrations of people to the region and secondly during the reorganization of the Akan beginning in the seventeenth century. In particular, the forest zone region witnessed numerous changes and transformations due in part to the high number of people entering the interior from all directions along with expansion of political and economic influence from emerging states. As these people converged on the forest zone they brought along with them culture and ideas, all of which had an immediate impact on the interior region during these centuries. Nonetheless, the changes experienced in later centuries were numerous but not unlike those which occurred in the same region between 700 and 1000 AD, also due in part to an increase of people entering and moving throughout the vast interior forest zone.

The early alterations between 700 and 1000 AD were based upon migrations into the hinterland and the development of a new advanced system of political and economic life which is much earlier than scholars such as Ivor Wilks suggests. Albeit, the continued development of these political and economic conditions within the forest zone in the later centuries also had an immediate effect on those who came into contact with peoples of the various states. Unlike the alterations to Gold Coast economy and region, which were discussed in the previous chapter, occurring along the coastline due to the arrival of Europeans in the fifteenth century, the interior zone was completely uninhabited by foreigners from outside Africa. Nonetheless, during this early era, European contact with the interior forest zone was done through middlemen who were in trade agreements with along the coastline. Moreover, the interior region remained off limits to European traders until well after the start of eighteenth and nineteenth centuries when the first outsiders began treks into the forest zone and establish their own trade partnerships. Therefore, the changes which occurred in the interior region of the Gold Coast before and after the start of eighteenth century were based solely upon the movement of indigenous people, culture, religion and the continual development of a political and economic institution from within the hinterland.

Furthermore, many of these changes which occurred in the forest zone were underscored by the arrival of earliest Akan settlers, known as the Oyoko and their constant movement throughout the region. This initial group of Oyoko states, the Mampon, Dwaben, Kokofu, Kekwai and Nsuta, in the vicinity of Kumasi shared borders with their neighbors, Adanse, Esumegya Ejisu and Offinsu.[1] These early travelers consisted largely of a loose confederation of states stretching from the hinterland to the coastline. The former mentioned states shared a common language with one another, twi, as well as economic linkages, a similar political system and were a part of the ruling families of the Oyoko. As the states continuously grew throughout the centuries, these ruling families were important to the later transition experienced in the seventeenth century. Nonetheless, these loose states were each within four thousand square miles of one another with the capital of each sitting within a thirty five mile radius of Kuamsi, a central trading city.[2] Centuries later, several of these states were consolidated under the power and direction of Oseit Tutu, the first Asantehene of the Asante state after its creation.[3]

As variations continued to occur within many of indigenous populations of the Gold Coast, the evolving Akan people who called the forest zone home were able to make a significant impact on the economy of the interior region. As the economy of interior began to expand, this resulted in an increase in both trade over routes and waterways, the use of captive labor and the transition from hunting and gathering state to one based upon a sedentary life. Choosing to call one place home also leads to greater forms of protection, new modes of production and growth of its population, which impacts the internal economy and continuously develops the political system. Albeit, this impact on the economy stretched to the north, east, west and south toward the coastline before influencing the global economy with the arrival of Europeans. Although much of this changeover began before the development of the Asante state, their eventual establishment in the later stages of seventeenth century continued to build upon the political and economic transition the region began experiencing with the arrival of the earliest Akan in the forest zone.

With many changes continuing to occur to the interior region due to constant migration, variations to trade patterns and partnerships, the growing presence of Europeans along the coastline caused several more internal shifts as the forest zone states altered their trading routes to take advantage of this new opportunity and partner. Although new paths emerged in several directions to account for the changes on the coastline, the interior economy thrived in the previous centuries. Combining changes experienced along the coastline with those among the hinterland areas shows the interior region and its growing population of indigenous and foreign people were in a prime position to enter the growing commercial economy of West Africa and the Americas. Most importantly, their access to the most sought after items, particularly gold and later captives, made the interior forest zone a lucrative trading partner. Furthermore, these changes which occurred were not only strengthened by the emergence of the Akan but also the eventual expansion of the Asante at the latter stages of the eighteenth century.

As groups trekked into the hinterland, the Oyoko or early Akan were not only in a position which allowed them to trade in all directions, including toward the coastline, they were also protected from any outside invasion due to their location. Seemingly, the forest zone acted as a natural barrier allowing the interior people access to the most fertile land in region and keeping unwanted visitors out. Throughout the interior, numerous fortifications were found which allowed people use these hills and forests to create defensible sites proving warfare had become a common threat in the region.[4] The Akan upon their formation in the forest zone in the fifteenth century made particular use of this natural defensive system to protect themselves from enemies trying to invade the region. Kumasi itself was situated atop a rocky hill surrounded by fertile soil and a natural forest which allowed the region to stay relatively mosquito free, providing a healthy environment for those leaving in the region.[5]

This natural dense barrier while providing protection to the fast developing states also proved to be a defender of trade routes and traders which only those calling the region home could navigate in the earliest centuries. Albeit, those within the region in the earliest years of eleventh century were able to successfully establish a trading link to the north and in the coming centuries these links stretched in each direction from the interior. This trading network to the north with those on the edge of the Sahara Desert was heavily dependent on commodities such as kola nuts grown in the interior and salt from the coastline. Moreover, kola a stimulant and one of the most valuable goods and an important economic crop and salt used in food preservation were viewed as key commodities in trade to the north.[6]

With trading beginning to increase from the interior region, the push for a consolidation of power by the ruling elite of the Oyoko was well under way. This process entered a new stage by the latter half of the seventeenth century as the Akan was in the process of reorganization and the Asante were being established as a dominant interior state. Ivor Wilks, whose numerous works on the Akan and the Asante are heavily critiqued, refers this reformation period in his work *Forests of Gold* during the early fifteenth century as a "big bang theory," suggesting several changes gave way to a stronger and more influential economic system based upon an elite class.[7] According to Wilks this happened in three phases: (1) a change to agricultural production, (2) reorganization of society and (3) emergence of new political system and structure.[8] Importantly, it was this transformation in these phases Wilks suggests converting the economic system from one dependent upon hunting and gathering to one which was based on the production of goods, namely crops.[9] This transformation, Wilks suggests' occurred within two centuries of its initial start and was liked closely to the arrival of Portuguese ships and the trade of captive labor.

Nevertheless, as Wilks suggests the changeover which occurred in three phases began in the fifteenth century with the arrival of the Portuguese several other scholars dispute this timeline. While his theory regarding the phases of transition has proved accurate, this transition occurred much earlier than Wilks himself suggests in his works according to both Anatole Norman Klein and Gérard Chouin, a point which is emphasized in the coming paragraphs. This region of West Africa began trading very early with local indigenous groups, Muslims trekking south across the Sahara bringing goods from as far away as Western Europe, North Africa and the Arabian Peninsula. Many of these contacts made between people of the forest zone and foreigners entering the region occurred much earlier than the fifteenth century as Wilks suggests.

Ivor Wilks' work accounts for only those coming in the beginning of the fifteenth century as foreigners and does not account for those entering prior to this century. A hunter-gatherer society, as Wilks refers them, was incapable of successfully incorporating themselves into an advanced trading network within two centuries or between the fifteenth and seventeenth centuries, such as the system linking the forest zone and Northerners and later the trade network created along the coastline with the arrival of European traders.[10] Wilks in his work states:

> A necessary . . . condition of the establishment of agriculture in the Akan country was, we have seen, the demands of external bullion markets, and the flow of Akan gold into the later medieval Europe was undoubtedly one among the very many factors facilitating the emergence of mercantile capitalism. . . . European capitalism, however, developed in such a way that the Akan economies became over determined by it: by its requirements first for gold, later for labour in the period of the slave trade. . . . It was, however, precisely this access to capitalist markets, as suppliers, that enabled the dominant classes in Akan society to deprive a great part of their revenues from the management and manipulation of trade in exported and imported commodities.[11]

Archaeologists have especially been critical of Ivor Wilks timeline and sources which he has used, especially those which are European in nature. While, few argue such a transition took place, A. N. Klein suggests a similar theory, but instead believes Wilks dates for this transition are incorrect. Her work argues that, Wilks thesis contains several holes which are based upon his analysis of the mode of production. She instead insists such a mode of production as the one seen in the Akan state could exist only among an advanced state, which occurred in the earlier centuries.[12] A. N. Klein in her work writes about Wilks and his thesis statement:

> Wilks's myth is beset by many problems . . . which supports the assumption that a mode production based on large-scale slave labor could exist among hunters-becoming-agriculturalists. . . . Moreover, these hunter-early agriculturalists would seem to have been in an especially weak position to control slaves. . . . Hunters, even those who have initiated food production, are regularly away from their campsites to hunt for game. . . . According to Wilks, Akan kingship and marriage, rather than the policing power of Akan military units, provided the instruments that effectively "controlled" and "administered" this large immigrant, alien labor force[13]

Similarly, to Klein, Gérard Chouin provides his own assessment of Wilks giving a far different interpretation of the timeline and idea of the "big bang" theory, writing:

> The "big bang" theory incorporates the most substantive historical facts known for the late fifteenth and early sixteenth century. Akan forest and shapes them into interpretative hypotheses: the existence of the world bullion market. . . . Drawing mainly on Asante oral traditions, Wilks proposes an appealing model . . . he tries to fill the gap between an alleged society of hunter-gatherers and a kinship-based society already attested in European sources . . . however, his theory is constrained by limited source material, and by retro-diction, that is writing history by glossing later sources. . . . In fact, archaeological and historical data do not suggest that before the fifteenth century, people living in what is now the land of the Akan, were hunter-gathers.[14]

Both A. N. Klein and Gérard Chouin studying both the local terrain and the historical artifacts believe the hunter-gatherer transition discussed by Wilks occurred well before the time period which he suggests in his work.

Those of the Akan linguistic group migrated into the forest zone as early as 1000 AD[15] and therefore the changeover from the hunter-gatherer society referenced to a state based upon large scale labor and trade began upon their initial arrival in the interior and not five centuries later as suggested by Wilks. Therefore, during the period in which Wilks discuss, the Akan, the state was much more advanced than the state and peoples calling the region home some 500 years earlier. The use and trade of captive labor, Wilks discusses in the fifteenth century, is also useful in earlier centuries among people with an extensive system of trade and well-organized state. Captive labor was useful in clearing land and maintaining farms which grew crops traded to the north and south.[16]

Moreover, by the seventeenth century the region and area of the forest zone continued to experience growth and development, still well before the arrival of Europeans who were looking to explore the interior. As much of the region continued to see foreigners trekking into the area, and with this the constant transition steadily incorporated these new-comers. Nevertheless, many new-comers were not as willing to link themselves to the new states they were coming into contact with. These new-comers entered the region gradually and peacefully, hoping to acquire their own territory along trade routes, but often became captives of war, as they often antagonized those who were well-established states.[17]

The many changes occurring within the forest zone region of West Africa and the Gold Coast should not be viewed from the context of a transition into a trading partner for arriving Europeans or acceptance into the world economy as Wilks suggests. Studying their development only as a trading partner for arriving Europeans limits the scope and value of those people calling the forest zone home. Instead this region should first be studied as an emerging region with several thriving groups all with a strong economy prior to the arrival of Europeans. Thereafter, with the arrival of Europeans, the forest zone should be analyzed as one which expanded and shifted its trading network to fit the growing demands of an emerging international market.

Furthermore, these states were able to develop a system of exchange along with a strong cultural, social, political and economic order. In the period which Wilks refers to as the development of the region, the start of the fifteenth century, instead should be referred to as the second era of interior expansion. This second period of expansion of interior borders lasting from the fifteenth to seventeenth century is also a period which groups sought to control trading though through military campaigns. The third era of expansion occurs in the mid-1700s with the growth of the Asante into a dominant military power and eventual changeover to legitimate commerce after the start of the nineteenth century.

Shortly after the arrival the Akan in the forest zone region, they emerged as a group with a strong social order. Furthermore, combined with the social order, they developed a functioning family structure, religious ceremonies, cultural celebrations and long distance trading markets, linking them to the routes of the Trans-Saharan Trade. Moreover, the development of such a structure shows the Akan began its transition into thriving economic state with political and economic system in the earliest centuries of their emergence. The Akan settlers after arriving in the region traded gold, manufactured items and agricultural goods with empires and states to their Northern borders and eventually to those who surrounded them in all directions. In the coming years, trading routes and the value of goods was altered with the arrival of Europeans to their Southern border along the coastline.

The overwhelming appearance of European traders and merchants caused many of these arriving nations to construct several forts along the Gold Coast, placing them in an even closer proximity to many of the Akan trade routes which crisscrossed the interior. These forts also a part of the economic changes occurring along the coastline of the region were key in the growing Atlantic commercial system in which the Akan directly contributed goods. Nevertheless, the arrival of Europeans and the construction of numerous forts allowed the Akan to actively seek out new trading partners to expand their already thriving interior commercial market. The presence of Europeans resulted in a shift of trading patterns and partners, away from the Trans-Saharan Trade, and eventually leading to gold, manufactured items and agricultural goods reaching Europe for both trade and sale, well before the European desire for African slaves. The Atlantic commercial system, which the region of the Gold Coast became involved continued to expand as the Akan, the largest group continued to develop and reorganize itself first as traders of gold and secondly with the start of the Trans-Atlantic Slave Trade, traders of captives.

In discussing the early Akan people and the forest zone, another critical development is the formation of the Asante in the late stages of the seventeenth century into a powerful state within its first 100 years of existence. Nevertheless, soon after this state was created several trade routes were extended further connecting the region to trading grounds to its north and south, seemingly establishing even greater economic partnerships. During the first 150 years, 1650–1800, as the trade in captives from the Gold Coast continued to grow, the forest zone region also witnessed an increase in the number of Africans exported partly due to the reformation of the Akan and growth of the Asante. Ultimately, with the start of the Trans-Atlantic Slave Trade and the growing Atlantic Commercial market, the Asante were able to enter this new market.

This expansion of the trade in captives between the sixteenth and eighteenth centuries was partly due to changes within the Akan social organization but also the emergence of Asante and their dominance over the central Gold Coast region leading to a steady surplus of captives within the state. As the Asante continued to expand and control the central area of the Gold Coast or forest zone, this region became known as Greater Asante, with its most recognized cities being Kumasi and Salaga. As a member of the Akan social structure, the Asante challenged several other neighboring groups and many other smaller states of their respective areas. This was done before the Asante were able to gain complete control over the interior of the Gold Coast and becoming one of the most powerful states in West Africa. Eventually, Asante dominance over the region left many who surrounded the forest zone in a state of captivity or sold into the captivity. Those who remained became enemies of this newly expanding interior state.

Although, the early years of the Asante are well documented, through oral traditions and from visitors to the Greater Asante region and cities of Kumasi and Salaga between the eighteenth and nineteenth centuries, the origins of the Akan people themselves who were established much earlier are very much obscure and debated. This is evidenced in the writings of Joseph Dupuis, T. E. Bowdich, Thomas Beecham, Brodie Cruickshank and M. J. Bonnat. In 1821, T. E. Bowdich published a pamphlet describing his experiences on a mission to Asante State, ultimately concluding their origins linked them to Ethiopia.[18] Bowdich also suggests he only heard this history contradicted only once, which suggested they came from a country or region near the waterside.[19]

Thomas Beecham and Brodie Cruickshank in 1841 and 1853, respectively, visited the interior of the Gold Coast and agreed with Joseph Dupuis who visited the region in 1824. Each concluded after visiting the central territory that the Akan originated from the north and were driven south by the advancement of Moors.[20] Joseph J. Williams over one hundred years later in 1925, like Bowdich before him, argued the Akan originated from the Abyssinian region.[21] This debate surrounding the origins of the Akan continued well into the 1950s and 1960s as colonialism began to come to an end, especially in the region of the Gold Coast soon known as Ghana.

Scholars such as J. D. Fage[22] in 1955 argued the Akan descended from the empire of Ancient Ghana. In a series of four books and articles published between 1952 and 1962 Eva Meyerowitz[23] argued the Akan were not of Negro origin but instead of Libyo-Berber origin. Unlike previous works published in the nineteenth century by early travelers, Osei Kwadwo argued they migrated from the former West African empire of Ghana. Furthermore, he also suggests oral traditions of the Akan believe they came from Mesopotamia where they shared boundaries with the Isrealites.[24] Although these individuals lend greatly to debate on the origins of the Akan, much of the attention today focuses on the works of Ivor Wilks, Kwame Arhin, T. C. McCaskie, Larry Yarak, K. Y. Daaku, Ray Kea, K. B. Dickinson, A. Norman Klein and Ann Stahl. Debates over these origins have played out among these scholars in books and journals published around the world.

Nevertheless, as the first major West African Empires of Ghana, Mali and Songhay all began to decline; small loose confederations of people near the region of the Niger Bend comprised of several groups began to call the region home. The early groups who moved into this region filled the numerous voids left behind by these declining empires.[25] The earliest impact made by this early confederation of states was in the realm of agricultural development of the forest zone. Filling this void left by those declining empires of West Africa resulted in development of an extensive trading system consisting of numerous routes and traders.[26] During the thirteenth century as the Empire of Ghana continued into its final decline, people began to move further south into areas of Northern Ghana, just south of the Pra and Offin Rivers, still far from the coastal region. This extended the trading links between the forest zones and connected them to the routes of the Trans-Saharan Trade.[27]

The migration of these early groups who became known as the Akan, into the forest zone served as a pivotal point in not only the history of the group, but also the Gold Coast in the coming centuries. Akan migration into the area resulted in the formation of sociopolitical groups organized for trade, state rituals, and a system of labor and eventually the creation of numerous thrones. As these interior communities continually developed into larger more bureaucratic states, the coastal region to its south, as trading routes began to increase initially remained small, but also began to experience its own population growth during expansion.[28]

Once finally moving further south and reaching the area of the Pra and Offin Rivers, during the thirteenth century, the Akan quickly made a significant impact establishing a number of villages and communities. The earliest villages of the Akan in this area were known as Adansemanso, Abuakwa Atwumamanso, Asantemanso, Asenmanso and Abankeseso all of which were in the Adanse and Amansie regions.[29] Nevertheless, in the coming centuries the Akan became a much more centralized series of peoples and states. Ultimately, after the Asante state was established, nearly four centuries later the central region became the source of the vast state.[30]

In these early villages, the Akan people consisted of both matrilineal and patrilineal sects. Matrilineal divisions of the Akan consisted of Ekoona, Oyoko, Asona, Asenee, Agona, Bretuo, Asakyiri, Asuana, Atwea and Aberade. Early patrilineal divisions consisted of Bosommuru, Bosompra, Bosomtwe, Bosommaram, Nketia, Poakwa, Afram and Abankwaade.[31] Moreover, as they became a more centralized state, each of the Akan matrilineal and patrilineal groups continued to rely upon their common language, twi, developed by their predecessors. Each operated with a common calendar, religious beliefs, naming ceremonies and marriage institutions.[32] The creation of a calendar, religious practices, naming and marriage ceremonies along with a common language represent the emergence of a strong social organization.

The social organization of the developing Akan state during the period as well as their growing economy based on the trade of gold and the ability to produce agricultural goods created a setting for the absorption of foreigners into the state.[33] As the Akan economy continued to develop further, they made contact with numerous groups and cities, including the Wangara, Mande, Hausa, Timbuktu, Jenne, Hausaland and the Bight of Benin.[34]

The increased presence of Akan settlers and later arriving foreigners brought along with them a skill set, which was crucial to the growth of agricultural products in the area, namely kola nuts. As the Akan state continued its further development and witnessed the increased demand for kola nuts during in thirteenth, fourteenth and fifteenth centuries, this led to a greater need for labor. By the fifteenth century, the Akan themselves turned to captives a source of labor for their expanding empire and trade routes.

Moreover, as the large empires continued to decline in West Africa and new Muslim states emerged in their place, in conjunction with an increase in kola production and gold trading, population shifts continuously occurred in the region of Northern Ghana. These population shifts created a distinct social organization, which constantly changed as more people entered the area, with a central administration making use of captives.[35]

The use of captives in the Akan has been one of great debate among numerous scholars of Akan history. Ghanaian History Professor Akosua Perbi studies the use of captives in these earliest centuries of the Akan society, and notes their contribution to agriculture, industry, commerce and the administration of the state. Captives within the Akan were not only crucial to the development of the state, but they were also key contributors to the family unit. Moreover, as a captive became private property and a member of the owner's family and lineage, they had no right to determine the life or death of an individual.[36] In the later centuries, the use of captives became a crucial element of the state and its development and ultimately became a central issue of contention among the Asante and British as they expanded into central areas of the region.

Albeit, with the creation of this new state the Akan social hierarchy was overseen by a ruling class of military elite who were in complete control of each patrilineal and matrilineal sect within the forest zone. The first kings of the Akan were all military leaders, who were chiefly concerned with the protection of trading and trade routes to and from the forest zone.[37] Several of these early military leaders ruled on their ability to militarily and economically dominate the lower classes of other Akan groups.[38]

Nevertheless, many of these Akan military leaders also worked to keep up the maintenance of trade routes connecting the forest zone with the declining Trans-Saharan Trade routes to their Northern borders. The later arrival of Europeans along the coastline increased the areas and routes which needed protection to include those to the south. These massive trading routes resulted in the large scale movement of both agricultural and manufactured commodities as well as iron and gold.[39]

Soon after the arrival of the first Portuguese merchant ships in the fifteenth century trading to and from the central region of the Akan territory was immediately impacted by their coming and the construction of São Jorge da Mina in 1482. The construction of this fort also served to protect the commercial enterprises for Portuguese merchants.[40] With the arrival of Portuguese merchants and later the coming of more European traders, this shifted the vast majority of Akan commodities away from the north, instead south of the forest zone along the emerging trade routes which crossed toward the coastline. Their arrival altered trade in the region. The Royal African Company and the Dutch West Indies Company both traded along the Gold Coast for thirty years prior to the emergence of the Asante state in the late stages of the seventeenth century.[41]

Prior to and after the construction of Elmina Castle in 1482, the Portuguese traders used canoe men to ferry goods and people back and forth between ships and the coastline. The role of these canoe men continued to expand even further with the arrival of more European nations and the construction of more castles along the coast. [42] Making contact first with the coastal people, the Portuguese became one of many European nations to trade along the Gold Coast between the fifteenth and eighteenth centuries. Moreover, after their arrival and trek into the interior, the Portuguese soon came to realize the linguistic, commercial and cultural connections between the coastal and interior regions of the Gold Coast.[43] This realization of the commercial connections proved a valuable asset as trading increased and with the arrival of more European nations.

Moreover, with the arrival of more European traders between the sixteenth and eighteenth centuries, the exact location of the Akan became documented by Dutch explorers traveling to the various coastal territories of what was known as the Gold Coast. The first Dutch ships reached the Gold Coast in 1593–1594, nearly 100 years after the contraction of Elmina and became an ambitious nation in accumulating as much wealth and territory as possible.[44] In 1629, a Dutch map of the Gold Coast (see Figure 2.1) outlined the exact location of numerous groups. In addition to documenting the various locations of people, they also included a brief description. In their description of Acanij they write, "Here live the most principal merchants who trade in gold with us."[45] Politically the Dutch upon their arrival and travel along the

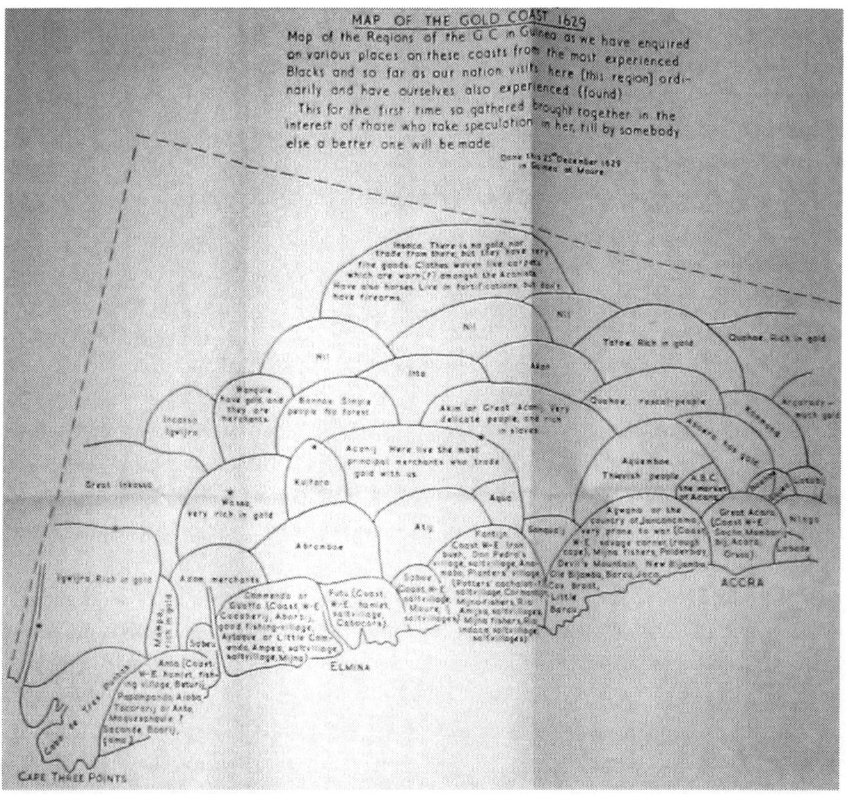

Figure 2.1 1629 Dutch Map of the Gold Coast, showing the exact location of the various places and people whom they made contact with. Map is an early outline of the Gold Coast prior the formation of the Asante state. *Source*: *Ghana Notes and Queries*, No. 9 (November, 1966), p. 71.

coastline, believed it to be no fewer than twenty states located in the Gold Coast.[46]

Today, this map is well known among historians and anthropologists who study peoples and states of the region. Since the origins of the term Akan are unclear, Portuguese, Dutch and English travelers all mention several different groups with names similar to that of the Akan. Portuguese who later arrived in the mid-sixteenth century along the coast referred to the areas as Acanes Grandes and Acanes Pequanos.[47] Later documents published after the release of the 1629 Dutch Gold Coast Map by Portuguese, Dutch in English all reveal several similar names including Akan, Arcanny, Arcania, Akanis Accanny, Heccanny and Accanists.[48]

Although consisting of several groups, the early Europeans considered the Akan to be a loose confederacy of states that were prohibited from marrying one another.[49] Unknown to early travelers, these eight matrilineal and patrilineal groups shared a common lineage, language, culture, naming practices and religious ceremonies.[50] This becomes very evident as later Europeans hoping to establish trading partnerships traveled across the territory visiting the areas and towns closer to the interior of the region. The Akan class structure is also very important to the origins of the earliest states of the forest zone.[51] Of this loose confederacy of states consisting of the matrilineal and patrilineal groups in the Akan people, the Denkyira and the Okoyo became the strongest and well organized of the forest zone region ruling over Kwaman, later known as Kumase.

The Denkyira, once defeating Adanse and prior to the formation of the Asante, became the most powerful of the many people who called the interior regions of the Gold Coast home as well as one of the most feared states. This state, between the 1660s and the 1690s, contributed to the export of gold and captives and the import of European guns and ammunitions.[52] As the Denkyira sought to expand their state, this brought them along with their ruler Ntim Gyakari into a conflict with Osei Tutu of Kwaman, the leader of the Oyoko.[53]

In the final sixty years of the earliest patrilineal and matrilineal entities of the Akan state, there remained problems between several groups, leading to several inter-state wars.[54] The Oyoko group, under its final three leaders Nana Twum Kwabia Amanfi (1640–1660), Nana Antwi Oti Akenten (1660–1680) and Nana Kobia Obiri Yeboa (1680–1701), like the Denkyira became one of the strongest Akan groups of the forest zone. During this period, the Oyoko also began to expand its reaches to nearby areas pushing for the unification of several key groups with whom they made contact with during expansion.

This urge for the unification of all the Akan began under the rule of the last Okoyo, King Nana Kobia Obiri Yeboa. Moreover, this idea of unification reached new heights as the Okoyo formed its own loose confederation of states as Yeboa himself ruled over Kwaman and revealed his plans for this association to another nearby leader, Okomfo Anokye.[55] Because Nana Kobia Obiri Yeboa had no children or direct brothers, only a niece, meant that Osei Tutu became the successor the Oyoko group.[56]

This is a key point, as it reveals the role of lineage and the importance matrilineal descent among the people even prior to the formation of the Asante state. Yeboa, the maternal grand uncle of Tutu, established the direct link between the formation of the Okoyo group and the beginning stages of the Asante.[57] Immediately after the death of Yeboa, the Okoyo now under the rule of Osei Tutu began to transform themselves into the Asante, a process aided by his maternal grand uncle's ally, Okomfo Anokye. To create this link in the transformation from the Okoyo to the Asante, Anokye called a meeting of all the Akan chiefs, and began praying to the ancestors for guidance.

This meeting of chiefs and prayer led by Okomfo Anokye is believed to have resulted in the gods sending down the "Golden Stool" (see Figure 2.2), and whomever chief it landed upon was ultimately to be the king of the unified Asante people or Asantehene.[58] The "Golden Stool" or *Sika Dwa* is believed to contain the spirit of all the Asante people and is to never be sat upon by anyone including the Asantehene himself.[59] Nevertheless, this ceremony and the "Golden Stool" landing upon the lap of Osei Tutu serve as the beginning stages of the history of the modern Asante people.[60] The "Golden Stool" unified all of the Asante people of the former Oyoko under one ruler, although they were initially in different states. Describing the day upon which the "Golden Stool" descended from the sky Osei Kwadwo states:

> On the appointed day, the chiefs, each waiting to be the paramount chief elect. . . . Okomfo Anokye appeared amidst drumming and dancing. After some magical dances, he paused a little, jumped here and there and began to call something from the sky. Drumming started again and the priest conjured. The sky became tense and a deafening noise was heard. Then a stool studded with gold descended on the laps of Nana Osei Tutu. It therefore meant that he had been chosen by the ancestors and the gods as the unquestionable king of the kings of the Asante Nation.[61]

To commemorate the Golden Stool, ancestors and loyalty to the Asantehene, the Akan routinely met at the Odwira festival in Kumasi.

Through the Golden Stool, the Asante believe this gave them a connection to the spirits of their ancestors, whom they believed had a direct connection to God who created the world. The spirits of the ancestors within the Asante belief system were also believed to be connected with the deities that connected them with the natural resources in their surrounding territory. In Asante the belief system, deities and spirits needed to be in constant contact with items on earth, which included the animate and inanimate items.[62]

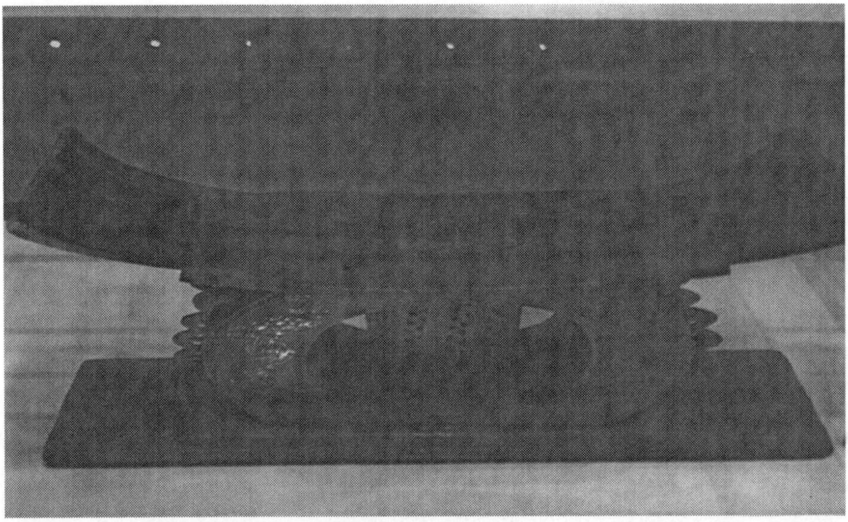

Figure 2.2 Example of Asante Golden Stool. Example of the Asante Golden Stool on display at the British Museum of History in London, England. This stool is made of wood. The original is made of gold. Photo provided by author.

The Asante also believed human beings also consisted of a spirit or "ntoro" which they inherited from the father.[63] Although the belief systems within the state vary from one Akan to the next, they all descended from a similar system.

Similarly, in the years after the formation of the Asante, the state continuously relied on the early history of the Akan as they developed their own religious rituals, philosophy and its own unique history. Beyond the Golden Stool, which the Asante believed connected them to their ancestors religion was a central feature of the state and its people. Although the new Asante developed their own uniqueness, they remained very much aware of their ancestors and the links to previous, Okoyo group.

Within the Asante, the Supreme Being known as Onyankopon also referred to as Onyame, Nyame, Odomankoma was the power source of Asante cosmology. The power of Onyame was rooted in the two varying theories of spirituality and religion which existed throughout the Asante state. As a matrilineal society, the Asante linked religious practices of the state to women.

The Akan, after the descent of the Golden Stool, transformed from its small traditional sects into several sub-groups consisting of the Akwamu, Guan, Fante, Denkyira, Brong, Akyem, Kwahu, Sefwi, Wassa, Asante, Akwapim and Assin.[64] Although the Akan were unified, after 1650, the Akwamu, and Denkyira were seen as the most powerful and feared of the states. The Denkyira state, one the most powerful of the Akan, expanded and grew wealthier than any of the other states. As Akwamu gained wealth and power they also expanded, invading the Anlo state of the upper slave-coast.[65] As both expanded, they also became two of the most feared states, resulting in numbers of people migrating into the Asante territory.

The new inhabitants who came to Asante also brought along with them military skills learned in the Denkyira and Akwamu. As the Asante state was formed and began its process of expansion, they came into direct contact with the Denkyira state to their south, resulting in the Asante-Denkyira war in the early stages of the 1700s.[66] Making use of its developing military, the Asante were able to defeat the Denkyira, and achieve several key economic and political goals. Afterward, the Asante used their army to conquer neighboring states, expanding their empire even further.[67]

Defeating the Denkyira set in the motion the earliest stages of Asante expansion and formation of Greater Asante and its capital Kumasi. This also eliminated any interference for the Asante opening a clear path between the interior and coastal trading routes. Ultimately, this early war set in motion Asante contact with the coming European nations, especially the Dutch and British merchants with whom they actively traded. The defeat of Denkyira also allowed the Asante to transform their coalition of military states into a large political union under the guidance of the Asantehene, Osei Tutu.[68] This early expansion of the Asante in the 1700s created a new political and economic power in a region with several small states in the states' path. Under this political and economic expansion this state was able to spread 100,000 square miles and incorporate some three million inhabitants. Furthermore, this also included the incorporation of numerous roads to and from Kumasi, to both its north and south.[69]

This newly created independent state, with its large military, remained on friendly relations with its closest neighbors because of the commercial success of the period. This peace along trading routes lasted until the late 1700s and their contact with another Akan group, the Fante.[70] Although the expansion process of the Asante was carried out with a military campaign, much of the expansion also took into account the cultural identity of the Asante.

The Asante, after their transition from the Oyoko, maintained a cultural identity which not only linked them to their ancestors, but also established a political and economic system for future generations to follow. Similar to the patrilineal and matrilineal groups that made up the early Akan, the later Akan states adopted a similar system of matrilineal succession and identity in their societies. According to Robert Dodoo, ". . . blood transmitted through the mother, the individual was made a member of his mother's kin group and of his mother's lineage, which consisted of all the descendants of both sexes who traced their genealogy through the female line to a common ancestress."[71] This determines the wealth, social and political standing of individuals and members of the state.

The Asante, who call the region of Greater Asante home, are a matrilineal society in which only the women can transmit blood to the descendants, whether they are male or female, while men can only transmit "ntoro" or their spirit.[72] Just as property is transmitted via the female in the society, so is the position of the Asantehene or chief of the Asante people. Accordingly K. A. Busia who discusses the lineage of Asante people writes, "Ashanti chiefship is based on the lineage system . . . the blood . . . is inherited from mother and spirit from the father."[73] Although the Asantehene is given control over the Asante because he holds the Golden Stool, the Queen Mother or Ohema also takes a substantial role both in the government and the enstoolment of a chief.

In a state such as this, matrilineal succession was fundamental as it assigned kinship to those within the state and royal status of the ruling elite. Although the passage of lineage through males in the state was a secondary concern, this did not limit their role within the state in terms of succession. Specifically, naming practices were passed down through male blood lines and included both great names and by names.[74] Matrilineal succession was a key concept practiced within the Asante once established and passed down continuously through each Asantehene. This is another point which A. N. Klein is critical of Ivor Wilks as she states in a 1979 paper presented at the Department of Anthropology Seminar in Cambridge. She writes, "Wilks denies the centrality of matrilineal kingship and the relevance if the lineage to nineteenth century Asante political organization."[75] Matrilineal succession is a point which has been discussed in later works about the Akan and the Asante.

Matrilineal succession is an important facet of the Akan and the Asante as every aspect of the individuals of the state can be traced through their blood line. These aspects of Akan and Asante social life which can be traced through succession include status, right to political office, citizenship and inheritance of property. Marriage gave the husband sexual rights, claims to domestic services and rights to economic support for his wife and his children.[76]

Nevertheless after its initial establishment, the first two lines of the Asante kingship during the latter stages of the seventeenth and early years of the eighteenth centuries were passed down by patrilineal succession. This short-term solution included the passage of succession from Asantehene Osei Tutu and Asantehene Opoku Ware I. Even after their deaths there still remained challengers from within these families to the throne of the state. Under Kwakua Dua any remaining challengers were eliminated through the practice of cross-cousin marriages.[77]

Once the practice of matrilineal succession was firmly established, women took on an even greater role, notably the Queen Mother. In Asante, the Queen Mother (see Table 2.1) accompanies the chief everywhere except to war and

Table 2.1 Asante Queens (Queen Mother). Reign of Asante Queens Begin with the Reign of Osei Tutu

Guarku Kussi Amua
Inkatiar Otim Abamu
[Kofiae] Akuafriae
Kwandu Yardom
Aduma Akosua
Ambah Sewah
Ya Difiae
Afua Sapon
Afua Cobbi
Yachia

Source: The History of Ashanti Kings and the Whole Country Itself and Other Writings by Otumfuo, Nana Agyeman Prempeh I (London: Oxford University Press, 2003).

Table 2.2 Asante Kings (Asantehene). From Kumaseman to the Asantehene (1640–Present). Last Kings of Oyoko Abohyen Dynasty

Kumaseman	*Date of Rule*
*Otumfuo Nana Twum Kwabia Amanfi	(1640–1660)
*Otumfuo Nana Antwi Oti Akenten	(1660–1680)
*Otumfuo Nana Kobia Obiri Yeboa	(1680–1701)

*Refers to last the Kumasemans of the Oyoko Dynasty.

is present for ceremonies connected to both birth and puberty and ultimately chooses the senior wife, or one to replace her after death. The status of the Queen Mother is so important that without her the Golden Stool cannot exist.[78] Because women in Asante are backed by a united family, they are protected from all ill-treatment from men and all family property and children belong first to her and the entire group.[79]

While men are seen as the leaders of the society, only certain aspects of their bloodline can be tied to the children they bear. Women through the bloodline of this matrilineal society transmit descent to the children they bear, while the bloodline of men in the state carries the religious and educational ties of the children.[80] In the complete structure of the Asante society, the ancestors or deceased members are seen as the center of the state that are followed by the traditional elite of the society, heads of families or lineage heads and simple folks.[81]

In a matrilineal state such as the Asante a head of the household, a husband or father had less control over his own wives, children and grandchildren in his blood-related kin group. Thus, a head of a household controlled his younger brothers and sisters, his sisters' children, the grandchildren by his sons who married uterine nieces (i.e. cross-cousin marriages), his household captives, the children of female and male captives and under certain circumstances pawns and debt servants. A household head is responsible for his uterine nieces and nephews, their debts and dependents. Such is the case that men also profited from the labor of nieces and nephews and could ultimately choose their spouses. Even after marriage, an uncle still remained the legal guardian of his niece, which is responsibility that fell to her eldest brother if the uncle was not alive.[82]

Several different visitors to Asante discussed the structure of the state and the day-to-day relationship within families. R. S. Rattray, notably discussed this in his early work on the Asante state and its laws, custom and constitution. Among his many observations, he discovered a preference or order dependents were listed as under the head of the household. This included married sister or married niece, unmarried sister and niece, nephew, brother, mother and finally captive.[83]

Another facet discussed of the Asante was the structure and architecture of the settlement and its role in hierarchy of the society, which was established prior to the creation of the state. The interior region had a well-developed plan of settlement with a broad main street with divided with narrow streets and several foot-paths. Furthermore, main street, as it is referred to extended along the north-south axis with housing compounds lying on each side. Along the center of this main street sat the palace of the Omanhene, the eldest traditional ruler, and farther north lay the residence of Juanbenhene, who oversaw the court system.[84] With numerous towns surrounding Kumasi Joseph Dupuis described the streets which ran through the city as:

> main-street being about two furloughs in length, broad, clean, and regularly formed. This street cuts through the village at right angles, and intersects a number of little lanes and passages formed by rows of houses, which are closely erected, although generally detached from each other by a space of several feet.[85]

The continued construction of towns and streets also shows the constant evolution of the state well after its creation.

The Gold Coast from the fifteenth century to the start of the seventeenth century went through several changes which ultimately impacted not on the indigenous population of the region but the coming European nations as well. Stretching from the Northern fringes of the country to its coastal points, the changes which occurred on the Gold Coast impacted the economy throughout. The Akan people, led by the Asantehene (see Table 2.3), over the same period experienced several changes as well, which impacted the local indigenous population, African states coming across its Northern border and the Europeans trading on the coast. The major change which occurred during the era was the formation of the Asante nation. Over a one-hundred-year period from the interior of the Gold Coast, the Asante nation, beginning as the small

Table 2.3 Asante Kings (Asantehene): From Kumaseman to the Asantehene (1640–Present)

Asantehene	*Dates of Rule*
Asantehene Kwame Osei Tutu	(1697–1717)
Asantehene Opoku Ware	(1720–1750)
Asantehene Kusi Obodum	(1750–1764)
Asantehene Ose Kwadwo	(1752–1777)
Asantehene Kwame Panin	(1777–1803)
Asantehene Osei Fofie	(1803–1804)
Asantehene Osei Bonsu	(1804–1823)
Asantehene Osei Yaw Akoto	(1824–1834)
Asanatehene Kwaku Dua Panin I	(1834–1867)
Asantehene Kofi Kakari	(1867–1874)
Asantehene Osei Mensa Bonsu Kumaa	(1874–1883)
Asantehene Kwaku Dua II	(1884)
^Owusu Kofi, Chairman	(1884)
^Akyampon Panyin, Chairman	(1884–1887)
~Owusu Sekyere II, the Manmponghene	(1887–1888)
Asantehene Prempeh I	(1888–1931)
Asantehene Osei Tutu Agyeman Prempeh II	(1931–1970)
Asantehene Opoku Ware II	(1970–1999)
~Osei Bonsu II, the Mamponghene (1999)	(1999)
Asantehene Otumfuo Osei Tutu II	(1999–Present)

^Beginning in 1883 and lasting through 1888 the Asante were involved in a Civil War. During this period the Asante were overseen by an interim council.

~Mamponghene oversees the finances of the Asante state.

Source: Several works were used to compile the list of Asantehene's. Works used include: Margaret Preistly and Ivor Wilks, "The Ashanti Kings in the Eighteenth Century: A Revised Chronology," *The Journal of African History*, Vol. 1, No. 1 (1960); also see Osei Kwadwo, *An Outline of Asante History* (Accra, Ghana: O. Kwadwo Enterprise, 1994).

Oyoko group, transitioned from being an undersized state to one of the largest nations in both the Gold Coast and the West Africa. The extent of this change and growth became more evident between 1701 and 1808 as the Asante influence on the trading from the Gold Coast stretched from the interior to the coastal points of the region.

Beginning first as a small group of matrilineal and patrilineal states, between 1701 and 1808, the Asante were formed and were involved in several wars between themselves and other Akan groups. Their influence over the indigenous population during the era was felt culturally, politically and economically. Asante influence also impacted the day to day operations of the Dutch and British, who by the period were the largest traders on the Gold Coast. As the changes continued from within the Gold Coast interior, both Britain and the United States set in motion laws to officially make the Trans-Atlantic Slave Trade illegal. British and American abolition laws affected the Trans-Atlantic Slave Trade from the Gold Coast just as the Asante push toward the coast affected Dutch, British and American trading patterns from the region.

The Asante state, between 1701 and 1808, continually developed becoming one of the largest groups within the Akan. Covering nearly one hundred years, the emergence and growth of the Asante affected not only the trading patterns of people calling the Gold Coast home, but European nations entering the region as well, as they also hoped to establish their own commercial network. The formation of the Asante undoubtedly contributed to the final one hundred years of the Trans-Atlantic Slave Trade as captives leaving the region increased during the period, but their formation also helped sustain a developing economy of manufactured and agricultural goods as the trade in captives was ultimately closed by the largest slave trading nations of the day in the nineteenth century.

NOTES

1. Edmund Abaka, *Kola is God's Gift: Agricultural Production, Export Initiatives and the Kola Industry of Asante and the Gold Coast, 1820–1950* (Athens, OH: Ohio University Press, 2005), p. 11.
2. Thomas J. Lewin, *Asante Before the British: The Prempean Years, 1875–1900* (Lawrence, KS: The Regents Press of Kansas, 1978), p. 9.
3. Ibid., 10.
4. Martin A. Klein, "Defensive Strategies: Wasula, Masina, and the Slave Trade," in *Fighting the Slave Trade: West African Strategies*, ed. Sylbiane A. Diouf (Athens, OH: Ohio University Press, 2003), p. 66.
5. Lewin, *Asante Before the British*, 10–11.
6. Jon D. Carlson, *Myths, State Expansion, and the Birth of Globalization: A Comparative Perspective* (New York: Palgrave MacMillan, 2012), pp. 82–83.
7. Ivor Wilks, *Forests of Gold: Essays on the Akan and the Kingdom of Asante* (Athens, OH: Ohio University Press, 1993), p. 94.
8. Ibid.
9. Ibid., 71.
10. Ivor Wilks, *Asante in the Nineteenth Century: The Structure and Evolution of Political Order* (New York: Cambridge University Press, 1989), p. xxx.
11. Ibid.
12. A. N. Klein, "Slavery and Akan Origin," *Ethnohistory*, Vol. 41, No. 4 (1994), pp. 627–656.
13. Ibid., 629.
14. Gérard Chouin, "The 'Big Bang' Theory Reconsidered: Framing Early Ghanaian History," *Transactions of the Historical Society of Ghana New Series*, No. 14 (2012), p. 23.
15. Mary McCarthy, *Social Change and the Growth of British Power in the Gold Coast: The Fante State, 1807–1874* (New York: Lanham Books, 1983), p. 1.
16. Carlson, 83
17. K. Y. Daaku, "Pre-Ahsanti States," *Ghana Notes and Queries: Historical Society of Ghana*, No. 9 (November 1966), p. 13.

18. T. E. Bowdich, "An Essay on the Superstitions, Customs and Arts Common to the Ancient Abyssinians and Ashantees" (Paris: 1821). In Adu Boahen, "The Origins of the Akan," *Ghana Notes and Queries*, No. 9 (November, 1966), p. 4.

19. T. E. Bowdich, *Mission from Cape Coast Castle to Ashantee with a Descriptive Account of that Kingdom*, New Edition (London: Griffith & Farran, 1873), p. 179.

20. For an explanation on the move of the original Akan people from north of the forest zone see: Joseph Dupuis, *Journal of Residence in Ashantee* (1824); Thomas Beecham, *Ashantee and the Gold Coast* (1841); Brodie Cruickshank, *Eighteen Years on the Gold Coast* (1853) In Adu Boahen, "The Origins of the Akan," *Ghana Notes and Queries*, No. 9 (November, 1966), p. 4.

21. Joseph J. Williams, *Hebrewisms in West Africa*, 2nd ed. (New York: Biblio and Tannen, 1967).

22. J. D. Fage, "Vanished Negro Civilization, Review of *African Glory in Universitas*," Vol. 1, No. 5 (1955), *Transactions of the Historical Society of Ghana*, Vol. III, Part 2 (1957). In Adu Boahen, "The Origins of the Akan," *Ghana Notes and Queries*, No. 9 (November, 1966), p. 5.

23. E. L. A. Meyerowitz published four books on the subject titled: *Akan Traditions of Origins* (1952), *The Akan of Ghana* (1958), "The Akan and Ghana" (1957), *Akan Divine Kinship* (1962) and "Akan Oral Traditions" (1962) in Adu Boahen, "The Origins of the Akan," *Ghana Notes and Queries*, No. 9 (November, 1966), p. 5.

24. Osei Kwadwo, *An Outline of Asante History* (Accra, Ghana: O. Kwadwo Enterprise, 1994), p. 1.

25. Eva L. R. Meyerowitz, "The Akan of Ghana," *Man*, No. 99, Vol. 57 (June, 1957), pp. 83–84.

26. J. K. Fynn, *Asante and Its Neighbors, 1700–1807* (Evanston, Ill: Northwestern University Press, 1971), p. 1.

27. Ibid., 4.

28. Trevor Getz, *Slavery and Reform in West Africa: Toward Emancipation in 19th Century Senegal and Gold Coast* (Athens, OH: Ohio University Press, 2004), pp. 5–6.

29. Ivor Wilks, *Forests of Gold: Essays on the Akan and the Kingdom of Asante* (Athens, OH: Ohio University Press,1993), p. 91.

30. Adu Boahen, "The Origins of the Akan," *Ghana Notes and Queries: Historical Society of Ghana*, No. 9 (November, 1966), p. 10.

31. Ibid., 4.

32. Ibid.

33. Naomi Chazan, "The Early State in Africa: The Asante Case," *The Early State in African Perspective, Culture, Power and Division of Labor*, Vol. 3, eds. S. N. Eisenstadt, Michel Abitbol and Naomi Chazan (Netherlands: EJ Brill Publishers, 1988), p. 64.

34. Ibid., 62.

35. Akosua A. Perbi, *A History of Indigenous Slavery in Ghana: From the 15th to the 19th Century* (Legon, Accra, Ghana: Sub-Saharan Publishers, 2007), p. 18.

36. Ibid., 5–7.

37. Chazan, 64.

38. Ibid.

39. Timothy F. Garrard, *Akan Weights and the Gold Trade* (New York: Longman Group, 1980), pp. 2–7.

40. Albert van Dantzig, *Forts and Castles of Ghana* (Accra, Ghana: Sedco Publishing Limited, 1980), p. 3.

41. Magaret Preistley and Ivor Wilks, "The Ashanti Kinds in the Eighteenth Century: A Revised Chronology," *The Journal of African History*, Vol. 1, No. 1 (1960), p. 83.

42. Peter C. W. Gutkind, "Trade and Labor in the Early Pre-Colonial African History: The Canoemen of Southern Ghana," *Cahiers d'Études Africaines*, Vol. 116, No. 115 (1989), pp. 25–27.

43. Harvey M. Feinberg, "Africans and Europeans in West Africa: Elminans and Dutchmen on the Gold Coast During the Eighteenth Century" (Philadelphia, PA: The American Philosophical Society, 1989), pp. 7–9.

44. Georg Norregard, *Danish Settlements in West Africa,1658–1850*, Translated by Sigurd Mammen (Boston, MA: Boston University Press, 1966), p. 3.

45. *Dutch Map of the Gold Coast 1629*, Map, *Ghana Notes and Queries*, No. 9 (November, 1966), p. 71.

46. Feinberg, 10.

47. Letter from the Acting Governor of Mina to the Queen, April 18, 1557, and Anonymous Report on Mina, September 29, 1557m see A. Teixeira da Mota and P.E.H. Hair, *East of Mina: Afro-European Relations on the Gold Coast in the 1550s and 1560s* (Madison, WI: African Studies Program, 1988), p. 64, 86 in Wilks, *Forests of Gold*, 91.

48. D. Kiyaga-Mulindwa, "The Akan Problem" *Current Anthropology*, Vol. 21, No. 4 (August, 1980), pp. 504–505.

49. K. Y. Daaku, *Osei Tutu of Asante* (London: Heinemann Publishers, 1976), pp. 9–10.

50. Ibid., 9–10.

51. Boahen, 4.

52. T. C. McCaskie, "Denkyira in the Making of Asante, 1660–1720," *The Journal of African History*, Vol. 48, No. 1 (2007), p. 1.

53. Ibid., 2.

54. Kwadwo, 2–3.

55. Ibid., 3.

56. Daaku, 15–18.

57. Kwadwo, 4.

58. Ibid., 5.

59. Ibid.

60. Daaku, 17; This is often accepted due to the writings of Dutch slave trader William Bosman.

61. Kwadwo 5.

62. Robert Dodoo, "Ashanti Cultural Resource Elements and Their Relevance to the Perception and Utilization of Resources," *African Studies Review*, Vol. 14, No. 1 (April, 1971), p. 58.

63. Ibid., 60.

64. Ibid., 1.

65. Sandra E. Greene, *Gender, Ethnicity, and Social Change on the Upper Slave Coast: A History of the Anlo-Ewe* (Portsmouth, NH: Heinemann Publishers, 1996), p. 24.; The Anlo state is located in the Southeastern region of the Gold Coast also referred to as the Upper Slave Coast.

66. J. Pashington Obeng, *Asante Catholocism: Religious and Cultural Reproduction Among the Akan of Ghana* (Netherlands: EJ Brill Publishers, 1996), p. 19.

67. Fynn, 32–33

68. Ivor Wilks, *Forests of Gold: Essays of the Akan of the Kingdom of Asante* (Athens, OH: Ohio University Press, 1993), p. 112.

69. Lewin, 12

70. Fynn, 124

71. Dodoo, pp. 60–61.

72. Captain R. S. Rattray, *Ashanti*, 2nd ed. (NY: Negro Universities Press,1969), p. 77.

73. K. A. Busia, *The Position of the Chief in the Modern Political System of Ashanti* (Oxford: Frank Cass and Company, Ltd., 1968), p. 1.

74. T. C. McCaskie, "Agyeman Prempeh Before the Exile," A. Adu Boahen, Emmanuel Akyeampong, Nancy Lawler, T. C. McCaskie and Ivor Wilks, eds. *The History of Ashanti Kings and The Whole Country Itself and Other Writings by Otumfuo, Nana Agyeman Prempeh I* (London: Oxford University Press, 2003), p. 4.

75. A. N. Klein, "The Two Asantes: Competing Interpretation of 'Slavery' in Akan-Asante Culture and Society," Paper Presented in Department of Anthropology Seminar, (May, 1979).

76. Chistine Oppong, *Marriage Among a Matrilineal Elite: A Family Study of Ghanaian Civil Servants* (London: Cambridge University Press, 1974), pp. 29–38.

77. Ibid., 4–5.

78. Rattray, 81–84.

79. Ibid., 79.

80. Busia, 1.

81. Dodoo, 62.

82. Beverly Grier, "Pawns, Porters, And Petty Traders: Women in the Transition to Cash-Crop Agriculture in Colonial Ghana," in Paul Lovejoy and Toyin Falola, eds., *Pawnship, Slavery, and Colonialism in Africa* (Trenton, NJ: Africa World Press, 2003), pp. 301–307.

83. R. S. Rattray, *Ashanti Law and Constitution*, Revised Edition (London: 1969 [1929]), p. 48 in Ibid, 306.

84. Tarikhu Farrar, *Building Technology and Settlement Planning in West African Civilization: Pre-Colonial Akan Cities and Towns* (Lewiston, NY: Mellen University Press, 1996), pp. 63–67.

85. Joseph Dupuis, *Journal of a Residence in Ashantee* (London: 1820) in Tarikhu Farrar, *Building Technology and Settlement Planning in West African Civilization: Pre-Colonial Akan Cities and Towns* (Lewiston, NY: Mellen University Press, 1996), p. 67.

Chapter 3

Slave Trading and Trade Routes on the Gold Coast

The Fight for the Coastline, 1770–1820

In the era which followed the Akan reorganization, Asante emergence and rising European presence, the Gold Coast and its many indigenous and foreign entities continued its course of political and economic restructuring. Much of this process began in the latter years of the eighteenth century through the first portion of the nineteenth century as more European nations, particularly the British, sought greater access to the region and the Asante hoped to expand its reach beyond the forest zone. As more European traders found their way to West Africa the trading patterns which focused on goods being exchanged toward the north and northeast were redirected to the more valuable markets of the south and southwest along the coastline. Across West Africa, the transition from trading across the Sahara Desert to one instead focused on the coastline began slowly by the start of the fifteenth century to expand greatly between the sixteenth and nineteenth centuries. On the Gold Coast, this transition to trading along the coastline was especially critical between 1770 and 1820. During this window which encompasses fifty years, numerous African and European states were actively exchanging gold prior to the start of the era, only to begin placing a greater emphasis on the exchange of captives. Nevertheless, the era also witnessed the transition to the exchange in legitimate commercial goods.

These years also prove to be the definitive period of the relationship between the Asante and Fante as well as the Asante and British. These relationships declined steadily during the era due to conflicts, the intent of the Asante to expand and the interior exploration and the eventual coming of colonialism in the latter half of nineteenth century led by the British. The relationship established between the three nations in this era only sped up the arrival and spread of the British Protectorate over the region and start of the colonial machine in the coming decades. Albeit, the Asante state and its acts of open diplomacy with coastal entities such as the coming Europeans were directly challenged by their decision to expand from interior to the coast to the interior. Instead these relationships or lack thereof between the nations over this fifty year span began to show the early cracks in a fragile connection in the political and economic well-being of the region only hastening its transition to a colonial territory. Although the cracks were forming, many within the Asante ruling elite hoped to maintain a relationship with the British prior to their push to establish a protectorate over the interior region. Moreover, these decades show, first, why the Asante desired to extend its empire beyond the forest zone, second, why the British began to increase their presence along the Gold Coast and, finally, the expansion of the British sphere of influence beyond the coast.

Therefore, the period between 1770 and 1820 is a critical era as it encompasses the initial spread of the Asante state, wars between African and European nations over coastal and interior territories and finally the start of British exploration of the interior region which set the stage for colonial rule in the nineteenth century. As the Asante hoped to expand toward the coastline and increase its status among European traders, the British pushed toward the interior hoping to intensify its reach across the entirety of the Gold Coast and West Africa. Although the history of Europeans along the Gold Coast dates back several centuries the Asante and British relationship which began much later in a positive manner in the sixteenth century turned negative in the later years of the nineteenth century.

Upon the arrival of the earliest British traders along the Gold Coast in the sixteenth century, the dominant states throughout the region included the Denkyira, Akyem and Akwamu. These states controlled portions of Western, Central and Eastern areas of the Gold Coast and therefore also controlled extensive portions of trade between the interior and coastline as well.[1] By the end of the seventeenth century, both the Asante and Fante states had emerged and either replaced or became the chief competition for these early states. As trading began to increase the coastal Fante, whom Europeans such as the British, Dutch and Portuguese actively exchanged goods with, and newly created interior Asante state, who hoped to acquire the coastal territory only decades after their creation were soon in competition with one another. The two Akan states, Asante and Fante, shared a common lineage with one another, but connections to European traders ultimately proved to be a significant part of the later conflicts between the groups.

By the middle of the eighteenth century with the Trans-Atlantic Slave Trade increasing from the region, the numbers of captives leaving the Gold Coast began to steadily escalate through the end of the period. Moreover, between 1700 and 1775, close to 740,000 thousand captives were being shipped from the Gold Coast to numerous locations throughout South America, the Caribbean and North America by European traders (see Table 3.1).

Table 3.1 1700–1775: Captives Leaving the Gold Coast

	Portugal/ Brazil	*Britain*	*Netherlands*	*U.S.A.*	*France*	*Denmark/ Baltic*	*Total*
1700	1,538	9,311	353	0	0	0	11,203
1701–1725	35,561	170,910	9,384	2,162	7,806	3,214	229,037
1726–1750	18,186	131,232	32,281	11,645	33,335	4,416	231,095
1751–1775	544	143,554	24,961	63,478	20,232	15,460	268,228
Total	56,228	455,008	66,979	77,285	61,373	23,089	739,563

Source: David Eltis et. al, *TheTrans-Atlantic Slave Trade Voyages Database*, http://slavevoyages.org/tast/assessment/estimates.faces?yearFrom=1700&yearTo=1775&flag=2.3.4.5.6.7&embarkation=4&disembarkation=205.204.201.203.202.402.403.401.404.405.804.702.805.703.701.801.802.803.305.304.307.100.306.309.308.311.310.705.704.501.502.600.301.302.303 (Accessed January 14, 2015).

This data shows during the period there was a substantial increase in the numbers taken from the Gold Coast in comparison to those between the years 1650 and 1699 as shown in previous tables, which is only witnessed slightly more than 95,000 captives leaving the region.[2] As the number of captives began to steadily increase between the two centuries, the numerous forts constructed throughout the region also saw constant changeover of ownership between European nations. This resulted in captives being transported to numerous locations based upon the owner of the fort.[3] Nevertheless, this caused numerous European nations who had already constructed forts along the coastline of the Gold Coast to take advantage of this trade by partnering with African states for captives; the greatest increase was among the British and Dutch. This increase in the number of captives had the greatest impact on the trade of gold leaving the region between eighteenth and nineteenth centuries.

Although the trade in gold began to decline at the turn of the eighteenth century, the Dutch continued to maintain their interest in the metal as well as maintaining a relationship with the interior Asante. Nonetheless, during the same period the British began to place a greater emphasis on the trade of captives unlike their European counterparts. While the Dutch in the first half of the century considered abandoning the region, they believed doing so gave the British a clear advantage in the trade of both captives and gold.[4] Examining gold trading in the region during the fifty-year span, 1750 to 1800 also suggests changes which coincide with the increase in captives and a decrease in gold trading. An analysis of the Gold Coast region between 1750 and 1800, suggests 10,000 ounces a year and 500,000 ounces over the fifty-year span of gold were transported out of the region. Furthermore, in the fifty years prior, 1700 to 1750, an average of 40,000 ounces of gold were transported a year and a total of 2,000,000 ounces over the same time span.[5]

During the period between 1699 and 1725, the Dutch West India Company carried away an average of 4, 652.73 ounces of gold. Gold carried away by the Dutch West India Company during this period had a total estimated value of fl. 4,700,000.[6] William Bosman writes,

> Thus I have a made a rough calculation of the quantity of gold . . . but those unacquainted with this trade, may, perhaps, think I have computed wrong: If I happen to see these gentlemen, I have shall civilly desire them to correct my computation; which no one having yet attempted . . . and to the best of my knowledge as near the truth as I could bring it. According to our reckoning then, there is brought hither and carried off exactly twenty three tunn of gold, reckoning three marks to one thousand gilders . . . the merchants can pass safe and uninterrupted; but when the Negroes are at war with one another, I do not believe that half this quantity is shipt off.[7]

Although the trade in gold carried on aggressively over the period the number of captives being transported by the Dutch began to increase as well. Nevertheless, the Dutch between December 1707 and November 1708 and again in 1725 and 1727 carried away more than 6,500 captives from the region. These four years represent a substantial increase in comparison to the overall number of captives taken from the region by the Dutch.[8]

Albeit, the increase in captive labor and decrease in gold leaving the region corresponds with Asante expansion in the mid to late stages of the eighteenth century along with the Fante who began their process of growth much earlier in the era. The expansion of the Fante, in the early 1660s, was already in full swing and the trade in gold was beginning to decline by the time slave trader John Barbot arrived in the 1680s. Although in decline, Barbot later wrote about this experience trading gold, ". . . I might have the judgment . . . of the mint of Paris . . . to know which of chief places of trade on the Gold Coast afforded the finest, and which afforded me the worst gold."[9] Barbot's analysis still proves gold was of such high value in the seventeenth century along the Gold Coast that it was considered some of the finest in the world. Moreover, this decline in gold trading from the region was impacted by the Fante expansion and the creation of Asante within the interior forest zone.

This expansion process by the start of the 1700s reached a new phase as the Fante began to consider the Asante a serious threat to their coastal state and power, forcing the group to consolidate its on power into one. Although this expansion and consolidation process lasted for several decades, by the latter half of the century, the republic which they had created began to break apart into independent units completely separated from one another. The fear of the Asante encroaching upon their region served as the only unifying force of each city.[10]

As more European nations entered the region and constructed forts, partnerships were formed with African states to take advantage of the growing market for captives leaving the Gold Coast between the first and second half of the eighteenth century. The Fante received payments from Dutch and British traders along the Gold Coast adding to the wealth and power of the state.[11] Along the coastline, Dutch officials paid Fante for assistance against the British only to be ultimately out bribed by those officials for their position of neutrality.[12] The British during the eighteenth century became dependent upon surrounding Fante for essential survival skills and eventually protection against the invading Asante forces.[13] Albeit, as the Asante and Fante entered into a hostile relationship with one another in the eighteenth century, they became directly involved in the conflicts over trading grounds, especially those occupied by the British and Dutch.

The Dutch began its relationship with the Asante immediately after their defeat of the Denkyira; in the years which followed numerous Dutch emissaries were sent to Kumasi to meet with Asantehene Osei Tutu and ultimately his successor Asantehene Opoku Ware from their establishment through the 1720s. This positive trading relationship between the Asante and Dutch remained intact through the 1760s, just prior to their decision to sale their coastal forts to the British. Moreover, this relationship between the Asante and Dutch was so important that foreign emissaries were sent to attend the enstoolments of each Asantehene.[14]

With forts lining the entire coastline, each involved party played a major role in expanding the vast trading opportunities and later transitions which occurred: including first to the gold trade, second to the trade in captives and finally the transition to a trade in legitimate goods or commerce. This last transition to legitimate goods, defined in later chapters, in the earliest years of the century, left many along the coast and within the interior in a state of transition, not one of crisis, before entering trade agreements with European traders, only decades after the start of the eighteenth century.

Furthermore, by the start of the eighteenth century the exchanges between the Asante and Fante, still seemingly peaceful, after their creation, led to trade arrangements between the two nations. These trade arrangements prior to numerous conflicts between the two nations, by the start of the 1720s contributed to the growing Gold Coast economy, one which increasingly connected the region between the interior and the coastline to the ever-expanding European and Atlantic Commercial economy. Moreover, the trade relationship which first connected the two states beyond their Akan cultural heritage was based upon a mutual fear of invasion. Although both during the early years hoped to expand its borders, a strong military presence stopped both from doing so at the others expense. Albeit, as the Fante union began to decline, the Asante began its expansion process.[15]

The peace between these two nations was extended again when trade alliances were formed in 1750, which increased arms sales to Asante in exchange for captives.[16] Only 100 years after their establishment, by the middle of the eighteenth century, the interior Asante state was already one of the most powerful in all of West Africa and the Gold Coast, seemingly replacing the Denkyira, Akyem and Akwamu all whom they defeated in military campaigns. The Asante state by the middle of the eighteenth century proved they were a force in which coastal African states and the British needed to immediately concern themselves with as they pushed to expand their empire beyond its own established borders. In the years between the start of the American Revolution and its end, 1765 and 1783, and the turn of the century, evidence shown in later charts, suggests the trade in captive labor increased from the Gold Coast. Just prior to the eventual passage of abolition laws closing this trade, between 1801 and 1807–1808, the trade in captives began to slowly decline. Furthermore, it is this time period between the American Revolution and the closure of the slave trade also coincides with the eventual push by the Asante toward the coastline in hopes creating an even more powerful state only to be met with opposition from the Fante and British crown.

Trading partnerships formed between African states were also impacted by the presence of European traders and the closure of the slave trade. Albeit, Britain in particular between the eighteenth and nineteenth centuries played a critical role on the Gold Coast as they partnered with African states, namely the Fante to acquire goods from the interior. Prior to the Asante attempt to encroach upon the coastal region, the Fante served as middlemen between Asante and British merchants along the coastline. The desire of the Asante to expand its borders and the British push to control the coastline and later its protected territory in the nineteenth century resulted in two competing strategies of expansion. These two strategies placed the coastal Fante state, whose power and authority was beginning to dwindle, at the center of these extension theories. In this interior process of expansion, the Asante began by attacking several other African nations in their path, which included the Fante state whose empire location gave them access to traders on the coast. With the British expanding along the coastline and the Fante in particular beginning to benefit from their presence this impacted the relationship between the two nations. As the Asante undertook its own expansion, the high profits the Fante began acquire through trade with the British ultimately served as point the state was willing to protect.[17]

The Fante for more than a century were the preferred middlemen of both nations, but by the start of the nineteenth century they were placed in the center of two expanding theories; one, the British hope to expand its sphere of influence, and the other, Asante push to further develop its empire. Moreover, these competing strategies by the mid-nineteenth century placed the Asante and British in direct conflict with one another resulting in several wars between the two nations throughout the nineteenth century. By the start of the nineteenth century, the relationship between the two African states was altered by the desire of the Asante to expand. This period also brings forth many of the root causes of declining relationship between the Asante and British before later creation and extension of the British Protectorate into the interior Gold Coast region.

The Akan people and the Asante state throughout the nineteenth century were heavily involved with coastal traders. Along the coastal market, Asante merchants exported and imported goods to and from interior region and despite the considerable amount of power concerning the economy of Greater Asante held by these traders, the more powerful elites were able to stop the development of a new independent middle class. Moreover, in doing so, the Asantehene, his chiefs and other subordinates were able to split any wealth finding its way into the hinterland, beginning with the formation of the state in the late seventeenth century. This growing economic dependency on one another continued for several centuries until the eventual coming of colonial rule. Albeit, in the coming decades of the eighteenth and nineteenth centuries, the region continued to witness changes in trading. Those revolutionary changes occurring throughout the centuries along the Gold Coast gave rise to increased trading which greatly impacted the interior exchanges.[18] Much of the interior changes which occurred were in response to the market, a point emphasized in later chapters.

As a result of the Asante rise and expansion, the state developed into the dominate traders within the region, often seeking out free trade with other Akan states and Europeans. Four groups had particular interests in the coastline of the Gold Coast:

1. The Asante, who want to promote unfettered free trade with the coast;
2. Other African states such as Fante or Denkyira that thrived precisely because of their status as profit-taking middlemen;
3. Europeans and local allies favorably inclined toward Asante goals (i.e. the Dutch and the Danes, who had concern over increased British monopoly);
4. Europeans opposed to increased Asante control over the coastal markets (i.e. the British)[19]

The Fante state, by the start of the nineteenth century, hoped their partnership with the British limited any attack from the Asante.

Europeans trading and living on the Gold Coast were well aware of the happenings in the interior states, especially those of the emerging Asante state. Both the Dutch and the British, the leading slave trading nations on the Gold Coast by the late 1600s into the early 1700s, were well aware of the formation of the Asante and their impending war with the Denkyira people.[20] The Asante expansion toward the coast and the wars that came along with it also increased the numbers of captives the state eventually sold into the

Trans-Atlantic Slave Trade in the eighteenth century. Beginning with their early decision to expand and their effects on the rise in the slave trade, Rebecca Shumway writes:

> During these years of Asante expansion, large number of war captives were sold into the trans-Atlantic slave trade. The volume of Ghana's export trade in slaves, relative to other parts of West Africa, was higher during the 1720s through the 1740s than at any other time during the slave trade. The Asante Empire continued to produce the bulk of enslaved Africans that were sold on the Ghana coast even after their initial wars of expansion ended . . . states in the empire were required to pay taxes in the form of human beings . . . states rebelled several times during the eighteenth century, causing a renewal of war and the generation of more captives.[21]

As the Asante began their expansion process toward the coastline in the middle of eighteenth century and engaged in conflicts with the Fante and neighboring states in the same area during the era, the number of captives also increased and evidenced by the previous chart. This resulted in an increase of 635,000 captives leaving from the Gold Coast between the two centuries. Moreover, the significant increase in the numbers of captives leaving the region increased just before the laws passed by the British and Americans became official.

As the position of the Asantehene passed through the generations, under the leadership of Asantehene Bonsu (1799–1824), encompassing the period prior to and after the passage of abolition laws, the Asante continued to wage several wars during their expansion from the region of Greater Asante. Although these wars of expansion began much later than the earliest years of this process, his reign shows the lasting impact of the initial Asante leaders on the final years of the Trans-Atlantic Slave Trade and the beginning of the era of legitimate commerce. The expansion process affected people not only within the state but also the neighboring nations and ultimately affected trade with Europeans to the south as well.[22]

Including those captives taken to the Spanish Americas, the number of total disembarking victims in areas across the Atlantic Ocean rises above 300,000. Prior to the turn of the century, the newly independent United States and Britain, by then two of the largest slaving nations increased their involvement in the Trans-Atlantic Slave Trade as well as in other African commodities. Furthermore, between1767 and 1807–1808, the Trans-Atlantic Slave Trade from the Gold Coast, like similar locations in West Africa, saw an upturn in trading along their coastline as more Europeans entered the area, which coincided with Asante expansion. (See Table 3.2.)

Thirty years prior to the closure of trading in captives (1807–1808), the Asante began to make their initial push toward the coast in several directions.

Table 3.2 Captives Leaving the Gold Coast during Asante Expansion, 1776–1808

	Mainland North America		*British Caribbean*		*French Caribbean*	
	Embarked	*Disembarked*	*Embarked*	*Disembarked*	*Embarked*	*Disembarked*
1776–1780	0	0	27,658	25,114	7,963	7,056
1781–1790	6,119	5,075	60,207	54,311	39,533	34,529
1791–1800	4,818	4,143	54,261	50,218	9,074	7,890
1801–1808	12,025	10,489	40,415	35,996	627	554
Total	22,962	19,706	182,541	165,639	57,198	50,029
	Dutch Americas		*Danish West Indies*		*Total*	
	Embarked	*Disembarked*	*Embarked*	*Disembarked*	*Embarked*	*Disembarked*
1776–1780	2,246	2,001	3,299	2,864	41,166	37,035
1781–1790	12,041	9,955	13,629	11,129	131,530	115,000
1791–1800	11,014	9,365	11,513	10,035	90,679	81,652
1801–1808	3,555	3,190	2,478	2,135	59,100	52,364
Total	28,856	24,512	30,919	26,164	322,476	286,050

Source: David Eltis et al. *The Trans-Atlantic Slave Trade Voyages Database*, http://slavevoyages.org/tast/assessment/estimates.faces?yearFrom=1776&yearTo=1808&embarkation=4&disembarkation=205.305.204.304.307.306.309.201.308.311.203.310.202.402.501.403.502.401.404.405.600.301.302.303 (Accessed December 20, 2010).

Similar to the expansion process the Asante experienced after their formation nearly eighty years earlier, the group began its move towards the coast. This push from Greater Asante began first toward Denkyira in 1701 and by 1765 Asante state's attention turned to the Fante state, Elmina and Cape Coast which had a heavy impact on the slave trade.[23]

Many of the earliest Fante connections to the Gold Coast region predate the arrival of any Europeans. Oral traditions of the Fante suggest their connection to the region is directly linked to earliest ancestors, known as Oburumankuma, Odapagyan and Osun.[24] By the seventeenth century as the trade in gold from the region began to increase coastal warfare between neighboring states also began to emerge. These conflicts between the Eguafo, Asebu, Agona and Fante resulted in the emergence of established connections between Europeans and African states. Furthermore, these wars fought over several years between these nations resulted in the exchange in trade routes, which proved very valuable to the growing Gold Coast economy linking the coastline to the interior states.[25]

As discussed in the previous chapter, between 1697 and 1701, the Asante State, encompassing the area Greater Asante[26] as it is often referred, formed as the Akan consolidated its power. Combining an economic and political expansionary process the Asante were able to establish themselves as a dominate state in the interior region of the Gold Coast.[27] Furthermore, as a result of this expansionary processes, the Asante were able to influence the economies of neighboring states in the region. In doing so they impacted the interior region along with neighboring states outside the realm of the Gold Coast to its north and also those to its south; which included Europeans. While the boundaries which surrounded the state were both well established and protected, the trade routes linking the various states and regions to one another were just as important to the structure of Greater Asante. These routes crisscrossing the entire region linked the interior state with the coastal markets consisting of Europeans and the African states along with Muslims to the north.

Moreover, the system of maintaining these numerous routes was developed under the leadership of Asantehene Osei Tutu. Under his early guidance, the state experienced several significant contributions in its formative years, all of which contributed to the expansionary process toward the coast. Asantehene Osei Tutu in these formatives years: (1) created a strong union replacing the loose military alliance, (2) after receiving the golden stool Kumasi was made the new capital, (3) introduced the Odwira festival, (4) mediated quarrels within the state, (5) and finally turned the Asante into a dominant military power.[28] Also between 1697 and 1717, under Asantehene Osei Tutu, using the established routes of trade led the Asante into several military campaigns against many of the surrounding indigenous groups, which bordered Greater Asante.

Using these established routes, traders were able to transports goods from the coastline into Greater Asante and well into the Northern region reaching the Mossi and Hausa. As trading increased cities were formed along the numerous routes. Garcia Clarke argues that, "Control of trade routes and regulation of trade played a primary role in the formation of indigenous empires . . . in the Gold Coast."[29] As with various areas across West Africa, states and empires were created along these trade routes each playing a vital role in the extension of trading. These routes leading from Kumasi, the center of the Asante state, were vital to the expansion process of the nation and ultimately the conflict with the British.

The Asante, realizing the value and importance of trade created a system of policing and maintenance of these routes from the interior, and as they expanded so too did the system of protection. This system of policing and maintenance of routes was important to the economy, military and the bureaucratic control of the Asante over the region and neighboring states.[30] Nevertheless, these routes were a crucial life-line to trade not only for expanding Asante State, but as more Europeans arrived and began residing and trading on the coast their need and use of roads increased. Moreover, European goods later became a constant presence along these trade routes. As the presence foreigners and their goods traded increased throughout the Gold Coast, the use of these routes became linked to expansionary goals, namely the British in the nineteenth century.

Of the numerous conflicts which resulted, several were due in part to the Asante decision to expand first to their Northern and second to their Southern boundaries. Furthermore, during the process of expanding the Asante sphere of influence in the eighteenth century this put several groups in their path, namely the Tekyiman and Wassa to their north and to the south, Akyem, Akwamu, Akras, Aowin and Ga.[31] Many of these states had trading relationships with Europeans residing along the coastline, often hosting them in their own villages as well as residing near the forts which they constructed.[32] Once defeated, several of states became tributaries of the Asante and were forced to pay taxes to the conquering state. These taxes were placed in the state treasury to be used in numerous capacities, including the maintenance of very trade routes their conquerors used to economically, politically and militarily to force them under their control.

Nevertheless, after the first Asante-Denkyira war, there were several conflicts among many of the indigenous populations of the region as well as wars between the Asante and other African nations on the Gold Coast. Once the Asante were able to defeat the Denkyira, they politically and economically controlled the forest zone region from 1701 to 1874 when the British invaded Kumasi and established a protectorate over the area.[33] Until 1731, Osei Tutu continued to lead the Asante in these campaigns against many of the indigenous groups, which surrounded Kumasi and Greater Asante. Conflicts of tributaries also became conflicts of the Asante, and one of the major conflicts on the coast resulted between Akyem, an Asante tributary and the Akwamu. This resulted in a conflict with the Asante army as they marched toward the coast, returning from a somewhat successful campaign at Koromante [Koromantin]. The resulting conflict did little to slow the Akwamu, who afterwards still remained one of the leading slave trading nations.[34] Expanding their Southern boundaries gave the Asante access to the coastal areas of the region and important trading locations, namely to Europeans and their trading forts.[35]

In the aftermath of Asantehene Osei Tutu's death, he was formally succeeded by his nephew, Opoku Ware, as the leader of the Asante people. Nonetheless, Asantehene Opoku Ware during his reign continued the expansion plans of the state established first by his uncle Osei Tutu. Albeit, under the leadership of Asantehene Opoku Ware, the expansion process resulted in several more wars fought between nations in the region from 1731 and 1745. Asantehene Opoku Ware was able to expand the Asante state further than his uncle or any of his later successors in all directions before his death in 1750.[36] Under Asantehene Opoku Ware, the Asante push to expand its borders coincided with the growth of internal and external commerce, realizing the importance of the trading with Europeans along the coast. Hiring the Fante, a member of the Akan, a state along the coastline, to act as middlemen aided in Asante expansion of commerce. By 1740, they too were in the direct path of expansion plans of the states' political boundaries. Although once hired by the Asante, the two fought against each other throughout the 1700s. Albeit, the Fante received substantial support from the British during the period, which became turning point on several occasions over the lifespan of this continuous conflict between the two Gold Coast states.

The need for expansion toward the coast by the Asante was attributed to the growing presence of Europeans on the coast who desired goods from the interior as well as the growing overseas markets for African goods in the nineteenth century. The Asante state at the start of the century funded their expansion process, in two different ways, first at the height of its power the Asante were able to tax traders who used trade routes.[37] This ability to tax traders who used trade routes resulted in a substantial source of revenue to the Asante state. Thereafter, the Asantehene and his surrounding regional governors collected taxes from traders to use both in the maintenance of these routes and expansion. While state traders were free to easily move along these routes, taxes were collected from private Asante and foreigners who trekked through the interior region.

Secondly the Asante state was able to pay for this expansion with the acquisition of guns and ammunition from Europeans on the coastal areas. The early guns that were introduced into the Gold Coast in early years of the seventeenth century were flint lock muskets.[38] Guns brought into the Gold Coast by the Portuguese continued over several centuries that by the eighteenth century the constant introduction of foreign weapons into the region began to dramatically impact conflicts between nations and states along with the economy. The continuous introduction of these guns into the Gold Coast in the eighteenth century by European traders also coincides with the Asante decision to expand trading in the region.[39] Guns and ammunition were acquired by non-slaving states and used for protection, while slaving states used weapons to conquer territories and slave-gathering.[40]

By 1742, the Dutch residing along the Gold Coast believed the Asante had 5,000 musketeers which by the eighteenth and nineteenth centuries included a complex system of military specialists.[41] These military specialists were crucial to the protection of the state in the nineteenth century as British forces got closer to the Asante state. Of the guns imported into the Gold Coast, the square musket proved to be the most popular of the guns.[42] Beginning with the reign of Osei Tutu, the Asante used guns and ammunition gained from trading captives for both warfare and expansion.[43]

The 107-year period, from 1700 to 1807, is important in the evolution of the Asante; so too is the period crucial to the development of the Fante. While the Asante controlled the interior of the Gold Coast, the Fante, another

Akan nation, controlled the coastline of the region. Their closeness to the coastline gave the Fante access to some of the twenty-six forts previously built along the region as of 1702.[44] The Fante, using already established trade routes along the coastline and those linking the area to the interior, created a direct trading link between both territories. Moreover, this allowed the Fante to become the key trading partner with several African states in the Gold Coast and Europeans, namely the British. The group became the key trading partners with several indigenous African groups nearby and Europeans at nearby Cape Coast Castle. Acting as middlemen, the Fante brought Asante goods and captives to the coast to the awaiting European ships.[45] Between 1700 and 1724, the Asante traded peacefully with the Fante, soon afterwards the relationship changed.

Between 1724 and 1806, as the Asante expanded, they came closer to encroaching upon the trading relationships the Fante established between themselves and European nations. Once hired by the neighboring Asante, this era proved the Fante were now in the direct path of their expansion plans. While there were several early conflicts near the coastline, the Asante defeat of Akyem in 1742 left only the Fante as the last state keeping the interior state away from total control.[46] As the Asante got closer to their territory, the Fante began to restrict the flow of guns and ammunition finding their way to the Asante. This process of restricting the weapons allowed into the Asante nation began as late as 1765, but this did little to affect their trading relationship with one another in the 1770s.[47]

The Asante using trade routes moved toward the coast and eventually moved closer to the Fante territory and Cape Coast Castle. The Asante began to move toward two locations on the coast, first Cape Coast and second toward Accra.

By the start of the 1740s, the Asante controlled the entire coast region except for the Fante area near Cape Coast Castle, and between 1770 and 1806, another era of the ever complicated relationship between the Fante and Asante began. Moreover, the Asante control of the entire coastal region except for the Fante area near Cape Coast Castle, a British fort, brought on more conflicts between the former partners in trade. Asantehene Osei Kwadwo, Asantehene Kwame Panin and Asantehene Opoku Fofie pushed the Asante directly onto the cusp Fante territory on the coast. As the trading relationship between the Fante and the Europeans along the coast continued to develop, namely with the British, they too began to fear the coming an Asante army. Some believed the coming of Asante armies could possibly invade the Europeans forts on the coast and stretch their empire from the interior to the coastline. British forts stretched from Dixcove to Cape Three Points and encompassed forts at Cape Coast, Accra, Tantum,

Winnebah and Annamaboo. British merchants on the coast saw these forts as an essential component to British trading.[48] Danish traders on the other hand saw this as an opportunity to oust any other Europeans along the coast gaining even more access to goods from the interior. They began supplying the Asante with weapons.[49] The Anglo-Dutch rivalries that were playing out in Europe found their way to the Gold Coast prior to the turn of the century.

Although the Asante did not gain a key victory over the Fante until 1806, Europeans along the coastline, especially the British, were well aware of this growing state and their coastal interests prior to their invasion. Several British traders along the coast began to take steps to ensure both themselves and the Fante were protected against invasion from the Asante. In 1765, 1767 and again 1772, the Council of the Company of Merchants, British traders, at Cape Coast Castle adopted policies to aid the Fante if the Asante invaded the territory.[50] Even though these policies were adopted to protect the Fante from Asante invasion, they decided only to aid them with military support when the case presented extreme emergency. In doing so they hoped to avoid unnecessarily making the Asante an enemy.[51] British merchants on the coast saw the Fante as an essential element to the survival of their economy, even though the British commercial entities in London did not agree with the assessment of the Council of the Company of Merchants.[52]

Encamped in the Fante state, Abora, the Asante finally invaded the Fante territory in 1805, eventually returning victorious in 1806, under Asantehene Osei Bonsu. During Asantehene Osei Bonsu's reign, the Asante nations made their first contact with Europeans living along the coast. Moreover, as the Asante invaded the Fante territory and in a matter of time had pushed them back to the sea, forcing them to surrender their grip on the coast. The Asante acquisition of portions the Fante territory gave them access to the entire coastline of the Gold Coast, stretching their empire from the interior to the coast, cutting out its one-time trading as middlemen. According to Osei Kwadwo, the war started after the Fante chiefs decided to protect the chiefs of Assin, an Asante tributary, which the Asantehene saw as an offence against the Asante state. Kwadwo states:

> The cause of this war was the offence committed against the Asantehene by two Assin chiefs, Otibo and Aputae . . . the chiefs bolted away to Fanteland and asked chiefs to protect them . . . therefore they decided not to give up the chiefs up . . . they would fight the Asante Nation to halt their superiority. War therefore broke out. Soldiers were sent from the Cape Coast Castle to help the Coastal force. Though the battle was fierce, the Asante army were victorious. The defeat of the coastal forces earned the Asante Nation the papers of the other forts at the Coast. . . . The defeat of the coastal states extended the Asante Empire to the sea. The then governor at Cape Coast, Colonel Torren recognized

> Asante Nation as far as to the seas but the coastal states, especially the Fantes, did not recognise this.[53]

This conflict resulted in a number of deaths and people being taken into the Trans-Atlantic Slave Trade, just prior to its closing. This was only the first of several more skirmishes fought between the Asante and Fante.[54]

By the middle of the nineteenth century several more large scale conflicts between the Asante and Fante were narrowly avoided, but this did little to repair the relationship between the two states. Ultimately, conflicts between the Asante and British during this period began to increase. Furthermore, by the middle of the century, the relationship between the British and Fante entered a new contract, as the African state or Confederacy as it became known thereafter relinquished several of its rights to the emerging colonial entity. Albeit, during this same period the Fante state had begun to give up several of its judicial rights to the British crown in the Bond of 1844. This led to the British assertion of judicial authority beyond the coastline and into the Fante territory.[55]

Once established, the Fante hoped creating their own confederacy could help them achieve modernization, an extension of internal self-government and importantly, greater security to keep away the danger of the expanding Asante. Agreeing to the Bond of 1844, limited the power of Fante kings and chiefs abolished their judicial system in favor of the British system and later began payment to caboceers.[56]

Although European nations and America were in the process of abolishing the Trans-Atlantic Slave Trade, this did little to slow the expansion hopes of the Asante state well into the nineteenth century. Their expansion toward the coastline beginning in the eighteenth and nineteenth centuries was done at the expense of several other African states, namely the Fante. The results of this expansion brought about changes across the Gold Coast which had a lingering impact well into the twentieth century after the start of colonial rule. Moreover, as numerous changes occurred due to laws passed, this did little to slow the Asante expansion. The Asante while expanding during the period they were able to adapt to the fluctuations across the region as a result of the rise in legitimate commerce.

NOTES

1. Walter Rodney, "The Guinea Coast," in J. D. Fage and Roland Oliver eds., *The Cambridge History of Africa,* 1600–1790, Vol. 4 (United Kingdom: Cambridge University Press, 1975), p. 302.

2. David Eltis et al., *The Trans-Atlantic Slave Trade Voyages Database* http://slavevoyages.org/tast/assessment/estimates.faces?yearFrom=1650&yearTo=1699&embarkation=4 (Accessed January 14, 2015).

3. Albert van Dantzig, *Forts and Castles of Ghana* (Accra, Ghana: Sedeco Publishing, 1999), pp. i–ix.

4. Walter Rodney, "Gold and Slaves on the Gold Coast," *Transactions of the Historical Society of Ghana*, Vol. X (1969), pp. 16–17.

5. N. R. Junner, *Gold on the Gold Coast* (Colchester, 1935), p. 14.

6. Harvey M. Feinberg, *Africans and Europeans in West Africa, Elminans and Dutchmen on the Gold Coast During the Eighteenth Century* (Philadelphia, PA: The American Philosophical Society, 1989), pp. 53–55.

7. William Bosman, *A New and Accurate Description of the Coast of Guinea, Divided in the Gold, the Slave and the Ivory Coasts* (London: J. Knapton, et al., 1705), pp. 89–90.

8. Feinberg, 54–55.

9. John Barbot, *A Description of the Coasts of North and South Guinea* (1732) in Elizabeth A. Bohls and Ian Duncan, eds. *Traveling Writing* 1700–1830*: An Anthology* (Oxford: Oxford University Press, 2005) p. 186

10. Mary McCarthy, *Social Change and the Growth of British Power in the Gold Coast: The Fante States,* 1807–1874 (Lanham, MD: University Press of America, 1983), pp. 6–7.

11. Ibid., 9.

12. W. W. Claridge, *A History of the Gold Coast and Ashanti*, 2nd ed. (New York: Barnes and Noble, 1964), p. 150.

13. Rebecca Shumway, "Palavers and Treaty Making in the British Acquisition of the Gold Coast Colony, West Africa," in Saliha Belmessous, ed., *Empire By Treaty: Negotiating European Expansion,* 1600–1900 (New York: Oxford University Press, 2015), p. 170.

14. Feinberg, 131–132.

15. McCarthy, 7.

16. Ibid., 8.

17. Mary E. Wiesner-Hanks, William Bruce Wheeler, Franklin M. Doeringer and Kenneth R. Curtis, eds. *Discovering the Global Past: A Look at the Evidence, Volume II: Since 1400*, 4th ed. (Boston, MA: Wadsworth, 2012), p. 210.

18. Christine Oppong, *Marriage Among a Matrilineal Elite: A Family Study of Ghanaian Senior Civil Servants* (London: Cambridge University Press, 1974), p. 38.

19. John D. Carolson, *Myths, State Expansion and the Birth of Globalization: A Comparative Perspective* (New York: Palgrave Macmillan, 2012), p. 89.

20. Ivor Wilks, "On Mentally Mapping Greater Asante: A Study of Time and Motion," *The Journal of African History*, Vol. 33, No. 2 (1992), p. 111.

21. Rebecca Shumway, *Between the Castle and the Golden Stool: Transformation in Fante Society in the Eighteenth Century* (Unpublished Dissertation: Emory University, 2004), p. 44.

22. Osei Kwadwo, *An Outline of Asante History* (Accra, Ghana: Monarch Publications, 1994), pp. 19–20.

23. Shumway, *Between the Castle and Golden Stool*, 44.

24. Rebecca Shumway, *The Fante and the Transatlantic Slave Trade* (University of Rochester Press: Rochester, NY, 2011), pp. 34–35.

25. Ibid., 42–43.

26. The term Greater Asante is often used to refer to the Asante Empire, see: Kwame Arhin, "The Structure of Greater Ashanti, 1700–1824," *The Journal of African History*, Vol. 8, No. 1 (1967), p. 67.

27. Ibid.

28. Elizabeth M. Halcrow, *Canes and Chains: A Study of Sugar and Slavery* (Oxford: Heinemann Educational Publishers, 1982), pp. 42–43.

29. Garcia Clark, "Class Alliance and the Class Fractions in Ghanaian Trading and State Formation," *Review of African Political Economy*, No. 49 (Winter, 1990), p. 75.

30. Ivor Wilks, "On Mentally Mapping Greater Asante: A Study of Time and Motion," *The Journal of African History*, Vol. 33, No. 2 (1992), pp. 175–177

31. Naomi Chazan, "The Early State in Africa: The Asante Case," in Eisenstadt, S. N., Michel Abitbol and Naomi Chazan, eds. *Early State in African Perspective, Culture, Power and Division of Labor*, Vol. 3 (Netherlands: EJ Brill Publishers, 1988), pp. 78–79

32. Rodney, "The Guinea Coast," 309.

33. Emmanuel Akyeampon, "C. C. Reindorf on the Cultural Articulation of Power in Pre-Colonial Ghana—Observations of a Social Historian," in Paul Jenkins, ed., *West African Past: African Pastors and African History in the Nineteenth Century*, 2nd ed. (Basel, Switzerland: Basel Mission Archive, 2000), p. 107.

34. The Akwamu state after its defeat of Anlo used the coastal region to export captives into the Trans-Atlantic Slave Trade. Sandra Greene's work *Gender, Ethnicity, and Social Change on the Upper Slave Coast: A History of the Anlo-Ewo* (London: Heinemann, 1996), p. a 24, discusses the impact of the Akwamu conquering of Anlo and the increase in captives afterward.

35. C. C. Reindorf, *History of the Gold Coast and the Asante, Based on Traditions and Historical Facts, Comprising A Period of More than Three Centuries From About 1500 to 1860* (London: Kegan Paul, Trench, Trubner & Co., 1895), pp. 68–69.

36. Ibid., 90.

37. Wilks, "Mentally Mapping Greater Asante," 175–177.

38. Trevor Getz, *Slavery and Reform in West Africa: Toward Emancipation in the 19th Century Senegal and Gold Coast* (Athens, OH: Ohio University Press, 2004), p. 13.

39. Joseph E. Inikori, "The Import of Firearms into West Africa 1750–1807: A Quantitative Analysis," *The Journal of African History*, Vol. 18, No. 3 (1977), p. 341.

40. Ibid., 351–352.

41. R. A. Kea, "Firearms and Warfare on the Gold and Slave Coasts from the Sixteenth to Nineteenth Centuries," *The Journal of African History*, Vol. 12, No. 2 (1971), p. 202.

42. Inikori, "Import of Firearms into West Africa," 355.

43. Kwame Arhin, "The Financing of the Ashanti Expansion, 1700–1820," *Africa: Journal of the International African Institute*, Vol. 37, No. 3 (July, 1967), p. 283.

44. Getz, *Slavery and Reform in West Africa*, 16.

45. James Sanders, "The Expansion of the Fante and the Emergence of Asante in the 18th Century," *Journal of African History*, Vol. 20, No. 3 (1979), p. 350.

46. Ibid., 351.

47. Ibid.

48. John Adams, *Sketches Taken During Ten Voyages to Africa, Between the Years 1786 and 1800*, Reprint (New York, Johnson Reprint Corporation, 1970), pp. 5–6.

49. Chazan, 79.

50. Margaret Priestley, "The Ashanti Question and the British: Eighteenth Century Origins," *The Journal of African History*, Vol. 2, No. 1 (1961), p. 36.

51. Ibid., 55.

52. Ibid., 57.

53. Osei Kwadwo, *An Outline of Asante History* (Kumasi, Ghana: O. Kwadwo Enterprise, 1994), p. 19.

54. Ibid.

55. Francis Agbodeka, *African Politics and British Policy in the Gold Coast: A Study in the Forms and Force of Protest,* 1868–1900 (Longman Press: New York, 1971), p. 15.

56. Ibid., 16–23.

Chapter 4

The Gold Coast, Abolition Laws and the Era of Illegal Slave Trading, 1776–1842

With the Trans-Atlantic Slave Trade already in full swing, the 1770s proved to be a pivotal turning point in the Asante relations with other nations on the Gold Coast. Just as the Asante were hoping to expand, a pivotal turning point occurred also for the economies of the British and the Dutch at home as well as in West Africa and in the Caribbean. Just as the Asante made their final push into Fante territory, ultimately capturing parts of the coastal state in 1806, Denmark (1803–1804), the Britain (1807) and America (1808) governments took the necessary steps to abolish the slave trade from the west coast of Africa to its citizens. These simultaneous actions, Asante expansion as discussed in the previous chapter, the passage of abolition laws, set the stage for an extension of British settlements well into the interior of the Gold Coast. Taking the initial steps necessary to close the Trans-Atlantic Slave Trade affected all parties involved including Africans trading along the coast and this was especially evident along the Gold Coast. Moreover, the passage of abolition laws begins the era of illegal slave trading for these nations and its citizens, but it also proves to be the start of the trade in bulk export commodities,[1] commonly referred to as legitimate commerce.[2]

The many worldwide events which occurred during the period from 1776–1842 were interconnected with one another and had lingering effects on all parties involved. Not only does the period include the Asante expansion toward the coast but also the American and Haitian Revolutions, the passage of laws to close the trade in Africans and the start of naval squadrons by the British and Americans to slow the trade. The roles of both the British and United States' naval squadrons, known as the West Africa Squadron[3] and the Africa Squadron,[4] respectively, patrolled waters near the Gold Coast. The British squadron started in 1807–1808 and was permanently put on the West Coast of Africa in 1816, while the American squadron started after the passage of the Webster-Ashburton Treaty in 1842. Both squadrons, especially the powerful British Royal Navy, have been viewed as necessary components to the slave trade's closure.

With the start of these naval fleets, both the British and American fleet faced issues that were similar and obvious. Seemingly, both squadrons faced (1) the shortage of ships and (2) the lack of men to serve on board. Although both were seen as essential and effective units in closing the slave trade, I contend that the primary concern omitted in previous studies is the use of both the British and American squadrons for the protection of commercial interest in American, Caribbean and West African waters. This primary concern is emphasized by the importance of establishing what has been referred to as legitimate commerce. Along the Gold Coast the extension of legitimate commerce in the nineteenth century served as the foundation for the creation of a British Protectorate in the last quarter of the century. Another glaring omission is the active involvement of the Kru people of Liberia's Kru Coast,[5] many of whom settled in British trading towns throughout West Africa, including the Gold Coast, eventually helping lead the way into the interior of the region in the decades following their arrival.

Beginning in the latter half of the eighteenth century, as mercantilism began to decline the world began transitioning to the new economic system of capitalism. In this transition, the West Indies served as one of the first locations to suffer decline due to changes in economic perspectives. The slave trade was vital to British industrial growth and as the population of the New World grew, capitalism expanded.[6] Eric Williams, in his classic work *Capitalism and Slavery*, points to the period from 1783 to 1833 as the rise of capitalism and the end of slavery for the British Empire. This period covers a number of important dates in regard to the slave trade. Williams pointed out that the growth of industry during this period ended the slave trade and slavery in the British Empire, saying simply "Mercantilism had run its course."[7]

The Haitian Revolution served as one of the first major blows to the Trans-Atlantic Slave Trade. Albeit, the region was once viewed as a key component to the continually developing Caribbean slave economy, by the start of the Haitian Revolution, the area proved to be home to a turning point in history, as it proved to be the starting point for the decline in slave trading. David Brion Davis writes, "The Haitian Revolution impinged in one way or another on the entire emancipation debate from the British parliamentary move in 1792 to outlaw the African slave trade to Brazil's final abolition of slavery in ninety six years later."[8] The Haitian Revolution was a contributing factor to the decision of the British and the United States to abolish the slave trade as it sparked fear among many Europeans and Americans. Furthermore, the images of the Haitian Revolution were on full display when nations began the process to abolishing the slave trade.[9]

Another major blow dealt to the Trans-Atlantic Slave Trade was the start of the American Revolutionary War, which Selwynn H. H. Carrington argues was both traumatic as well as devastating for the British West Indies because eventually it was the beginning of the decline for the sugar colonies of the region.[10] This decline was further advanced by the passage of the United States Constitution. Passed in 1787, the United States Constitution abolished the trade in Africans to take effect in January 1, 1808, twenty-one years later. As Article 1 Section 9 of the United States Constitution reads:

> The migration or importation of such persons as any of the states now existing shall think proper to admit, shall not be prohibited by the Congress prior to the year one thousand eight hundred and eight, but a tax or duty may be imposed on such importation, not exceeding ten dollars for each person.[11]

Thereafter, the United States began passing several laws that lead to the complete closure of the slave trade to its citizens. Several state governments passed similar suppression laws to that of the United States which went into effect immediately. In 1787, New Jersey and Rhode Island became the first states to abolish the slave trade with Massachusetts following in 1788 and by 1794 states began prosecuting its citizens for illegally trading captives.

In 1794, the United States passed the first of its slave trade acts, to prohibit its citizens from engaging in the trade, although it was weakly enforced. This act prohibited United States citizens or foreigners residing in the country to serve as master or owner of a ship as well as build, fit, equip or load any vessel to transport Africans. Those captured and found guilty would be forced to pay a fine of two thousand dollars.[12] Albeit, this act was further strengthened by the Slave Trade Act of 1800 which gave district courts power to put suspected slave traders on trial, prohibiting the bringing of people into states which allowed the slave trade and forfeitures would be sold on behalf of the United States.[13] Three years after the implementation of the Slave Trade Act of 1803, this allowed for the forfeiture of captured ships.[14]

Captured slave traders were punished to the fullest extent of the law according to the slave trade acts passed. The implementation of the law, in many cases, was at the discretion of the judge they faced. Even though these laws were passed, they did little to slow traders. One of the largest slave trading families in the United States, the De Wolf's, continued to exploit the Gold Coast on numerous occasions before the trade was closed and even after slave trade acts were passed. In a 1790 letter to James De Wolf, Captain Ganver wrote him immediately after arriving at Cape Coast Castle, ". . . I immediately went to shore and then made a barter for eight Benin slaves. . . . I will buy also some prime men. . . . Hundred and twenty knives for one prime slave . . ."[15]

Immediately following the completion of the American Revolution and the start of the Haitian Revolutions, Denmark, took several steps to change its economy in the eighteenth century. The country expanded several of its colonial possessions and increased the role of its private owners in its territories.[16] By this point, although accounting for small numbers of captives being transported to the West Indies, between 1733 and 1802, the Danes introduced 123,000 captives into the Caribbean.[17] During the period, several American traders also sailed into the Danish Caribbean to acquire captives, especially from the area of St. Croix.[18]

In the final years of the Denmark involvement in the slave trade, war and free trade increased the numbers of traders and captives. While the number of captives they acquired was still relatively small as compared to the Dutch and British, the nation became the fourth largest trader in Africa prior to the closing of its trade.[19] Much of the market for Danish captives included other territories in the Caribbean and in the Americas.[20] Even with this small increase, the Danes in 1792 began a push to close the trade in Africans, due in part to the increased numbers of private owners participating in the developing Danish free-trade market. As a result of these, Denmark officially became the first nation to close the slave trade to its citizens. According to Joseph Beldam, who discusses the decision of Denmark to close the trade:

> The King of Denmark, by an edict, dated Copenhagen, so early as the 16th of March, 1792, decreed, that the slave trade carried on by his subjects, should with the beginning of the year 1803 cease on the African coasts and elsewhere out of the West Indies. By an articles in the treaty of Kiel, of the 14th of January, 1814, the King of Denmark engaged to prohibit all his subjects in the most effect manner, and by the most solemn laws, from taking any share in that traffic.[21]

As the Danish traders along the Gold Coast began to transition into the era of legitimately traded goods on the Gold Coast, they established a number of plantations in the region do so.[22] Moreover, the creation of such plantations and the use of slave labor causes pause in the use of such a term as legitimate commerce. The former Danish traders, who exclusively traded in captives along the region, began to export crops produced on these plantations located in the Southeastern portion of the Gold Coast near the Akuapem Mountains.[23]

The Danish plantations of the Akuapem Mountain region consisted of both domestic slaves who were acquired through the pawn system and enslaved workers, who fulfilled production needs. Slaves on Danish plantations Bibease and Frederiksgave, working four days a week, were responsible for the production of commercial crops and their transport to Accra.[24] These plantations grew crops such as plantain, citrus, cassava, sugar cane, banana, cotton, coffee and bean for export.[25]

The American Revolution also had damaging effects on the Dutch trading in not only Africa, but also in the Caribbean and American waters as well and by the 1780s they watched as their trading in the Atlantic region continued to decline further. Although they backed the Americans during the 1780s, the start of the Fourth Anglo-Dutch War (1780–1784) watched as many of their merchant ships were captured by the British. This war brought an end to the Dutch slave trading as many of their slave ships were captured by the British.[26] After 1795 to 1815 the Dutch slave trade continued to fall to low numbers and many of the slave traders decided to go into other ventures after peace was restored.[27]

Over this same time period, Britain passed laws similar to those of the United States as they pushed toward abolition.[28] Its campaign against closing the slave trade, many have argued, began in 1787 with the foundation of the Committee for the Abolition of the Slave Trade.[29] Thomas Clarkson along with Oludah Equiano became two of the first individuals to write about the horrors of the slave trade as well as two of the founding members of the Committee for the Abolition of the Slave Trade. Two years later, William Wilberforce delivered his first speech arguing for the closure of the slave trade in 1789, also refuting the claim that Liverpool commerce would eventually go into a decline.[30]

The early British laws regulating the slave trade limited the number of captives on board but were intended to maximize the number brought and profits made in the final years of the trade. According to the British act to regulate the shipping and carrying of slaves, no more than five slaves were permitted on board per ton with the ship not to exceed 201 tons.[31] In 1793, this act was amended to allow five slaves per three tons[32] and by 1799 this act determined the space slaves were allotted on board to a perpendicular height of five feet.[33] This early act determined how captives were carried onboard British vessels throughout the final years of the trade, which affected both the slave trade and other commerce. Over the final years of the British slave trade, Parliament amended this act several times through 1799 before the trade was completely closed in 1807, which unlike the previous acts did not refer to tonnage.[34]

Portions of the Gold Coast between 1793 and 1810 were exclusively divided between the Americans and British, with the latter controlling more than three-fourths of the trading. Although the Anglo-Dutch Maritime War of 1793 slowed trading slightly, by 1810 the English were exporting nearly 55,000 captives a year, up from the 38,000 they acquired prior to the Revolutionary War. The only nations during the period with the ability to acquire captives at such a high number were the Portuguese, who acquired nearly 20,000 captives a year and the Americans, who acquired nearly 15,000 captives yearly.[35]

The British Slave Trade Act of 1807 was passed on March 25, 1807, and was to take effect on May 1, 1807. It read:

> that from and after the first day of May one thousand eight hundred and seven, the African Slave Trade, and all manner of dealing and trading in the purchase, sale, barter, or transfer of slaves, or of persons intended to be sold, transferred, used, or dealt with as slaves, practiced or carried on, in, at, to or from any part of the coast or countries of Africa, shall be, and the same is hereby utterly abolished, prohibited, and declared to be unlawful[36]

Unlike the previous British laws which focused on the number of captives and the tonnage of the ships, this act directly prohibited the trade to its citizens.

Well into 1806–1807 and prior to the passage of the British laws closing the slave trade, William Wilberforce continued to discuss the impact of suppressing the trade on all involved parties. Wilberforce argued that African nations involved in the trade wanted it closed. According to Wilberforce:

> We have the evidence of several most respectable officers of the navy, to prove, that wherever they touched . . . in the widely distant countries of Senegambia and the Gold Coast . . . all that appeared . . . worthy of a remark; and it was from this record that the Committee read the affecting account which has been mentioned, in which one of the African Kings, with every appearance of sincerity, repeatedly expressed his deep remorse for having been instigated, in a season of intoxication, into which he had been drawn by the Slave merchants, to oppress and pillage his subjects.[37]

Ultimately the British finally began the steps to close the trade in captive Africans.

With its foundation laid by the United States Constitution, the United States passed its abolition to law on March 2, 1807, to take effect in 1808. Finally on January 1, 1808, after twenty-one years, the slave trade to the United States was suppressed by federal laws, making it illegal for any American citizen to transport Africans into the United States or equip ships to do so.[38] The passage of both British and American laws would officially begin the era or "legitimate commerce."

Prior to the passage of the 1808 laws abolishing the Trans-Atlantic Slave Trade to American shores, the United States patrolled its own shoreline in pursuit of ships traveling near the eastern seaboard trading goods illegally. The ships patrolling the American coastline, known as the Revenue Cutters, specifically kept a close eye on ships heading for American port cities. The Revenue Cutters served under the United States Treasury Department. They were created in 1790 by Alexander Hamilton.[39] By 1793, the Revenue Cutters had officers from several of America's earliest states, including New

Hampshire, Massachusetts, Connecticut, New York, Virginia, Maryland, South Carolina and North Carolina.[40] Three years later, President George Washington called for new ships. In a September 1796 letter, George Washington stated to Oliver Wolcott:

> Having considered your report of the fifth instant, I do hereby authorise you to take suitable and legal measures for procuring by contract or otherwise as shall appear to be most for the public interest, four Revenue Cutters, to be employed on the Pennsylvania, Maryland, Virginia and South Carolina Stations. And I do hereby direct you to cause the Revenue Cutters belonging to the United States on the Maryland, Virginia and South Carolina Stations to be sold at public Auction, and to cause the proceeds of such Sales to be paid into the Treasury of the United States; and for so doing this shall be your warrant.[41]

Increasing the Revenue Cutters did little to slow the slave trade by Americans.

Serving as a forerunner to the United States Coast Guard (Created in 1915), the Revenue Cutters patrolled waters to do just as the name implies—protect American revenue. This small fleet, initially consisting of ten ships but never attaining more than seventeen ships, was sent out on American waters to capture those illegally smuggling goods into American ports. With a combined fleet of ten ships (i.e. Massachusetts, Argus, Scammel, South Carolina, Virginia, etc.), the Revenue Cutters protected American revenue along its shoreline, but lacked the number of ships needed to suppress the slave trade.[42]

Capturing slave traders and ships illegally smuggling in Africans eventually became a top priority of the Revenue Cutter Service with the passage of the 1794 Slave Trade Act. If found in violation of the 1794 Slave Trade Act, an individual could face possibly the forfeiture of property, namely his ship and all goods onboard. Truman R. Strobridge and Dennis L. Noble write, "As early as 1794, the Revenue Cutters had been instructed to prevent the importation of new slaves ("contraband" in revenue terminology) from Africa to the United States. The further prohibition against the foreign slave trade in 1807 enlarged this effort. Before the Civil War ended, the cutters had captured numerous ships and freed almost five hundred slaves."[43]

The protection of American revenue was further tested after the US Congress gave President John Adams permission to use the Cutter Service, after a conflict between the French and Americans upon the French seizure of United States mercantile ships and the fallout of the XYZ Affair.[44] This served as one of the first attempts to interfere in American trade, a point that in later years became the biggest topic of suppressing the slave trade.

Protecting American commerce from foreign invasion (i.e. right to search and seizure) became the biggest issue in the era of illegal slave trading after 1807–1808 as the British threatened to seize suspected American slavers. This would become one of the biggest disputes between the American and

British leading to the War of 1812. This dispute also affected the suppression effort of both until 1862, when a treaty signed between Britain and the United States allowed a for limited right of search and seizure of American ships on the high seas and off certain coasts during the Abraham Lincoln administration. The signing of this treaty led to the creation of a mixed court system established in New York, similar to those already in Freetown, Cape Town, Havana, Cape of Good Hope and Luanda.[45]

Another factor leading to the creation of the Revenue Cutters and the final closure of the slave trade was the Haitian Revolution. Don E. Fehrenbacher writes:

> Adding to the pressure for curtailment of slave trading . . . was the black revolution in Haiti. . . . In 1794, after having ignored the problem for several years, Congress . . . with its first slave-trade law . . . prohibited citizens and other residents of the United States from carrying on such a trade to any foreign country.[46]

The Haitian Revolution in 1791 became a major factor in the decision of the United States to follow through on its efforts to ban the transportation of Africans from West Africa. It later played a role in the efforts of American Colonization Society to transport free blacks back to West Africa leading to the establishment of Liberia in 1822.[47]

The United States abolition of the slave trade law affected a number of industries in a country that was only thirty-two years old. Even after its passage, the United States continued to use the Revenue Cutters to slow the flourishing slave trade industry. By the time of the War of 1812 the use for the cutter service was again revised. Many of the ships considered old and obsolete would be used in the War of 1812 and de-commissioned afterward. The ships of the Revenue Cutters, unfit to chase slave traders fifty years prior, faced a similar problem, when used in the Africa Squadron. This became the subject of a heated debate among crew members serving on the ships and Congress members who supported the efforts of the African Squadron to subdue the illegal trading of African captives.[48]

Much of the American fight against the Trans-Atlantic Slave Trade during the earliest years also coincided with the colonization of both West African territories, Sierra Leone and Liberia. Could the final closure of the slave trade be due to the African and West African Squadrons making progress or could there be another factor, perhaps one on land that should garner more attention than it has previously received? Often overlooked is the impact of the colonization of Sierra Leone and Liberia by free blacks. There since 1811, the West Africa Squadron made very little progress in slowing the illegal slave trade, nonetheless commerce developed due to their presence in Sierra Leone. Much of this slow progress was the result of several diplomatic disputes, namely over the right to search and seizure. The right to search and seizure reappeared numerous times as the British pressured nations into abolishing their slave trade. In the United States, Liberia was seen as an essential element for the expansion of legitimate trade to and from West Africa.

The lack of success that the British Royal Navy experienced in West Africa capturing a large number of slave traders did not deter the British government from further expanding its hopes of commercial success from Africa. Established in 1787, Sierra Leone and in particular Freetown became crucial elements to British trading and efforts to close the slave trade. After finally passing laws to abolish the Trans-Atlantic Slave Trade, the British freed former slaves from England, Nova Scotia, and Jamaica returning them to Sierra Leone. Afterward many of the intercepted slave ships were also taken to Freetown, Sierra Leone, where captives were ultimately set free.[49]

After the passage of laws to abolish the British role in the Trans-Atlantic Slave Trade, the Royal Navy, considered the strongest naval force of the day, was commissioned to subdue the British involvement in this trade. Initially beginning with two ships in 1808 and growing to five in 1811, ships were especially at a premium during the Napoleonic Wars. Although, the British Royal Navy had a fleet of 795 ships, they were spread out to other areas including: the Mediterranean, the Caribbean and the Indian Ocean.[50] It was not until 1816 that a permanent British force was placed on the coast of West Africa. In a recent study on the British Royal Navy and its suppression effort Chaim D. Kaufmann and Robert A. Pape argue:

> For sixty years almost all of the costs of suppression were borne by Britain, which took the initiative to cajole, bribe, and, where possible, coerce the other slave-trading nations into compliance. It also provided nearly all of the naval strength needed to police slave trade suppression, maintaining squadrons off West Africa, South America, and in the Caribbean for this purpose.[51]

Although the British campaign lasted sixty years, their efforts received mixed success. Successful on the West African coast was in sharp dissimilarity to their success in Cuba.[52]

In the early years of the illegal era of slave trading, the West Africa Squadron after becoming a permanent force of the coast of West Africa, between 1814 and 1822, recaptured over 11,000 captives from ships trading captives. Of the 11,000 recaptured, over 10,000 were delivered to the British colony of Sierra Leone.[53] Conversely, over this same period, more than nearly 680,000 captives were transported across the Atlantic Ocean.[54]

With a permanent force in place on the African coast, the British and its West Africa Squadron became the largest naval force engaged in abolishing the slave trade from West Africa. Like the British, several other European nations with a navy established a patrol squadron for the closure of the slave trade, namely France, Spain and Portugal[55]; they also pressured the United States into establishing a navy for the suppression effort, with the Webster-Ashburton Treaty.

Previously, the United States had employed the Revenue Cutters in the suppression of the slave trade, giving them the task of capturing traders trying to evade paying taxes on its shores. The initial laws to suppress the slave trade with the use of American ships were passed in 1819.[56] This law directed the President of the United States James Monroe, ironically the same man for which the capital of Liberia (Monrovia) is named, to use cruisers to patrol the West coast of Africa to suppress the trade.[57]

Despite lacking the support from the black population in the United States and the American government, the newly formed Liberian colony played a role in damaging the efforts of slave traders in the region. After reaching the Liberian coasts free blacks began making contacts with several African groups that would further their efforts against slave traders. The work of the American Colonization Society in the United States continued to push for the repatriation of these newly freed blacks even as the government's suppression laws captured minimal numbers of slave traders.

Liberia in its early years was a key component to the suppression of the Trans-Atlantic Slave Trade and one could argue was a part of protecting American revenue. The Slave Trade Act of 1819 gave money to the American Colonization Society to aid recaptured Africans in the colony of Liberia even though much of this money did not go to its intended purpose. Liberia made several key contacts with groups in the surrounding region and neighboring countries that were vital to their efforts against slave traders, and thus played a substantial role in slowing the trade in Africans.[58]

A few months after the passage of the 1819 Slave Trade Law, President Monroe in a letter to Congress and the House of Representatives places two agents in Liberia with a salary of $1,500 and $1,200, respectively.[59] The American agents sent to suppress the trade arrived in Liberia 1820, and in two years made five visits to Africa. By 1823 there were no ships spotted on the coast of Africa even though the laws passed in 1819 were still in effect.[60] According to the United States African Agent Ayres, "Although for some years the coast had been occasionally visited by our cruisers, their short stay and seldom appearance had made but slight impression on those traders, rendered hardy by repetition of crime, and avaricious by excessive gain."[61]

Joseph Bryan, a representative from the state of Alabama, in his 1849 remarks on the colonization of free blacks in Liberia and their value to the efforts in suppressing the trade and speaking about the American Colonization Society wrote:

> The colony of Liberia was first established in the year 1820, by free colored emigrants from the United States, who were sent out by the American Colonization Society. . . . The objects of this society are:
>
> 1. To rescue the free colored of the US from their political and social disadvantages.
> 2. To place them in a country where they may enjoy . . . free Government . . .
> 3. To spread civilization, sound morals, and true religion throughout the Continent of Africa.
> 4. To arrest and destroy the Slave Trade.
> 5. To afford slave owners, who wish, or are willing to liberate their slaves an asylum for their reception.[62]

The individual goals of the American Colonization Society were helpful to the United States and were particularly beneficial to the suppression effort. Although not supporting the colony and its free black population in any way, the American government, as previously stated, with the establishment of the Revenue Cutters and later the African Squadron, became interested in protecting its commerce and revenue.

The trade coming from Liberia fell within the American sphere of influence. With the establishment of Liberia, Americans were now able to trade directly with African groups, especially those along the coastline.[63] In transitioning to "legitimate commerce" the American Navy sent several ships to protect commerce. Although ships were also sent to capture slave traders, none were very successful in slowing the slave trade. In the latter years, Liberia became important not only to American and British commerce but also to the Africa Squadron as a place to take captured ships.

Combining the naval squadrons, legitimate trade would place an emphasis on the protection of commercial interests and not the slave trade. Several factors on the mainland contributed to this closure: (1) transition in traded goods, (2) another being the free black colonies of Liberia and Sierra Leone who accepted many re-captives, and (3) Kru people of West Africa, who served on both the British and American naval ships.[64]

The African Squadron was created by the United States following a dispute with the British over the slave ship *Creole*. Traveling from Virginia to Louisiana, the *Creole*, after a slave revolt in Caribbean waters, finally arrived at the port of Nassau, Bahamas. On its arrival, the slaves were set free by British laws which abolished slavery in 1833. A dispute over the return of these slaves to the United States finally resulted in the Webster-Ashburton Treaty. The passage of the Webster-Ashburton Treaty resolved remaining border disputes and stipulated that Americans should aid the British in suppressing the slave trade from Africa with a naval fleet.

Wilbur Devereux Jones, regarding negotiations leading to the Webster-Ashburton Treaty, writes, "In one way or another most of the minor problems of the conference concerned slavery. There was the question of the *Creole*, a ship that wrecked, and ultimately had its slave cargo and brought into port at Nassau, where British authorities gave the slaves their freedom."[65] After disputes were settled, Articles 8 and 9 of this treaty required that both the United States and Britain will prepare, equip and maintain on the coast of Africa a sufficient and adequate squadron for the suppression of the slave trade. A second group of stipulations to which these squadrons was to adhere to, carrying no less than eighty guns and these squadrons were to be vigilant in capturing slave traders using fraudulent flags.[66]

> Article 8 of the Webster-Ashburton Treaty reads: The parties mutually stipulate that each shall prepare, equip and maintain in service, on the coast of Africa, a sufficient and adequate squadron, or naval force of vessels, of suitable numbers and descriptions, to carry in all not less than eight guns . . . to act in concert and cooperation, upon mutual consultation . . . copies of all such orders to be communicated by each Government to the other respectively.[67]

The treaty continues in Article 9, which states:

> Whereas, notwithstanding all efforts which may be made the coast of Africa for suppressing the slave trade, the facilities for carrying on that traffic and avoiding the vigilance of cruisers, by the fraudulent use of flags . . . while a market can be found for slaves . . . all markets but shut against the purchase of African negroes . . . and . . . all such Powers the propriety and duty of closing such markets effectually, at once and forever.[68]

The African Squadron patrolled the shores of West Africa from Arguin in modern day Mauritania down to Cape Lopez in modern day Gabon.[69] By the 1850s, the patrolling ground stretched from the Madeira Islands in the North to Cape Frio in the south. A depot was located on Cape Verde. The United States later transferred it to St. Paul de Loando in present day Angola in 1859.[70]

J. S. Mansfield commented on the African Squadron saying the squadron had little effect on the slave trade. Mansfield first analyzed the number of captives leaving West Africa and, in addition, those arriving and sold in American, Caribbean and South American territories. In his assessment of the trade during the period, Mansfield believe that the trade to Cuba had slowed but overall it increased dramatically. Between 1845 and 1848 100,000 to 110,000 Africans were transported across the Atlantic.[71] Mr. Hutt, the chairman of the select committee of the House of Commons, stated on the March 19, 1850, ". . . the number of slaves exported from Africa had sunk down in 1842, the very year of the negotiation of the Ashburton treaty, to very nearly 30,000. In 1843 it rose to 55,000; in 1846 it was 76,000; in 1847 it was 84,000, and was then in a state of unusual activity."[72]

Nevertheless, the Africa Squadron, several have argued, was essential to protecting American commerce from the African continent, as it was still in its growing stages. There are several instances which refer to the Africa Squadron and American commerce. Referring to commerce and the West African coast, Mr. Bayard from the Committee on Naval Affairs stated before the United States Senate:

> It gathers its rich returns from the coast of Africa. . . . To protect this commerce, and to maintain the security and dignity of the nation, the wisdom of Congress has provided a naval establishment, consisting of eleven ships of the line, seventeen frigates, eighteen sloops of war, two brigs, four schooners, and four steamers, with six store-ships and receiving-vessels and five small schooners. The employment of this force is a matter left entirely to the discretion of the President, under his constitutional power as commander-in-chief of the Navy. The second section of the act of Congress of the 21 April, 1806, expressly authorizes the President "to keep in actual service in time of peace so many of the frigates and other public armed vessels of the United States as in his judgment the nature of the service may require." . . . He proposes additionally to employ on the African coast one frigate and four sloops and brigs[73]

In a separate letter to the United States Senate, President Tyler continued he thoughts on African commerce, stating:

> Another consideration of great importance has recommended this mode of fulfilling the duties and obligations of the country. Our commerce along the western coast of Africa is extensive, and supposed to be increasing. There is reason to think that in many cases those engaged in it have met with interruptions and annoyances, caused by the jealousy and instigation of rivals engaged in the same trade. Many complaints on this subject have reached the Government. A respectable naval force on the coast is the natural resort and security against further occurrences of this kind.[74]

The jealousy, President Tyler was referring to, was the increasing contact among the British and American traders. United States Naval Commander A. H. Foote, in his assessment, also believed that the squadron was essential to protecting American commerce but would be more effective with the use of smaller/faster steamers.[75] This offers a question, was the Africa Squadron put in place to suppress the slave trade or protect American commerce?

Several problems faced the United States Navy following the creation of its African Squadron. The first problem was the right to search and seizure.

While they established relations with Spain regarding the right to search and seizure, they had no such policy with Great Britain, the very country with which they made arrangements in the Webster-Ashburton treaty to maintain these vessels off the coast of Africa to suppress the slave trade. There were many concerns among American officials regarding the right to search vessels by the British. Many in the government believed this was a tactic to acquire an advantage regarding commercial trading by slowing the movement of American ships and goods.[76] Donald Canney writes:

> There was little hard evidence to back up this line of thinking, but it was popular nonetheless . . . evidence to that effect was seen in the many treaties with African tribes where the tribes' agreement to end the trade was accompanied by . . . a virtual British protectorate over the treaty tribe . . . there were objections. . . . The fact that the British . . . abolished slavery, while the American South regarded the institution as its key to prosperity . . . exacerbated the negative feelings considerably south of the Mason-Dixon Line . . . the treatment of slaves from the vessels *Hermosa* and *Creole* who were . . . taken to the British West Indies . . . and . . . freed. Later, in the 1830s, there were certain British abolitionist activities in Texas prior to its annexation by the United States.[77]

While all Europeans engaged in the slave trade reached agreements with the British over the right to search and seizure, the American government never reached such an agreement. However, later arrangements between the African and West African Squadrons to help one another capture slave traders were reached but no formal agreements were made between the two governments.

Analyzing the two years of a journal of Master's Mate Lawrence kept from 1844–1846 as a member of the Africa Squadron crew, C. Herbert Gilliland offered a critical final analysis of the squadron. In his work, he concluded that between 1843 and 1862 the African Squadron captured 34 ships rescuing 3,617 captives. Over this same time, Gilliland estimates more than a half a million captives were brought to the Western Hemisphere. The number of captive captured by the United States Navy was minuscule compared to the British West Africa Squadron who rescued 45,612 captives. Gilliland, like others, believed that the reason for this large discrepancy was the issue of search and seizure. Unlike the British who agreed to treaties with European nations to search their ships, the United States, because they did not want to inhibit private trading in any way, permitted no such action.[78]

With the right to search and seizure agreed upon by these nations, there was also the creation of a mixed courts system to try suspected slave traders. These courts sat in a number of locations including: Freetown, Luanda, Cape of Good Hope, Rio de Janeiro and Havana. The United States stationed its court in New York, but in trying suspected slave traders it proved to be a court very difficult to reach if captured on the West African Coast.[79] New York also became a safe haven to captured slave traders between 1857 and 1862. According to Robert Trent Vinson, "New York court districts provided a popular destination for slave traders because of the lenient judges."[80]

After laws were passed establishing the African Squadron, several other problems were encountered regarding ships used in stopping illegal slave traders. These questions focused on the size and style of ships, the numbers of guns on the coast and the numbers of ships to use, and finally how many crew members to employ on these ships. For example, the navy employed over 500 of its own men to the cause of suppressing the slave trade, and for those Africans recaptured from slave vessels to be taken to Monrovia as of 1842.[81] The Webster-Ashburton Treaty called for the American squadron to have a total of eighty guns on the coast, but by 1845 this number fell well short only reaching twenty-six.[82] Employing over 500 of its own sailors, this number fell well below the number of men they hoped to employ. The amount $440,000 was used to acquire the nccessary vessels, $240,000 for the maintenance of the vessels and $40,000 for any repairs that may have arisen.[83]

Prior to the passage of the Webster-Ashburton Treaty there were several estimates as to how much this squadron could cost to equip and maintain. Early estimates for the total cost of this fleet ranged from $3,500,000 to $1,500,000, in order maintain. The total annual cost to maintain the entire operation was estimated at $8,500,000, after the addition of the travel of mail steamships and the added cost of transportation and improvement of naval yards.[84] Knowing the total cost and the possible estimates, the number of crew members became the problem that most concerned the United States Department of Navy when they finally decided to set sail for the West African shoreline.[85]

Known by their distinguishing feature, "The Kru Mark," a broad blue or black stripe running from their forehead to the bridge of their nose and sometime extending to their lower lip and chin, the Kru became sought-after because of their seafaring abilities.[86] Although considered to be politically fragmented, the Kru were great travelers and were important in trading with Europeans and later Americo-Liberians,[87] and in fact, are linked together through Dako. The ancestral line links families whose ancestors settled in the region centuries earlier together.[88] They became the choice group of several Europeans to trade throughout the African continent because they traveled easily.

Though I refer to them as the Krumen from the Kru Coast, Jonas Ibo argues all African sailors, no matter their ethnic identity, were known as "Krouman."[89] Similar to Ibo, Frederick D. McEvoy believes the term Krumen emerged as a result of labor migration.[90] Both believe the ethnogenesis of the Kru is a result of their migrant labor and the major British areas they worked.

In contrast to their studies, L. B. Breitborde believes Kru ethnogenesis has both rural and urban roots.[91]

Many Kru were transported along the West African coastline after working on British naval and merchant ships, to settle in modern-day Nigeria, during the nineteenth and twentieth centuries as both skilled and un-skilled laborers. The Krooboys, another reference for the Krumen, served as skilled mariners as already mentioned. Jane Martin writes, "Mariners were first recruited . . . five towns which have become . . . identified with the Kru name—Settra Kru, Nana Kru, Little Kru, Krobah, and King William's Town."[92] The coastal area, referred to as the Kru Coast spanned 150 miles of shoreline, lies between the Cestos River and Cape Palmas, just east of the free black settlements.[93] Serving on European ships since 1750, Kru peoples were paid low wages serving as deckhands, woodcutters, middle-men, pilots, intelligence men, a jack of all trades.[94]

Kru involvement in the efforts to suppress the Trans-Atlantic Slave Trade can be linked directly to the colonization of free blacks on the West Coast of Africa in modern day Liberia as well as those freed by the British government in neighboring Sierra Leone. Initially hired by British traders as unskilled labor, the Kru worked on one to two year contracts on ships. Some would eventually settle in areas of the Gold Coast and Sierra Leone in later years.[95]

The Kru people have a long and rich history along the coastline of West Africa where they worked both with slave traders as against slave traders. The Kru have had a continuous contact with people of European descent since the fifteenth century which continued down through the nineteenth and twentieth centuries as they began with the Portuguese and continued with the British and the Americans. There are several pieces of evidence that highlight the Kru working with both slave traders and eventually against slave traders. One such slave trader that came into contact with Krumen and thanked them for helping save his life was slave trader Captain Canot.[96]

Although Europeans had been residing along the coast of Africa in forts and castles for several centuries, the continent was still referred to as the white man's grave. As a result of this lingering fear by countries and its sailors, both the British Parliament and the American government were concerned about the health of their sailors who traveled to West Africa onboard naval ships. This concern over health fears and death caused many white sailors to transfer to other squadrons and resulted in both governments turning elsewhere to fill the void of needed sailors.

Krumen served on board the West Africa Squadron and the Africa Squadron playing substantial roles in the British and American ships efforts to abolish the illegal slave trade from the West coast of the Africa. Both also hired Krumen to work as members on their merchant ships as well. As British ships moved further down the West African coast, the Kru also moved along with them, establishing settlements in the various British trading areas. In the United States Navy, Krumen and African Americans who served onboard American ships shared a similar experience.

By 1816, already working aboard on British merchant ships, the Kru population of Sierra Leone began to increase steadily. By 1819, there were already some 500 Kru people living in Sierra Leone. Many Krumen had come to the region initially on British merchant ships, eventually settling there as trading continually developed. This prompted the British to pass a resolution establishing designated Kru areas in Sierra Leone, ultimately leading many Kru to join the British Royal Navy already stationed in the region.[97] Through the 1840s at the height of the British suppression efforts, merchant trading and emigration system, Kru were continually recruited to fill the empty roles, especially those of the West Africa Squadron of the Royal Navy.[98] Many of the Kru who joined the West Africa Squadron were especially useful in navigating ships along West African coast and rivers.[99]

Many Krumen opted instead for the opportunity to work in suppressing the trade in the West Africa Squadron. Working in the British suppression effort, Krumen, as compared to working on merchant ships, were paid more in the navy.[100] Although told by naval captains their efforts went toward suppression, like African Americans who served in the United States Navy, the Kru were important to protecting commerce. Like the British, the American naval squadrons ultimately turned to the employment of Krumen on board their ships as a direct result of the fear of dying by white sailors.

The United States used African Americans in their navy from as early as 1803 in a number of different capacities. Similar to the African Americans, the Kru worked actively onboard ships in the closure of the slave trade as well. Because of their contact with British, French, Portuguese and ultimately Americo-Liberians, they also proved crucial to the protection of American commerce. Nevertheless, African Americans along with their Kru counterparts made their biggest impact on commerce trading ships, reaching ports around the world and in the United States serving onboard mixed crew vessels. Their involvement on mixed crew ships also meant they participated in all aspects of trade, notably commercial enterprises.[101]

Sailors in the United States Navy, mainly white, made substantial efforts not to be assigned to this Africa Squadron, seeking a reassignment as soon as they could to another squadron of their choice or another squadron seeking crew members and/or ships. One such squadron to gain transfers from the Africa Squadron was the United States Navy's

Mediterranean Squadron.[102] The effort to seek reassignment was in part due to the fear of death (see Table 4.1). Evidence presented before Congress on the deaths of white seamen would suggest otherwise:

The failure of the squadrons of the United States and England to abolish the slave trade cannot be imputed to the unhealthiness of the coast as a cruising ground. The document before us shows that the mortality on that station is less than the Home Squadron, or in the East Indies.

The following figures show the number of men and deaths in the Africa Squadron for four years:

Table 4.1 Deaths of Men Serving in the Africa Squadron

Year	*No. of Men*	*Deaths*
1845	631	5
1846	751	8
1847	639	7
1848	591	3

Source: American Colonization Society, *The African Repository and Colonial Journal* (Washington, DC: C. Alexander, Printer, 1850), p. 125.

This small number of deaths began a frenzy of transfer requests among white American sailors.

Starting in the 1830s, the use of quinine became wide spread among Europeans serving along the coast and especially those in the naval squadrons. Although this substantially lowered the death rates, the fear remained prevalent. According to Alexander Bryson and his study on the climate, diseases and death rates among British sailors on the African coast, he states:

The mortality figures for the Royal Navy's Africa Squadron on anti-slave trade duty are more significant. The numbers were much larger—several thousand sailors—but their death rates are not strictly comparable to those of troops permanently on shore. Shore duty was limited as much as possible because of the known danger from fevers. Death rates for the Africa Squadron nevertheless dropped by 58 percent between 1825–1845 and 1858–1867 and the sharpest part of that decline came in the mid-1840s.[103]

This significant drop in the number of deaths among white seamen in these anti-slave squadrons occurred just as the American crews arrived to start patrolling the coast with its small fleet. James Henry Matson, a British commander in its West Africa Squadron statement on his time patrolling for slave traders, also hints deaths were low. He states, "During the four years I commanded the Waterwitch . . . they never had a case of sickness. . . . "[104]

Under Commander Matthew C. Perry, several requests were made for additional crew. Perry established a system to hire Kroomen also known as Krumen. In his system, these men were hired as messengers, interpreters, boatmen partly because many believed Whites, due to the climate, were unable to spend extended periods of time on shore. The Krumen hired by the United States Navy were paid between $4 and $10 a month for their services.[105] In this system, between 20 and 30 were hired for the larger ships and no less than six for the smaller ships.[106] By 1843, the Kru began serving as members of the United States Navy and its Africa Squadron. This included 15 to 20 black seamen from the United States they believed could stand up to the hot African climate.[107]

The Kru people have had a continuous contact with people of European descent since the fifteenth century and continued down through the nineteenth and twentieth centuries as they began with the Portuguese and continued with the British and the Americans. There are several pieces of evidence that highlight the Kru working with slave traders and eventually against slave traders. One such slave trader that came into contact with Krumen and thanked them for helping save his life was slave trader Captain Canot.[108]

First arriving in West Africa in 1822, Americo-Liberians began to make several contacts with the local indigenous population. Eventually these early contacts caused portions of the Americo-Liberian population to move further down the coastline of Liberia. Eventually, in 1837, by the time the Mississippi Colonization Society established the area known as "Mississippi," free blacks had made direct contact with the Kru. This contact was furthered with the settlement of free blacks by Maryland Colonization Society, as they had a similar experience with the Kru people. Although making contact with free blacks settling in what would become known as Liberia, Merran Fraenkel argues it was fifty years before these settlements had any internal contact with the Kru.[109] Prior to this interior contact, their interaction with the Kru was restricted to the coastal trading areas Americo-Liberians called home.

The initial contact with free blacks led to Kru eventual appointment on board ships serving in the African Squadron.[110] While the exchange between these two groups altered over a short span of years, their initial contact with one another led to disputes, especially over annual tributes and the slave trade itself. Upon their arrival and contact with the local populations, the Americo-Liberians insisted on neighboring groups to refrain from participating in the slave trade.

The American Colonization Society and free blacks, calling the area home, found it difficult to make headway with the local population on a number of issues. One of the biggest obstacles they faced, prior to the emergence of the Africa Squadron, was the continued involvement in the slave trade by chiefs in the region, perceived as a detested commerce by recently landed blacks and the American Colonization Society. Both America and Britain wanted to end the slave trade and used Sierra Leone and Liberia to do so, pressuring groups into treaties. Settlers were persistent in their efforts to close the slave trade, by both treaties and later force.[111] In 1826, they began paying annual tributes to local chiefs and by 1845 with the growth of legitimate commerce, they began to stipulate, ". . . they must abstain indirect or direct from participation in the slave trade" to receive the annual tribute.[112] The 1845 agreement between then Americo-Liberians and local chiefs, referred to as the Treaty of Peace and Friendship, was finalized between the two sides three years after the creation of the African Squadron and two years after the Kru became members of the squadron.[113]

The free blacks forming Liberia came into contact with several groups along the coast including the Kru whom they actively traded with. According to Marie Tyler-McGraw, "The Krus . . . arrived at the coast in the about the sixteenth century and developed trade with the Portuguese and later with the Dutch, French and English."[114] The Kru known for many things had a specific knowledge of first the geography of the region and secondly the value of goods entering and exiting the region. Perhaps what made them a likely choice of the United States Navy was the Kru were also known as skillful mariners as well as skilled swimmers.[115]

The use of the squadrons to suppress the slave trade by both the British and the Americans, throughout their service, caused serious debate among the moralists and the economists of the day. Although the American squadron was ineffective in many regards, without the enrollment of blacks from the United States as well as Krumen, they would have been missing large numbers of crew needed. Much of the fear for white crew members was the fear of dying after making contact with the shoreline. The lack of numbers to fulfill all allotted spots in the squadron combined with the numbers of transfers by its own American crewmen, forced the United States Navy to look elsewhere to fulfill the crew requirements of the African Squadron. Just as the British Navy had done before them and unlike the French naval squadron who preferred to use Lebou and Wolof mariners,[116] the United States looked to a familiar group, the Kru.

Krumen again became especially important, once crews arrived and feared traveling further inland. Crew members of the Africa Squadron, feared dying from what they believed were incurable diseases. In many instances Kru, skillful swimmers, were used primarily to make contact with the people and recaptured Africans on the shore, because as previously stated the white crew feared they would die if the made contact with the land in any way.[117]

Even though the African Squadron was in direct contact with both the Kru and the free blacks of Liberia, the individuals sent there by the African Colonization Society often commented on the squadron. One of their many comments, many often referred to the lack of a presence from the squadron. Many of these same free blacks, colonizing the area, often complained they had not seen the ships sent to suppress the slave trade in several months. All the while, they continued to see ships trading illegally all of which they said were flying the American flag. [118]

Another problem observed was the use of American manufactured ships as W. E. F. Ward comments on this in assessment of the Royal Navy's efforts to close the trade by stating, "Many of the slave ships were especially built Baltimore clippers."[119] Many of these ships were built during the War of 1812 to fight the British, and were later altered to be used slave ships. Ward continues his argument of the American business interests in the slave trade even during the era of illegal trading. He argues that American businessmen continued to profit on the slave trade, "the South sought slave labor and the North built ships."[120] This furthers the notion of the ineffectiveness of the squadron in suppressing the slave trade and further points to a change in economic conditions on the land.

Visiting the coast of Africa for several years with other squadrons, the Brazil Squadron, North Atlantic Squadron, West Indian Squadron and South Atlantic Squadron were all unsuccessful in capturing large numbers of slave traders. Many traders used the American flag to illegally engage in the capturing and selling of Africans from West Africa in America, because it provided protection from other European squadrons.[121] Marie Tyler-McGraw writes, "The United States flag was flown by slave ship of many countries . . . its display meant that only a United States cruiser could board and search."[122] This contributed to the failure of the American squadron. Although its squadron was unsuccessful, declaring their independence from America in 1846, Americo-Liberians claimed to have successfully defended key territories against slave traders destroying barracoons in the process.[123]

By the start of the American Civil War, the need of navy shifted much of their attention back to the United States. Ultimately, the start of the Civil War put man power, ships and weapons at a top priority on the home front. Besides, it all but ended the need for African Squadron. By 1861, the squadron was brought home and the ships used to capture slave traders were put to other uses. Of the ships that served in the Africa Squadron, the sloop of war Constellation became the last ship to leave Africa reaching Baltimore.[124] Although American commerce on the African coast remained important, the use of the Africa Squadron to suppress the slave trade and protect commerce shifted to other squadrons.

Started by the United States government in 1842 under pressure from the British government the African Squadron joined the British West African Squadron patrolling the African shoreline. While they were there to capture potential slave traders their main objectives were to protect American revenue on the coast of Africa. Scholars argued that the abolition of the slave trade by Britain in 1807 and America in 1808 began the era of legitimate commerce from Africa and the slave trade to the Americas was completely stamped out by the 1850s only eight years after the arrival of America's African Squadron.

By 1861, the United States convicted only one slave trader to death for his role in illegally trading slaves.[125]

Kru became involved in patrolling the coast of Africa searching for slave traders, with European slave squadrons and on merchant ships namely the British, French and Portuguese. Many joined the British anti-slave squadron after settling in Sierra Leone's Krootown in 1816.[126] W. E. F. Ward writes, ". . . the first officer of a modern liner will tell you that he finds Kroo men better than Europeans at handling the ship's derricks."[127] Ronald Davis believes during this period, the dominance of British shipping tied the success of Krumen and the British together, partly because the British remained the largest traders in area of the Kru Coast. As the British slave squadron began making headway in areas near the Gold Coast and Nigeria, British commerce followed and so too did Kru peoples.[128] Working on these British ships, Krumen spread out to other areas beneficial to British trade, serving their needs in these areas.[129]

With the United States on the verge of splitting apart by the 1860s, the money and manpower used to maintain this squadron combined with the lack of success in capturing traders, all but ended the Africa Squadron. However, the British continued to use the West Africa Squadron, but by the 1860s its need shifted inland as well as to the Eastern seaboard of Africa and to the Caribbean territory. As late as 1860, fearing an Asante attack from the interior, the British employed thirty-two Krumen, throughout their Gold Coast forts.[130] Just as the British suppression effort expanded to the Eastern coastline of Africa, the role of the Kru people also extended. By 1863 nearly every ship on the east coast carried 100 Krumen on board.[131] Already used along the West African coastline, during the mid-nineteenth century nearly 2,500 Kru were transported to places such as Jamaica, Trinidad, Martinique and Guiana serving in the West India Regiment.[132]

The Gold Coast remained an important location to the British even as they expanded into other areas of Africa, in part due to the trade value of Cape Coast Castle and Elmina Castle. In 1873, the British government expanded their commercial enterprises to inland areas where they were in direct conflict with the Asante of the Gold Coast. According to Edward Reynolds, ". . . there is sufficient evidence to indicate that motives that let the British Government to maintain settlements and eventually to declare the country a protectorate were to promote and foster trade."[133] This idea of promoting trade also played a role in the start of the Asante Expedition and the burning of Kumasi.

Over a seventy-year period, the relationship between the British and the Asante had its ups and downs and was largely dependent on trade, but in 1874 came a blow during the Asante Expedition which resulted with the burning of Kumase in 1874. On their inland expedition into Asante territory, the British continued to employ Kru people, now many of whom resided in the

Gold Coast themselves. Another famous traveler in the British convoy was Henry Morton Stanley, well known for his later expeditions into the Congo leading to the "Scramble for Africa." Reaching Africa in 1873 as a part of the Asante Expedition, Henry Morton Stanley of the *New Herald* newspaper, described the Kru as a remarkable people with a good nature. Even as late as 1873, Krumen continued to hire themselves out to European steamers and sloops of war.[134]

Although having served for a number of years in the dangerous squadrons with a fear of never returning home H. M. Stanley provides an analysis of the Kru in contrast to others previous who argued the Kru were essential to the abolition campaign. He writes:

> The British General, in his search for allies to drive back the Ashantees from the Protectorate, has long before this time been informed that though the Krumen are invaluable aids on board British cruisers and trading steamers, they are useless as allies in war. The very name of battle is a terror to them, and they earnestly stipulate with all new-comers just now that they shall not be expected to go to war.[135]

Nevertheless the Kru had truly become essential labor and important to British commerce throughout Africa and their other territories.

With the abolition of the Trans-Atlantic Slave Trade and the start of the era of legitimate commerce, the British in search of new labor encouraged the migration of a number of peoples. Kru were encouraged to migrate to a number of places, including Sierra Leone, Liverpool and the Caribbean. Diane Frost writes:

> West Africans were also encouraged to migrate to West African countries where local labour was inadequate or unsuitable. Explanations to account for this migration are indeed complex and multifaceted involving factors that relate to the Kru themselves and the socio-economic and political positions they found themselves in Liberia. Yet the historical context of merchant capitalism and colonialism also played a significant role in the creation of a Kru diaspora. These provided the conditions within which Kru labour was encouraged to migrate to far and distant places such as Liverpool and the Guyana's as well as closer to home in Sierra Leone.[136]

Beginning as migrant communities in these various locations, in only a few short years several became established permanent settlements. They would also play a substantial role in British colonialism working in both lumber and palm-oil industries in Lagos and Accra.[137]

The Gold Coast proved crucial, first to the start of European gold trading, second the start of the Trans-Atlantic Slave Trade and ultimately the urge by nations to close the trade in Africans. As the Asante approached the coastline, the numbers of captives leaving the Gold Coast increased significantly enough to impact the Europeans trading along the coastline. This chapter examines the impact of the Asante on the final years of the legal slave trade, the start of the illegal era of slave trading as well as the impact of the passage of European and American abolition laws and the role of their naval squadrons.

Between 1807 and 1850, these naval squadrons were able to capture a number of traders, but were not as successful as once believed. This lack of success by these squadrons can be contributed to a number of factors including the lack of crew, lack of funding, the suppression courts lack of ability to prosecute high numbers of captured ships, and the inability to work with one another due to their nations' laws. While the British and American squadrons were unsuccessful in capturing high numbers of captives, they were seen as crucial to the promotion of free trade. Simultaneously, worldwide events were all interconnected with one another which had a dramatic impact on the slave trade, its closure and the eventual trek of Europeans into the interior of Africa. Along the Gold Coast, these events were also linked the Asante push toward the coastline to enter the slave trade as well as promote the trade of commercial goods with these worldwide events. In the coming years, conflicts and treaties were signed to promote trade and peace between the Asante and British which added a further complication to the era.

NOTES

1. Christopher Chamberlin, "Bulk Exports, Trade Tiers, Regulation, and Development: An Economic Approach to the Study of West Africa's Legitimate Trade," *The Journal of Economic History*, Vol. 39, No. 2 (June, 1979).

2. Robin Law, ed., *From Slave Trade to 'Legitimate' Commerce: The Commercial Transition in Nineteenth-Century West Africa* (New York: Cambridge University Press, 2002); this work consists of several conference papers which all argue against A.G. Hopkins notion of a 'crisis of adaptation' developed in his work *An Economic History of West Africa*.

3. For a better explanation of this see: Bernard Edwards, *Royal Navy Versus the Slave Traders: Enforcing Abolition at Sea, 1808–1898* (Great Britain: Pen & Sword Books, 2007), p. 46.

4. In 1789 with the creation of the United States Treasury Department, the Revenue Cutter Service was also created. Initially the Revenue Cutters were a group of customs collectors, but after the passage of the Slave Trade Act of 1794, this group became involved in enforcing regulations against the slave trade. This small fleet mainly patrolled the eastern seaboard of the United States, but did make trips into the Caribbean region and the West Coast of Africa. A permanent United States naval

fleet was finally created in 1842. Prior to the creation of the Africa Squadron the Revenue Cutter Service was largely responsible for protecting American interests in the slave trade. Liberia would also play an important role before the Africa Squadron was established. For a brief history of the Revenue Cutter Service, see: Florence Kern, *John Foster Williams' U.S. Revenue Cutter Massachusetts* (Washington, DC: Alised Enterprises, 1976).

5. In the nineteenth century the Kru Coast became known as the area between the Cestos River and Cape Palmas covering 150 miles of the Liberian coastline. See, Ronald W. Davis, "The Liberian Struggle for Authority on the Kru Coast," *The International Journal of African Historical Studies*, Vol. 8, No. 2 (1975), p. 222.

6. Joseph E. Inikori, "Slavery and the Development of Industrial Capitalism in England," *Journal of Interdisciplinary History*, Vol. 17, No. 4 (Spring, 1987), p. 786.

7. Eric Williams, *Capitalism and Slavery*, 2nd ed. (Chapel Hill, NC: University of North Carolina Press, 1994), p. 133.

8. David Brion Davis, "Impact of the French and Haitian Revolutions," in *The Impact of the Haitian Revolution in the Atlantic World*, ed. David P. Geggus (Columbia, SC: University of South Carolina Press, 2001), p. 4.

9. Ibid., 4–5.

10. Selwyn H. H. Carrington, "The American Revolution and the British West Indies' Economy," *Journal of Interdisciplinary History*, Vol. 17, No. 4, Caribbean Slavery and British Capitalism (Spring, 1987), p. 826.

11. United States Constitution Article 1, Section 9.

12. Slave Trade Act of 1794, Sections 1–4.

13. Slave Trade Act of 1800, Sections 1–7.

14. Slave Trade Act of 1803, Sections 1–3.

15. Thomas Norman DeWolf, *Inheriting the Trade: A Northern Family Confronts Its Legacy as the Largest Slave Trading Dynasty in U.S. History* (Boston, MA: Beacon Press Books, 2008), p. 115.

16. James A. Rawley, *The Trans-Atlantic Slave Trade: A History*, Revised Ed. (Lincoln, NE: University of Nebraska Press, 2005), p. 86.

17. Ibid., 87.

18. Ibid.

19. Ibid., 86.

20. Ibid., 87.

21. *The Foreign Slave Trade, A Brief Account of its State, of the Treaties Which Have Been Entered Into, and of The Laws Enacted for its Suppression, From the Date of The English Abolition Act to the Present Time* (London: John Hatchard and Son, 1837), p. 17.

22. Hugh Thomas, *The Slave Trade: The Story of the Atlantic Slave Trade, 1440–1870* (New York: Simon & Schuster, 1997), p. 691.

23. Yaw Bredwa-Mensah, "Landscapes of Slavery: The Danish Plantation Complex in the Akuapem Mountains, Southeastern Gold Coast (Ghana)." In *The Trans-Atlantic Slave Trade: Landmarks, Legacies Expectations*, ed. James Kwesi Anquandah (Legon, Accra, Ghana: Sub-Saharan Publishers, 2007) p. 148.

24. Ibid., 154.

25. Georg Norregard, *Danish Settlements in West Africa, 1658–1850* (Boston, MA: Boston University Press, 1966), p. 184.

26. Johannes M. Postma, *The Dutch in the Atlantic Slave Trade, 1600–1815* (New York: Cambridge University Press, 1990), p. 284.

27. Ibid., 289.

28. Thomas Clarkson, *History of the Rise, Progress and the Accomplishment of the Abolition of the African Slave Trade by the British Parliament* (London: John W. Parker, 1807), pp. 217–218.

29. Louis Taylor Merrill, "The English Campaign for the Abolition of the Slave Trade," *The Journal of Negro History*, Vol. 30, No. 4 (Oct., 1945), p. 385.

30. Ibid., 390–391.

31. British Foreign Slave Trade Act, An Act to Regulate, for a Limited Time, the Shipping and Carrying Slaves in British Vessels from the Coast of Africa 28, Geo 3 c. 54.

32. British Foreign Slave Trade Act, An Act to Regulate, for a Limited Time, the Shipping and Carrying Slaves in British Vessels from the Coast of Africa 31 Geo.3 c. 54.

33. British Foreign Slave Trade Act, An Act for Better Regulating the Manner of Carrying Slaves, in British Vessels from the Coast of Africa. 39 Geo 3 c. 80.

34. For the complete act abolishing the British Foreign Slave Trade see: An Act for the Abolition of the Slave Trade, 47 Geo 3, Session 1, c. 36. This act was passed on March 25, 1807.

35. Queries proposed by Viscount Castleragh to, and Answers of, the Africa Society in London, December 1816. In British Parliamentary Papers, *Papers Relating to the Suppression of the Slave Trade, 1818–1821*, Vol. 63 (Ireland: Irish University Press, 1970), pp. 16–17.

36. British Foreign Slave Trade Act, An Act for the Abolition of the Slave Trade. 47 Geo 3, Session 1, Cap. XXXVI.

37. William Wilberforce, *The Abolition of the Slave Trade: Addressed to the Freeholders and other Inhabitants of Yorkshire* (London: Luke Hansard & Sons, 1807), p. 48.

38. For the complete United States Abolition of the Slave Trade Act see: "An Act to Prohibit the Importation of Slaves into any Port or Place Within the Jurisdiction of the United States, from and after the First Day of January, in the Year of our Lord, One Thousand Eight Hundred and Eight." *American State Papers*, House of Representatives, 10th Congress 1st–2nd Session.

39. Irving H. King has written two works on the Revenue Cutters, see: Irving H. King, *The Coast Guard Under Sail: The US Revenue Cutter Service, 1789–1865* (Annapolis, MD: Naval Institute Press, 1989) and *George Washington's Coast Guard: Origins of the US Revenue Cutter Service, 1789–1801* (Annapolis, MD: Naval Institute Press, 1978). Also Florence Kern has written several pamphlets on ships in the Revenue Cutter fleet.

40. George Washington Papers at Library of Congress, 1741–1799: Series 4. General Correspondence, 1697–1799. Treasury Department, April 2, 1793, Officers of the Revenue Cutters.

41. George Washington to Oliver Wolcott, Jr., September 6, 1796. The Writings of George Washington from the Original Manuscript Sources, 1745–1799. John C. Fitzpatrick, Editor.

42. Florence Kern, *John Foster Williams' U.S. Revenue Cutter Massachusetts* (Washington, DC: Alised Enterprises, 1976), p. 2.

43. Truman R. Strobridge and Dennis L. Noble, *Alaska and the U.S. Revenue Cutter Service, 1867–1915* (Annapolis, MD: Naval Institute Press, 1999), p. 5.

44. Ibid., 6.

45. A Right to Search and Seizure Treaty was signed between Britain and the United States on June 7, 1862. For a brief explanation of this treaty see both: Donald L. Canney, *Africa Squadron: The U.S. Navy and the Slave Trade, 1842–1861* (Washington, DC: Potomac Books, 2006), p. 222; http://avalon.law.yale.edu/19th_century/br1862.asp

46. W. E. Burghardt Du Bois, *The Suppression of the African Slave-Trade to the United States 1638–1870*, 2nd ed. (New York: The Social Science Press, 1954), pp. 80–81, in Don E. Fehrenbacher, *The Slaveholding Republic: An Account of the United States Government's Relations to Slavery* (New York: Oxford University Press, 2001), p. 140.

47. Marie Tyler-McGraw, *An African Republic: Black & White Virginians in the Making of Liberia* (Chapel Hill, NC: University of North Carolina Press, 2007), p. 9.

48. Ibid., 38–39.

49. Assa Okoth, *A History of Africa, Volume One: African Societies and the Establishment of Colonial Rule, 1800–1915* (Nairobi, Kenya: East African Educational Publishers, 2006), p. 73.

50. Bernard Edwards, *Royal Navy Versus the Slave Traders: Enforcing Abolition at Sea, 1808–1898* (Great Britain: Pen & Sword Maritime, 2007), pp. 47–48.

51. Chaim D. Kaufmann and Robert A. Pape, "Explaining the Costly International Moral Action: Britain's Sixty-Year Campaign Against the Atlantic Slave Trade," *International Organization*, Vol. 53, No. 4 (Autumn, 1999), p. 634.

52. David R. Murray, *Odious Commerce: Britain, Spain and the Abolition of the Cuban Slave Trade* (New York: Cambridge University Press, 1980), p. 101.

53. An Account of the Number of Slaves Captures and Condemned at Sierra Leone, from 5th January 1814 to 21st April 1823; showing, The Number seized in each Year, how disposed of, and the Amount of all Money paid thereon to the Captor as Head-money or otherwise; so far as the same can be made up. *British Parliamentary Pāpers, Correspondence and Papers Relating to Slavery and the Abolition of the Slave Trade, 1823–24*, Vol. 66 (Irish University Press, 1971) p. 371.

54. http://slavevoyages.org/tast/assessment/estimates.faces?yearFrom=1814&yearTo=1822.

55. Lieutenant Henry Yule, *The African Squadron Vindicated* (London: James Ridgway, Piccadilly, 1850), pp. 2–5. Lieutenant Henry Yule in this work discusses the role and effects of the West Africa Squadron.

56. "Documents Relating to the United States and Liberia," *The American Journal of International Law*, Vol. 4, No. 3, Supplement: Official Documents (July, 1910), p.188, *Act* of March 3, 1819 Relative to the Slave Trade.

57. Du Bois, 120–121.

58. Tyler-McGraw, 160.

59. "Documents Relating to the United States and Liberia," 191–192.

60. Du Bois, 155.

61. Ayres to the Secretary of the Navy, February 24, 1823; reprinted in *Friends' View of the African Slave Trade* (1824), p. 31 in Du Bois, 125–126.

62. *Remarks on the Colonization of Western Coast of Africa, By the Free Negroes of the United States, and The Consequent Civilization of Africa and the Suppression of the Slave Trade* (New York: W. L. Burroughs Steam Power Press, 1850), pp. 6–7.

63. George E. Brooks, Jr. *Yankee Traders, Old Coasters and African Middlemen: A History of American Legitimate Trade With West Africa in the Nineteenth Century* (Boston: Boston University Press, 1970), p. 249.

64. Kaufamann and Pape, 634.

65. Wilbur Devereux Jones, "The Influence of Slavery on the Webster-Ashburton Negotiations," *The Journal of Southern History*, Vol. 22, No. 1 (February 1956), p. 48.

66. For the complete guidelines please see the Webster-Ashburton Treaty. This treaty is referred to as both the Webster-Ashburton Treaty and A Treaty to settle and define the Boundaries between the Territories of the United States and the possessions of Her Britannic Majesty, in North America: For the final Suppression of the African Slave Trade: and for the giving up of Criminal fugitive from justice, in certain cases. For the complete treaty see The Avalon Project from the Yale Law School: http://avalon.law.yale.edu/19th_century/br-1842.asp.

67. Boundaries, Slave Trade, Extradition (Webster-Ashburton Treaty), Article 8 in Charles I. Bevans, ed., *Treaties and Other International Agreements of the United States of America, 1776–1949*, Vol 12 (Washington, DC: Department of State Publication, 1974), p. 248.

68. Boundaries, Slave Trade, Extradition (Webster-Ashburton Treaty), Article 9 in Charles I. Bevans, ed., *Treaties and Other International Agreements of the United States of America, 1776–1949*, Vol. 12 (Washington, DC: Department of State Publication, 1974), p. 248.

69. Canney, 44; This is a map outlining the territories covered by the Naval Squadron known as the African Squadron on the west coast of Africa from 1842–1861.

70. Canney, 43; This also is a map outlining the territories covered by the Naval Squadron known as the African Squadron on the west coast of Africa from 1842–1861.

71. J. S. Mansfield, *Remarks on The African Squadron* (London: James Ridgway, 1851), pp. 8–9.

72. Mr. Slidell, The Committee on Foreign Relations, *Journal of the Senate of the United States of America, 1789–1873*, Tuesday, June 13, 1854.

73. *Journal of Executive Proceedings of the Senate of the United States of America 1841–1845*, May 16, 1842, pp. 69–71.

74. United States President John Tyler to Senate, *Journal of Executive Proceedings of the Senate of the United States of America 1841–1845*, August 11, 1842, pp. 119–124.

75. A. H. Foote, *The Africa Squadron: Ashburton Treaty and Consular Sea Letters Reviewed in an Address* (Philadelphia: William F. Geddes), p. 3.

76. Canney, 19.

77. Canney, 19–20.

78. C. Herbert Gilliland, *Voyage to a Thousand Cares: Master's Mate Lawrence with the Africa Squadron, 1844–1846* (Annapolis, MD: Naval Institute Press, 2004), pp. 292–293.

79. Leslie Bethell, "The Mixed Commissions for the Suppression of the Trans-Atlantic Slave Trade in the 19th Century," *The Journal of African History*, Vol. 7, No. 1 (1966), p. 92.

80. Robert Trent Vinson, "The Law as Lawbreaker: The Promotion and Encouragement of the Atlantic Slave Trade by the New York Judiciary System, 1857–1862," *Afro-Americans in New York Life and History*, Vol. 20, No. 2 (July, 1996), pp. 35–37.

81. Canney, 48.

82. Gilliland, 122.

83. Canney, 49.

84. Mr. Slidell, *Journal of the Executive Proceedings of the Senate of the United States of America, 1852–1855* (June 13, 1854), pp. 334–335.

85. Ibid.

86. George E. Brooks, Jr., *The Kru Mariner in the 19th Century: An Historical Compendium* (Newark, DE: Liberian Studies Association in America, Inc., 1972), p. 34.

87. D.C. Doward, "British West Africa and Liberia," In J.D. Fage, A. D. Roberts and Roland Oliver, eds., *The Cambridge History of Africa*, Vol. 7 (Great Britain: Cambridge University Press, 1986), p. 455.

88. Jane Martin, "Krumen 'Down the Coast': Liberian Migrants on the West African Coast in the 19th and Early 20th Centuries," *The International Journal of African Historical Studies*, Vol. 18, No. 3 (1985) p. 220.

89. Jonas Ibo, "Le Phénomène Krouman a Sassandra: la marque d'une institution séculaire," *Canadian Journal of African Studies*, Vol. 32, No. 1 (1998), p. 65.

90. Frederick D. McEvoy, "Understanding Ethnic Realities among the Grebo and Kru Peoples of West Africa," *Africa: Journal of the International African Institute*, Vol. 47, No. 1 (1977), p. 67.

91. L.B. Breitborde, "City, Countryside and Kru Ethnicity," *Africa: Journal of the International African Institute*, Vol. 61, No. 2 (1991), p. 191.

92. Martin, 402.

93. Ronald W. Davis, "The Liberian Struggle for Authority on the Kru Coast," *The International Journal of African Historical Studies*, Vol. 8, No. 2 (1975), pp. 222–224; In his work Davis gives an extensive description of the Kru Coast in the 19th century.

94. Ibid., 225–226.

95. Martin, 1.

96. Brantz Mayer, *Captain Canot; or, Twenty Years of an African Slaver Being an Account of His Career and Adventures of the Coast, In the Interior, or Shipboard, and in The West Indies, Written Out and Edited From the Captain's Journals, Memoranda and Conversations* (New York: D. Appleton and Company, 1854), p. 386.

97. Brooks, 38.

98. Rosanne Marion Adderley, *New Negroes: Slave Trade Abolition and Free African Settlement in the Nineteenth-Century Caribbean* (Bloomington, IN: Indiana University Press, 2006), p. 74.

99. Marika Sherwood, *After Abolition: Britain and the Slave Trade Since 1807* (London: I. B. Tauris, 2007), pp. 18–19.

100. Brooks, 38.

101. Martha S. Putney, "Black Merchant Seamen of Newport, 1803–1865: A Case Study in Foreign Commerce," *The Journal of Negro History*, Vol. 57, No. 2 (April, 1972), p. 167.

102. The Mediterranean Squadron received transfers from the Africa Squadron in both ships and crew members. See: Canney, 91, 118.

103. Alexder Bryson, *Report on the Climate and Principal Diseases of the African Station* (London: 1847), pp. 177–178, in Philip Curtin, The End of the White man's Grave? Nineteenth Century Mortality in West Africa, *Journal of Interdisciplinary History*, Vol. 21, No. 1 (Summer, 1990), p. 74.

104. James Henry Matson, *Remarks on the Slave Trade and African Squadron*, Knowsley Pamphlet Collection (1848), p. 32.

105. Brooks, 52.

106. Letters, Perry to Goldsborough, March 28, 1843; to Kennon, April 7, 1843; to Upshur, April 13, 1843, in Perry Letter Books, National Archives, M206 In Canney, 55.

107. Letters, Perry to Upshur, May 16, 1843; to Tatnall, May 20, 1843; to Upshur, in Perry Letter Books, National Archives, M206 In Canney, 55.

108. Brantz Mayer, *Captain Canot; or, Twenty Years of an African Slaver Being an Account of His Career and Adventures of the Coast, In the Interior, or Shipboard, and in The West Indies, Written Out and Edited From the Captain's Journals, Memoranda and Conversations* (New York: D. Appleton and Company, 1854), p. 386.

109. Merran Fraenkel, "Social Change on the Kru Coast of Liberia," *Africa: Journal of the International African Institute*, Vol. 36, No. 2 (April 1966), p. 156.

110. Ibid.

111. M. B. Akpan, "Black Imperialism: Americo-Liberian Rule Over the African Peoples of Liberia, 1841–1964," *Canadian Journal of African Studies*, Vol. 7, No. 2 (1973), p. 220.

112. Davis, 229.

113. George E. Brooks, Jr., *The Kru Mariner in the 19th Century: A Historical Compendium* (Newark, DE: Liberian Studies Association in America, Inc., 1972), p. 42.

114. Tyler-McGraw, 130.

115. Ibid., 141.

116. Ibid., 38.

117. Canney, 69; Canney's work also includes one of the only known pictures of the Krumen on board a ship of the Africa Squadron taken in 1867.

118. Tyler-McGraw, 160–163.

119. W. E. F. Ward, *The Royal Navy and Slavers* (New York: Pantheon Books, 1969), p. 101.

120. Ibid., 138.

121. Canney, 18.

122. Tyler-McGraw, 162.

123. Canney, 17.

124. Ibid., 203.

125. Captain Gordon became the only slave trader in the United States to convicted and sentenced to death for his role in illegally trading slaves. For a complete assessment of Captain Gordon and his hanging see: Ron Soodalter, *Hanging Captain Gordon: The Life and Trial of an American Slave Trader* (New York: Atria Books, 2006).

126. Diane Frost, *Work and Community Among West African Migrant Workers Since the 19th Century* (Liverpool: Liverpool University Press, 1999), p. 8.

127. Ward, 102.

128. Davis, 226.

129. Jane Martin, "Krumen Down the Coast: Liberian Migrants on the West African Coast in the 19th century," Working Papers, No. 64, African Studies Center (Boston, MA: Boston University Press, 1982), p. 2.

130. Letter Commodore Wilmot to Sir B. W. Walter, 14 April 1863, *British Parliamentary Papers, Papers Concerning the Gold Coast and Surrounding Districts, 1850–1873, Colonial Africa, Ghana*, Vol. 57 (Ireland: Irish University Press, 1971), p. 9.

131. Raymond Howell, *The Royal Navy and the Slave Trade* (London: Croom Helm Publishers, 1987), p. 42.

132. Monica Schuler, "Kru Emigration to British and French Guiana, 1841–1857" In *Africans in Bondage: Studies in Slavery and Slave Trade*, ed. Paul E. Lovejoy (Madison, WI: University of Wisconsin, 1986), p. 155.

133. Edward Reynolds, "Economic Imperialism: The Case of the Gold Coast," *The Journal of Economic History*, Vol. 35, No. 1 (March, 1975), p. 95.

134. Henry M. Stanley, *Coomassie and Magdala: The Story of Two British Campaigns in Africa* (London: Sampson Low, Marston & Company, 1891), pp. 7–9.

135. Ibid., 8.

136. Diane Frost, "Diasporan West African Communities: The Kru in Freetown & Liverpool," *Review of African Political Economy*, Vol. 29, No. 92, Africa, The African Diaspora and Development (June, 2002), p. 288.

137. Ibid., 290.

Chapter 5

Economic Transition within Greater Asante in the Mid-nineteenth Century

West Africa experienced a series of economic changes between the sixteenth and seventeenth centuries as the busincss of slave trading steadily increased and expanded to encompass areas stretching the entire coastline. Across the Gold Coast this led to an immediate increase in the number of captives exported from the region, as discussed previously in earlier chapters. These numbers began to decline into the first three decades of the nineteenth century as more economic changes began to occur. As the era of legitimate trade and commercial exchange was well underway by the middle of the nineteenth century, the numerous changes associated with this form of exchange began to stretch the entire coastline of West Africa. In particular, along the Gold Coast this commercial changeover had and immediate and dramatic impact on the coastal economy of the region before reaching into interior and affecting the Asante state. Nonetheless, the shift to a trade in legitimate and commercial goods began the second transition from the Gold Coast within a matter of two centuries.

By the middle of the nineteenth century with the region in the midst of its second changeover within a matter of two centuries, the largest states, along the coast and interior, were able to adapt and adjust to these numerous changes. The coastal area of the Gold Coast, like many which stretched the coastline of West Africa began as one which traded in legitimate items, i.e. gold, before transitioning to one of the largest captive trading regions, purchasing individuals from the interior. This transition back to legitimate trade was one of the greatest economic transitions experienced throughout West Africa and the Gold Coast, ultimately leading to a growth in family, individual fortunes as well as private wealth and ownership never experienced before in the region stretching from its coastline to the interior Asante state.

This changeover which began to take root in the mid-nineteenth century left the region and state largely engaged in the trade of captives transitioning to a trade which focused on both agriculture and manufactured mass produced goods. This transition to legitimate trade shows the economic adaptability of the people and the various states of the Gold Coast stretching from the coastal territory and the Fante state to the interior and beyond the Northern borders of the Asante state. Much of this transition experienced in West Africa focuses on the period beginning in the first half of the nineteenth century, or from the closure of the slave trade through the 1874 British decision to invade the area of Greater Asante and the city of Kumasi. Within the Gold Coast, these years, or mid-nineteenth century, are critical as they show the changeover from a region heavily engaged in the trade of captive labor to one invested in the exchange legitimate commercial goods.

This economic transition occurring along the coastline of West Africa not only impacted those coastal territories, home too many African groups and European forts, but adjustments being made stretched well into the interior regions of the numerous states as well. In particular the territory of Greater Asante, an interior state with access to the coastline through its numerous trade routes, was dramatically transformed by demand for specific items. Furthermore, as many of its goods, crops and manufactured items, found their way to merchants trading along coast of the region, this also increased the Asante States presence in the ever-expanding European and Atlantic commercial markets. In the coming years this demand for new bulk goods along the coast created a new class of citizens, traders and African merchants.

By the mid-nineteenth century, the Gold Coast region began the transition from an area which depended solely on trading captives across the Atlantic Ocean for economic survival to one which traded agricultural and man-made bulk goods; thus altering the family unit within the region. With this growth and increase in both the number of traders involved in the export of legitimate goods and the commodities shipped from the Gold Coast, the region and its people also began to acquire greater wealth. Moreover, this increase in wealth in the region impacted the state economy as well as increased the individual or family wealth. This is highlighted by the change in traded commodities also flowing into the central region of Greater Asante, especially into Kumasi and Salaga, two of the largest trading cities in the state.

Furthermore, this access to new capital in Greater Asante not only resulted in the growth of both individual and family private wealth, but also led to the increase in demand for captive labor that became an intricate part to mining and crop production in the aftermath of abolition. This emergence of individual and family private wealth greatly altered the structure of the state itself, the role of the chieftaincy and family unit. Nevertheless, these changes to the structure of the state played a significant role in changing the Asante-Gold

Coast economy during the period of the nineteenth century. Albeit, the significant family and individual accumulation of land and wealth ultimately altered the structure of the Asante family unit and role of the state. These changes also impacted the need and use of captives within the state as there was an increase in accumulation of private property, dramatically altering the economy well into the middle of the century and the decades which through the siege on Greater Asante and Kumasi.

In this transition to legitimate trade, lawful commerce or the trade in bulk export items, as the era has been commonly referred, the continent of Africa and West Africa in particular, were able to successfully navigate this transition. Albeit, as West Africa and the Gold Coast were able to successfully make such a transition they still experienced economic fluctuations which occurred in any economy of similar size and magnitude. Furthermore, the people of Greater Asante, well into the interior of the region, following the closure of the slave trade were able to successfully move away from this trade in captive labor between 1807 and 1874, which did little to stop the eventual British incursion into the hinterland. On the Gold Coast, this successful transition to bulk goods resulted in trade of numerous agricultural crops and manufactured goods.

Moreover, many of these changes although occurring following abolition of the slave trade continued until the expansion of the British Gold Coast Colony in the mid-1870s and the eventual sacking of Kumasi during the Asante Expedition. These successful and substantial changes to the economy beginning in the early years of the era showed officials, namely the British, were more than capable of being involved in the emerging capital system of the nineteenth century. Instead, explorations into the interior of Africa only proved to British officials that the region, economically, was much more valuable than any previous thought. These changes which began to occur bring forth numerous questions namely, what was the condition of the Asante family structure in the mid-nineteenth century, how was the family structure affected by the economy and what were the Asante relations with its neighbors like as the change to bulk goods occurred?

The era of trading which followed 1807–1808 decision to abolish the slave trade has brought much debate from scholars around the world. Considerable portions of this discussion have focused on the transition from the trade of captives across the Atlantic Ocean to a large scale import and export trade business in legitimate or bulk export goods. In the several decades since the publication of A. G. Hopkins early work, *An Economic History of West Africa* which began this debate, the controversy and discussion regarding this era in African history has only continued among historians. Although Hopkins work was revolutionary at its publication, his work focuses heavily on the production of manufactured mass-produced goods. Hopkins wrote in his work, ". . . the consumer imports of the nineteenth century were mainly cheap, mass-produced goods, which offered large numbers of inconspicuous . . . opportunities of material improvement. . . ."[1]

Hopkins early work, published in 1973, referred to this transitional period, from captives to legitimately traded items as one of a "crisis of adaptation," stating:

> The evidence indicates that West Africa's external trade experienced a crisis in the last quarter of the nineteenth century. Export producers had become caught in a staple trap: the barter terms of trade had turned against them, and attempts to increase the volume of exports had either failed or, where successful, had contributed to a further decline in terms of trade, with the result that growth had become self-defeating.[2]

Hopkins thesis has been challenged by several scholars since its initial first publication, most notably by Robin Law in his edited volume *From Slave Trade to "Legitimate" Commerce: The Commercial Transition in Nineteenth-Century West Africa*.

Scholars in Robin Law's edited volume of work have argued instead that West Africa was able to successfully manage this transition with very little disruption to the local states and their daily trading.[3] Albeit, this debate has continued among scholars who analyze the Trans-Atlantic Slave Trade, including economic historians, those who study slavery within West African states as well as individuals who study this transitional period and this era of African History. All these groups in their later analysis of the era refuted the claims of Hopkins early work. Similarly, many of these scholars also argued individuals, families and states throughout West Africa were able to successfully make this transition away from captive trading to legitimately traded items or bulk goods without doing much harm or disrepair to their societies.[4]

James Searing, in 1993, became one of the early scholars to look at this transitional period which occurred in West Africa from the perspective of a specific or localized area. In studying this transition on a local level, Searing argues Africa and Senegal River Valley went through a long period of structural adjustment leading to a transition from slave trading to legitimate trade.[5] This period of structural adjustment, as Searing refers to it, also coincides with the fluctuations in the prices on British imports from Africa and while the Senegal River Valley did experience a period of adjustment, this was not the crisis described by Hopkins in previous studies. Nevertheless, as Searing's work focuses on the Senegal River Valley his study suggests a similar analysis can also be applied to changes which occurred on the Gold Coast in the mid-nineteenth century.

As legitimate commerce expanded into the various areas of West Africa, its impact on the operations of the numerous states became much more evident. Moreover, this shift dramatically altered the need, purpose and use of captive labor in the various states. In discussing the Senegal River Valley James Searing writes:

> With the end of the slave trade, the slave-raiding, slave-trading economy continued to function, but the slaves were now diverted into the internal market, where their labor filled new demands for export commodities during the era of legitimate commerce. . . . The nineteenth-century consolidation of slave production was directly linked with the decline of the export slave trade and the expansion of "legitimate" commerce . . . its victims were now channeled into economies based on production for export.[6]

Similarly, captives on the Gold Coast experienced a similar transition, as they became an intricate part of the production of goods and commodities being exported from the region, namely the interior.

In the Gold Coast region, these changes or structural adjustments as James Searing has referred to them as resulted in commercial transformations which stretched from the coastline to the hinterland of the region. Furthermore, those commercial transformations also resulted in the changeover on the local level from captives to legitimate items, which in turn impacts those once involved in the trade of captives and those who were not. On the Gold Coast and across its hinterland, this transition resulted in the emergence of a successful cash crop economy, which relied heavily on the ability of the people of the state to produce goods for this growing economy.

In order to best understand the modifications which occurred on the Senegal River Valley and in Gold Coast, one must place those changes in the context of its region as well as its history, both of which shape the patterns of migration and settlement.[7] As these significant changes got underway along the coastline, within Greater Asante, migration, settlement, ownership and wealth patterns all shifted dramatically from the previously established traditional patterns. These modifications ultimately impacted all segments of society, changing the leadership structure within elite segments of the Asante state.

Immanuel Wallerstein, in an analysis of the changing economy of era argued the expansion of African commerce in the nineteenth century eventually led to the geographic growth of the European worldeconomy and its absorption of Africa into this system. This absorption came in three phases: 1750 to 1793 witnessed an increase in slave exports, 1790s to 1840s saw the steady increase in so-called legitimate trade and the 1840s to the 1880s gave way to an increase in the trade of primary products.[8] In analyzing the last two periods of Wallerstein's work, it is very important to note that African manpower in this emerging system was needed to produce cash crops in mass.[9]

Albeit, the changeover and the incorporation of West Africa into the world-economy between the 1790s and the 1880s, the last two periods discussed by Wallerstein, caused a large scale increase in the use of captive labor. Along the coastline of the Gold Coast but also within the interior as well, states began to rely heavily on the use of a captive labor force to meet the demands of European trading partners, as these areas produced the most desired crops and goods. Moreover, this increase in captive labor was also seen within the Asante and can also be connected with the increase in individual wealth and private land ownership. The mass production of agriculture and mass produced goods and their trade in the world economy placed the Gold Coast in prime position to take advantage of trading opportunities. Engaging in trade with two of the largest economies of the early and mid-nineteenth century, in the British and Dutch, the Gold Coast and its states, from those along the coastline to the interior, were forced to alter its own system and management of captive labor.

Absorbing Africa and the Gold Coast into the world economy led to the creation of a cash crop system within the region, which was well prepared to for the mass production of goods for export. While crops were previously produced within the interior for trade on a small scale, the closure of the slave trade led to an increase production of cash crops, forcing the interior traders look elsewhere. Along with the mass production of crops, manufactured goods also became the alternative to trading captives. The introduction of a cash crop system and the mass production of manufactured items, into a region which relied on previously relied heavily on the export of captive labor for sustainability, show the successful transition of the region.

With the passage of laws to abolish the trade in captive labor to the New World, the growth of legitimately traded items became the main concern of both Europe and the Americas. This term remained in the forefront of traders through the eventual start of colonialism in the latter stages of the nineteenth. Robin Law's edited volume *From Slave Trade to "Legitimate" Commerce: The Commercial Transition in Nineteenth-Century West Africa* argues that there was no crisis of adaptation but instead a smooth transition. Although this transition was smooth, the region also experienced its own highs and lows with the fluctuation in the imports and exports along with the prices of goods sold along the coastline.

Moreover, between the 1780s and the 1820s the value of exports from West Africa dropped from £31.7m to £27m. Accordingly, in the following years the value of trade, exports and imports, from West Africa prior to eventual expeditions into the interior and the ultimate start of colonialism, rose to £93.1m.[10] Although the nearly 23 percent decline in the value of

African exports between 1780 and 1820 caused some traders to leave the market altogether, this dip can be attributed to Britain's decline in imports. While this early decline caused many traders to leave the African market, its eventual rise in the middle of the century brought traders back. Albeit, as the British market for African goods rose again, legitimate items such as timber, ivory, groundnuts, palm oil and rubber were now the preferred imports into the European market.[11]

This fluctuation in exports along West Africa before its eventual rise coincides with the creation of trade partnerships and agreements between European nations and interior African states. Similarly, economic fluctuations also occurred on the Gold Coast and have been discussed in the previous chapter, relate specifically to those growing interior trade agreements. This increase in profits related to exports and imports of goods from West Africa highlights the successful transition many states and people were able to make away from the trade in captives to manufactured goods and crops. Although the trade in captives was slowly overtaken by the desire for other legitimately traded items, the era is still marked by controversy. In particular, the use of the term "legitimate trade" has been applied to all trade to and from Africa throughout the nineteenth century.

In a sentiment which expresses the eventual coming of colonialism to the region in the latter years of the nineteenth century, Arthur Pollock in the *United States Service Journal and Naval Military Magazine* wrote, ". . . on the Gold Coast . . . legitimate commerce is the most effectual means of civilization. . . ."[12] Pollock's remarks on the Gold Coast remind us of the saying, Christianity, Commerce and Civilization. Pollock's sentiment was common for the era regarding the connection between commerce and civilization. Nonetheless, at the height of the transition to legitimate commerce as Africa was being brought into the Atlantic world economy of the nineteenth century, a greater emphasis was placed on the goods generated and not the labor which produced those items.[13] This remained the views expressed among British traders, until the latter stages of the nineteenth century, just prior to the start of colonialism.

Moreover, several scholars have begun to look at how this term is defined as a result of these statements. The term legitimate commerce, which is commonly accepted among economists and historians who study this period, has been accompanied by controversy. Christopher Chamberlin became one of the early scholars to look at this wording and refers to the term legitimate commerce as being both a Eurocentric word and an outdated label from the nineteenth century that should be replaced with the bulk export commodities. He argues this is a term which many Africanist scholars employed up to the start of colonialism and should be therefore replaced by the concept of bulk export trade. Furthermore, he insists referring to commerce from this era, a term should encompass both the high and low values per pound of commodities.[14] Chamberlin writes:

> Legitimate trade is a hopelessly anachronistic label for the late nineteenth-century West African trade, but Africanists nonetheless employed it up to the onset of colonial rule. . . . More appropriate terminology would recognize the critical role of the transition from high value per pound to low value per pound products—from luxury export commodities to bulk export commodities. "Bulk export trade," therefore, is a sensible alternative to "legitimate trade . . ."[15]

Such a critique of the term from Chamberlin leaves open the question; is he right in questioning the use of the terminology? Albeit, scholars have continued to use the term freely as it has come to define the era of transitioning from the trade in captives to agricultural and manufactured goods.

The Gold Coast, like many portions of West Africa, entered the Atlantic commercial system specializing first in gold trading, but at the height of the Trans-Atlantic Slave Trade, it became more specialized in trading captives for profit.[16] After the British and American governments closed the slave trade and transitioned into the era of legitimate commerce, the Gold Coast began to use forts for trading goods other than captives and eventually saw the establishment of plantation systems and the coming of Afro-European traders.

Forts along the Gold Coast, some of which had been there since the fifteenth century, were crucial to the developing European influence in the region. As the British became the dominate nation in the region, they began to establish other goods as factors in trading, besides that of captive Africans. The need for these forts is further evident in a letter from Sir Nicholls of the Gold Coast treasury of the Parliament which discussing the maintenance of forts. In his letter he writes, ". . . to be made to the Lords of Treasury . . . for the sum of one thousand seven and fifty pounds . . . for the support and maintenance of forts and factories on the Gold Coast."[17] These forts during the era of legitimate trade took on a different responsibility from previous in which they were largely used to house captives prior to export.

As the British began the transition to legitimate trade or bulk export products in all of West Africa and the Gold Coast, the Kru people of Liberia served as a migrant labor force essential to trade. Diane Frost, who studies this migrant labor force, discusses this group extensively, stating the opening of trade partnerships in the eighteenth and nineteenth centuries led to the migration of the Kru. As the British expanded their desire for legitimate commodities on the Gold Coast, the Kru became a migrant labor force which followed the extension of trading. The Kru followed the British to a number of areas including the Gold Coast, working on merchant ships.[18]

Many merchants, along with the Asantehene himself, believed that the passage of abolition laws by the British and Americans could ultimately damage and eventually destroy the economy of the coastal Gold Coast region and interior Asante state.[19] Joseph Dupuis in his communication with Asantehene Osei Bonsu expresses this very concern in his 1820 work detailing his visit to the interior Asante state territory. Dupuis writes, "The king did not deem it plausible, that this obnoxious traffic should have been abolished from motives . . . that it lessened the number either of domestic or foreign wars."[20] Instead the Asantehene argues the state did not go to war specifically to gain captives, but this was an act which proved who was the strongest of men within their culture. Moreover, once war commenced many bad people were killed and many good people were sold into slavery; both acts were undertaken order to protect the Asante themselves from becoming victims of slavery or death.[21]

Once the slave trade was officially abolished on the Gold Coast, the British became the dominant European traders in the region due to wars back in Europe and the change to a more capitalistic economy. There were several commodities which quickly became the preferred choice of goods among traders. Palm oil became an especially crucial commodity shipped from the Gold Coast during the era following the closure of the slave trade. Beginning in 1814, only a few short years after the slave trade was abolished, palm oil, and between 1807 and 1842 the commodity played a role in altering the Gold Coast economy.[22]

Between 1850 and 1874, the trade in palm oil again went through up and down phases due in part to its supply.[23] As such palm oil came to define legitimate trade from the Gold Coast.[24] To cope with the impact of the abolition of the slave trade, the Asante began to use captives that once were shipped out as an export to grow agricultural products for the local economy and export. The Asante used these captives to produce food, collect rubber and carry kola nuts.[25]

As the slave trade was closed and slowly declined, kola nuts from the hinterland of the Gold Coast and Greater Asante also witnessed a similar growth in its trade value. This growth in the kola trade was most evident among those traders who traveled into the Northern markets interacting with Hausa, Mossi, Mande and eventually into the Sokoto Caliphate. Numerous conquests made by the Asante in the eighteenth and nineteenth centuries to both its east and west, to the Niger Bend and Volta Basin, opened up new trade markets for its kola nuts while incorporating these new states into the expanding economy. Moreover, this incorporation of new states into the Asante economy was referred to as central place theory, or the forcing of subordinates into a specific market to meet their needs, while the state provides services to its citizens.[26]

Kola in the nineteenth century was viewed as one of the many legitimately traded items which the Asante state depended heavily on for economic development. Edmund Abaka writes, "State kola supplies were obtained from kola plantations operated by state officials and worked by slaves) or by simply purchasing from producers."[27] Moreover, as kola was transported into areas of Salaga, this created to a substantial increase in the Asante treasury. These funds were used to both protect the state as well as maintain trade routes that were critical for the states' survival.

As previously discussed using Immanuel Wallerstein's *The Modern World System* and analyzing the final one hundred years of his absorption process which encompasses the increase in legitimate trade, cash crop commodities such as kola grew in value in the Gold Coast between the south and the north. This seemingly small nut became one of the many staple cash crops that altered the economy of the Gold Coast in the mid-nineteenth century. K. Y. Daaku, one of many to analyze this period, argues the loss in trade with the closure of the Trans-Atlantic Slave Trade did impact the Gold Coast negatively but the increase in kola trading by the turn of the century and into the mid-nineteenth century was able to offset this loss in commerce.[28]

While state traders whose sale of kola was overseen by the Asantehene, any profits from these specific individuals went directly to the state. With access to the early months of the Northern market, these traders were able to make considerable profits for the state. Moreover, controlling the early months of the market limited any form of competition that ultimately arrived from private traders who were also allowed to sale kola in later months.[29] Only after state traders sold their portion of the kola crop were private traders allowed to sale kola in the Northern market.

Private traders who entered the kola trade, without the labor force of the state, turned to family members as well as captive labor. Furthermore, for private traders they both used captives in the production of kola in the region of Greater Asante and exchanged the commodity for Hausa captives being sold in Salaga.[30] In order to gain access to these roads, private traders paid tolls to heralds who worked for the Asanthene and the state, which gave them access to the markets. Queenmother Abena Kete of Bekwai notes that heralds often took twenty-five kola nuts out of every 2,000 taken as a tax. Twenty were given to the Asantehene, and the rest were placed in the state treasury.[31]

Nevertheless, the emergence of a private class of traders and crop producers was instrumental to the transition of the state through the mid-nineteenth century. As the interior region linked to the growing Atlantic, commercial economy continued to expand, and private wealth also grew within the state. Private traders were able to capitalize on a market for their goods not only to the Northern Hausa markets but also to the Southern market of Europeans trading along the coastline. While the Asante state was able to acquire substantial wealth through tax collection, they became dependent of the growing class of professional traders who bought and sold goods wherever they were profitable. Thereafter, the Asante Empire relied on the ability of this emerging class to pay taxes, but this did not limit their growth as a state or individuals.[32]

As traders gained access to individual wealth the transition from the trade in captives to a trade in legitimate commerce or bulk goods, along the Gold Coast territory, created a development of private ownership and changing family structure. Both elements dramatically impacted not only the interior of the state but also its coastal trading partners. This continuous development of both the family private ownership and wealth also impacts the changing state and family structure of the Asante throughout the nineteenth century. Moreover, the changing state and family structure also alters the use of captives and their use in the production of goods and cash crops within the state.

Asante families who owned captives used them as field workers as well as domestic servants. Although the captives were generally accepted into the families of the owners, still they did not have the same social status.[33] While many of these captives could ultimately be adopted into a family, or marry into a family, elders of the family never forgot the roots of the individual. This is explained in family circles by the Akan proverb: "*Akoa ne ne wura ba edi agoro, a, na n'akoa wo̱ ne tirim.*"[34] Similarly, Rattray translated this as well, *Obi nkyere obi asi*, meaning one must not disclose the origin of another.[35] This is a sentiment, which all Akan follow, and is still a topic which is problematic when referenced by anyone in the society.[36] Free women who bore the child of a captive man in Asante allowed the family to circumvent the father's right to relation of anyone in the family, which also worked in the same manner in birth of a child to captive mother, but previous status was never disclosed.[37]

In a matrilineal state, such as the Asante, defining a child's status ultimately impacted the family and the operation of the state. As children bore between captives and free born persons became more of a reality in the Asante state, children of such exchanges needed to be identified. Children born to free men and captive women usually joined the fathers' line and grew up to consider themselves Asante, although this was in conflict with the Asante lineage practices. This practice also gave the father more authority over the child than the brother or uncle of the mother.[38] For free Asante men, captives provided a far greater advantage than pawns could give them as individual owners. This gave free Asante men the ability to take on more wives, for the purposes of inheritance and child-bearing.[39] Children born to free women and male captives became members of the mothers' line.[40]

Within the family, captives were entitled to fair treatment, and were governed by a set of rules: captives were deemed a part of the family, they were entitled to food, clothing and shelter, children were to be polite to them and captives could not be treated unfairly harsh.[41] Male and female captives were crucial to the extra-subsistence production; therefore the state made an effort to protect this labor force.[42] There has been a general sentiment among scholar that the value of the public sector cannot be underestimated in the nineteenth century. The public sector consisting of producers strengthened the state and attributed to the commercial transformation of the Asante beginning the nineteenth century.[43] Albeit, although the laws protected both captives and producers within the Asante state with certain rights, those captives of the first generation were often treated more harshly often bearing the marks resulting from scarification practices.[44] These marks or small incisions along the cheek or side of temple were given to those first generation captives and ultimately served as an identifier for those held within the state.[45]

Once formally held within the state, captives of Asante were commonly referred to as *odonko* a term that is tantamount with one being a foreigner in the society. The term *odonko* is defined as, ". . . to be without a free Asante mother is to be without the matrilineal ties which established an individual's formal and complete credentials certifying legitimate membership in

traditional Akan society."[46] This term was applied to those captured in warfare and purchased at one of the numerous markets for doing so in Greater Asante. A second term to refer to captives in the Asante was *domum*, which is often applied to those who were both captives of war and tribute arrangements.[47] Furthermore, within the Asante, a matrilineal society, having this connection to a free woman of Akan lineage legitimized any person within the state. A lack of any matrilineal connection to a free woman of Asante lineage within the state was ultimately perceived as a weakness. Therefore, many of those individuals without this matrilineal connection described as foreigners were held as captives.

Furthermore, those with an Asante blood line, who became pawns, were referred to as *awowa*. Someone who was a pawn was often given to another person to pay off any outstanding debts owed.[48] A person holding a number of captives, who also owed a debt to another, could use a captive to repay any debt that he or she may owe to another. Once this debt was paid in the full, the pawn quickly regained the status he or she held prior to their current status as a pawn, whether that be of captive or free status. Similarly, those who were born with one parent being of captive status in the Asante were quickly assimilated into the state.[49] This became a process of preservation and peace keeping as the previous status of one's captive ancestry became a taboo subject often not spoken of within family units.[50]

Thereafter, those captives were divided into three varying categories as distinguishing factor. First, those captured during a war effort, second those pawned by relatives or themselves to liquidate debts and last, those who voluntarily placed themselves in servitude for protection.[51] The division of captive labor was not a unique aspect only found within the Asante state, but among the people these principles governed the day-to-day lives of those held captive.

While the British and Americans made an effort to slow the Trans-Atlantic Slave Trade along the seas, this did very little to slow the trade in the interior. Although this trade was carried on at a much smaller rate, the market for their labor stretched from the Northern to Southern regions.[52] Albeit, captive labor has always been an integral part of the Asante economy, as these individuals were divided into classes and were used in both agriculture and mining industries. Most notably, T. E. Bowdich when traveling to the region witnessed the construction plantations or large scale farming units, with captives being the main source of labor.[53] Once the external slave trade was declared officially illegal, the internal trade in captive labor increased quickly to become the mainstay of the Asante economic system. Captive labor was doubtless the main factor behind the success of an ever-expanding farming system.

As a result of the developing farming units, wealthy elites began to emerge in and around Kumasi. Two types of elite could be detected within Greater Asante, in the years following the abolition of the Trans-Atlantic Slave Trade and the increase in the internal African Slave Trade. There were on one hand the rural producers of crops and on the other hand urban traders who conducted the slave trade and at the same time owned plantations. Jean Allman and Victoria Tashjian argue that the use of captives in the nineteenth century by Asante families transformed the wealth of the family aiding them in a successful transition to legitimate commerce.[54]

The development of an agricultural center to mainly export foodstuffs turned the Asante areas around Kumasi into major importers of captives and Salaga as exporters of captives. Furthermore, these captives were used in the development of an Asante cash-crop economy in the nineteenth century, contributing the growth of what has been defined as legitimate commerce. Families and individuals in Greater Asante, and to a great extent in the rest of Wet Africa, increased their traffic in the internal slave trade over an extensive network of commercial highways.[55]

Patrick Manning in his monumental work *Slavery and African Life* discusses the great increase in the number of captives in Africa following the abolition of the slave trade and the use of these individuals, which he adds puts pressure on the division of labor and social institutions. Manning first explains the various elements to which this trade operated, African, Oriental and Occidental over many centuries. Nevertheless, concerning years of the legitimate trade era and the rise of captives in Africa, Manning writes, “After about 1850, there were more slaves in Africa than in the New World. The nineteenth-century growth of the African slave trade not only expanded the scale of African slavery, but caused a new set of institutional transformations. . . . A slave mode of production flowered for a half-century, until it was ended under European colonization . . ."[56] This slave mode of production impacted the economy of the Greater Asante, especially in the areas of Kumasi and Salaga, stretching the entire Gold Coast region and ultimately the growing Atlantic commercial economy.

The transition into the so-called legitimate trade was not a crisis of adaptation as argued by A. G. Hopkins, as already explained. Instead the necessitated changes which occurred were predicated by alterations in three different systems of trade carried out in Africa and in the Gold Coast. First, there was the inter-state trade, that is, trade to markets within a particular region. Second, there was intra-state trade or trade conducted between two or more states. Third, there was long-distance trading, or trade covering a number of states over long distances.[57] Moreover, it was the development of these trade routes along with the consolidation of power by the Asante which led to the ascendancy of the state during the nineteenth century.[58]

As this trading pattern and format was altered, it forced the family unit and its emerging cash crop economy to also adapt to changes. As previously stated, the Asante family unit began to exploit its source of captive labor to an exhaustive amount. They began importing this captive labor from the surrounding areas but a considerable number arrived from Salaga. Indeed, ownership of captives in the Gold Coast and throughout Africa was a family business. Akosua Perbi writes:

> Labour in pre-colonial Ghana, as in most of Africa, was organized on the basis of households and slave complemented the labour requirements of families. . . . Indeed the development of legitimate trade in raw materials fuelled an extensive use of domestic slaves in local production to meet the demands of the international market. Farming expanded in scale and scope during the second half of the 19th century, partly to meet the demands of external markets. As farming expanded so too did the use of slave labour.[59]

Wealthy families in Kumasi maintained large numbers of captives in their farming units while the less fortunate were forced into a system of sharecropping.[60] Albeit, the acquisition of sizeable plots of land and the importation of a large number of captive labor turned the Asante economy into a commercial enterprise geared toward the export of goods.[61]

The rising demand for Asante agricultural products necessitated the introduction of an extensive farming system for the production of cassava, cocoyam, yam, plantain and maize.[62] Maize like many of these other commodities was critical to the changeover which occurred in the nineteenth century. Pieter de Marees who visited the region as early as 1602 discussed the introduction of several crops namely maize commenting on the prominent role it played after its introduction.[63] Moreover, maize became a staple crop grown in surplus for captive being sold into the Trans-Atlantic Slave Trade as well as those remaining to be sold. Not only did maize become a year round food source, but after the closure of the slave trade, it remained a crop grown in surplus on the Gold Coast.[64]

In the latter part of the nineteenth centuries kola, palm oil and rubber became the major items produced by captives. It is said that the production of palm oil toward the end of the nineteenth century was so great that it defined the era of legitimate commerce.[65] Moreover, trade in gold, which flourished in the eighteenth century, declined substantially by the nineteenth century giving way to agricultural goods.[66] Albeit, as this transition during the nineteenth century included this emerging system of goods and the work of captive labor, crop producers became the face of the changing economy. Nonetheless, the development of this class of producers and traders still entitled captives rights and fair treatment within their holding families.

Within the family, captives were entitled to fair treatment, and were governed by a set of rules: captives were deemed a part of the family; they were entitled to food, clothing and shelter; children were to be polite to them; and captives could not be treated unfairly harsh.[67] Although these were the laws of the Asante, captives of the first generation were often treated more harshly often bearing the marks resulting from scarification practices.[68] The practice of domestic and farming slavery within the Asante state continued until it was outlawed by the British in 1874. Moreover, the British "codified notions of the kinship of slaves by declaring all former slaves family members."[69]

The development of an agricultural center to mainly export foodstuffs turned the Asante around Kumasi into major importers of captives and Salaga as exporters of captives, which developed the Asante cash-crop economy of the nineteenth century. Families and individuals in Greater Asante, and to a great extent in the rest of Wet Africa, increased their traffic in the internal slave trade over an extensive network of commercial highways.[70] Patrick Manning discussing this increase in traffic during the era writes:

> After . . . 1850, there were more slaves in Africa than in the New World. The nineteenth-century growth of the African slave trade . . . expanded the scale of African slavery. . . . A slave mode of production flowered for a half-century, until it was ended under European colonization. . . . The abolition of slavery in the Atlantic world correlated in a broad fashion with the development of industrial capitalism . . . the abolition of slavery in Africa was an aspect of the world-wide movement for abolition. . . . The abolition of the slave trade in Africa . . . became in practice an aspect of European imperial conquest of Africa. . . . The abolition of slavery in Africa—quite a different matter from the abolition of slave trade—was slowed by the establishment of ties between European colonial rulers and African slave owners.[71]

It is stated above that Kumasi family units exploited captive labor imported from the surrounding areas but mainly from Salaga. Indeed, ownership of captives in the Gold Coast and throughout Africa was a family business. Akosua Perbi writes:

> Labour in pre-colonial Ghana, as in most of Africa, was organized on the basis of households and slave complemented the labour requirements of families. . . . Indeed the development of legitimate trade in raw materials fuelled an extensive use of domestic slaves in local production to meet the demands of the international market. Farming expanded in scale and scope during the second half of the 19th century, partly to meet the demands of external markets. As farming expanded so too did the use of slave labour.[72]

Wealthy families in Kumasi maintained large numbers of captives in their farming units while the less fortunate were forced into a system of sharecropping.[73] Albeit, the acquisition of sizeable plots of land and the importation of a large number of captive labor turned the Asante economy into a commercial enterprise geared toward the export of goods.[74]

While these sizable plots of land were equipped with captive labor they were not the traditional forms of plantations as described in the United States, the Caribbean Islands or South America. Nevertheless, as they were used in a form of sharecropping, they still maintained certain rights and standard living conditions. Many resided in small houses near the corners of the land living much like any other citizen in Greater Asante. Captives worked in small family groups, which also allowed them to both work under the supervision of an owner until the days end and also move freely thereafter.[75]

The Trans-Atlantic Slave Trade once formally closed at the start of the nineteenth, impacted all the regions of West Africa. This decision to formally close to trade in captives from West Africa first passed by Britain in 1807 and the United States in 1808 caused a ripple effect across the entire Western coastline of Africa stretching as far north as the Senegambia and as far south as Angola. Most notably, the economy of the area known as the Gold Coast witnessed a massive changeover resulting in fluctuations wealth and prices for goods in the numerous states of the region stretching well into the interior.

The formal decision to close the Trans-Atlantic Slave Trade at the start of the nineteenth century, thus, formally began the era of legitimate commerce. This era covering more than eight decades of the nineteenth century highlights not only the growth of European and American trading interests but also the involvement and growth of Africa a member of the new Atlantic world economy. Albeit, this growing economy in the nineteenth century incorporated states along the coastline as well as those regions and people well into the interior areas. The involvement of West African regions in the growing Atlantic commercial economy of the nineteenth century ultimately varied depending upon several factors: states, commodities, trading routes and agreements between partners.

On the Gold Coast, this shift from an exporter of captive labor at the start of the nineteenth century to a supplier of numerous agricultural items led to a large scale economic changeover across the entire region. This ability to successfully evolve into a series of states which legitimately traded items in the nineteenth century proves they were able to make this transition without causing much disruption. Within the state of Asante and the region of Greater Asante, much of this ability to successfully transition to legitimately traded items resulted in the rise of individual and family wealth. The emergence of this new family wealth altered the structure of this matrilineal society placing a greater emphasis on individuals and not the royal elites. Moreover, the fluctuations in the economy caused by the changeover to legitimate items did not leave any permanent damage to the state, but instead created a new class of citizens who benefitted from the emergence of new trading opportunities. By the mid-nineteenth century this included a new class of African merchant traders whose wealth allowed them new opportunities.

NOTES

1. A. G. Hopkins, *An Economic History of West Africa* (New York: Columbia University Press, 1973), p. 126.
2. Ibid., 135.
3. Robin Law, ed., *From Slave Trade to 'Legitimate' Commerce: The Commercial Transition in Nineteenth-Century West Africa* (New York: Cambridge University Press, 2002); this work consists of several conference papers which all argue against Hopkins notion of a "crisis of adaptation." Each paper instead argues the transition from the slave trade to legitimate commerce did not cause a severe disruption as Hopkins believed.
4. A. G. Hopkins, *An Economic History of West Africa* (New York: Columbia University Press, 1973); Christopher Chamberlin, "Bulk Exports, Trade Tiers, Regulation, and Development: An Economic Approach to the Study of West Africa's Legitimate Trade," *The Journal of Economic History*, Vol. 39, No. 2 (June, 1979); Robin Law, ed., *From Slave Trade to 'Legitimate' Commerce: The Commercial Transition in the Nineteenth Century West Africa* (New York: Cambridge University Press, 2002), all study this phenomena of trading following the abolition of the Trans-Atlantic Slave Trade. While Hopkins initially argued Africa experienced a Crisis of Adaptation in the transition from trading captives to bulk goods both Chamberlin and Law in later works proved Africa did not experience a crisis but instead this transition was smooth. Robin Law's edited this work consists of several conference papers which all argue against Hopkins notion of a "crisis of adaptation." Each paper instead

argues the transition from the slave trade to legitimate commerce did not cause a severe disruption as Hopkins believed.

5. James F. Searing, *West African Slavery and Atlantic Commerce: The Senegal River Valley, 1700–1860* (Great Britain: Cambridge University Press, 1993), pp. 167–168.

6. Ibid., 44–45.

7. Ibid., 1.

8. Immanuel Wallerstein, *The Modern World-System: The Second Era of Great Expansion of the Capitalist World-Economy, 1730–1840s* (San Diego: University of California Press, 1989), p. 148.

9. Immanual Wallerstein, *The Capitalist World Economy* (London: Cambridge University Press, 1979), pp. 27–28.

10. D. Eltis and L.C. Kennings, "Trade Between Western Africa and The Atlantic World in the Pre-Colonial Era," *American Historical Review*, Vol. 93 (1988), pp. 936–959 in Martin Lynn, "West African Palm Oil Trade in the Nineteenth Century and the Crisis of Adaptation," *From Slave Trade to Legitimate Commerce: The Commercial Transition in Nineteenth-Century West Africa*, Robin Law, ed. (Cambridge, UK: Cambridge University Press, 2002), p. 58.

11. Martin Lynn, *Commerce and Economic Change in West Africa: The Palm Oil Trade in the Nineteenth Century* (New York: Cambridge University Press, 1997), p. 12.

12. Arthur Pollock, *The United States Service Journal and Naval Military Magazine, 1838 Part II*, Vol. 27 (London: William Clowes and Sons, 1838), p. 207.

13. Jon D. Carlson, *Myths, State Expansion, and the Birth of Globalization: A Comparative Perspective* (New York: St. Martin's Press, 2012), p. 79.

14. Christopher Chamberlin, "Bulk Exports, Trade Tiers, Regulation, and Development: An Economic Approach to the Study of West Africa's Legitimate Trade," *The Journal of Economic History*, Vol. 39, No. 2 (June, 1979), pp. 420–421.

15. Ibid.

16. Joseph Inikori, "Slavery and Atlantic Commerce, 1650–1800," *The American Economic Review*, Vol. 82, No. 2, Papers and Proceedings of the Hundred and Fourth Annual Meeting of the American Economic Association (May, 1992), p. 155.

17. Letter from Sir Nicholls of the Gold Coast to the Lords of the Treasury, British Parliament, Received July 5, 1836. Letter Book, Sierra Leone and African Forts, Vol. 5, 1836, PRO British National Archives. CO 267/136

18. Diane Frost, "Diasporan West African Communities: The Kru in Freetown & Liverpool," *Reviews of African Political Economy*, Vol. 29, No. 92 (June, 2002), p. 289.

19. James Sanders, "Palm Oil Production on the Gold Coast in the Aftermath of the Slave Trade: A Case Study of the Fante," *The International Journal of African History*, Vol. 15, No. 1 (1982), pp. 49–50.

20. Joseph Dupuis, *Journal of a Residence in Ashantee, Comprising Notes and Researches Relative to the Gold Coast, and the Interior of Western Africa* (London: Henry Colburn, 1824), pp. 162–164 in William H. Worger, Nancy L. Clark and Edward A. Alpers, eds. *Africa and the West: From the Slave Trade to Conquest, 1441–1905*, Vol. 1 (New York: Oxford University Press, 2010), pp. 110–111.

21. Ibid.

22. Sanders, 49–50.

23. David Kimble, *A Political History of Ghana: The Rise of Gold Coast Nationalism, 1850–1928* (Oxford: Clarendon Press, 1963), p. 4.

24. Patrick Manning, "Slaves, Palm Oil and Political Power on the West African Coast," *African Historical Studies*, Vol. 2, No. 2 (1969), pp. 279–280.

25. Inez Sutton, "Labour in Commercial Agriculture in Ghana in the Late Nineteenth Century and Early Twentieth Centuries," *The Journal of African History*, Vol. 24, No. 4 (1983), p. 464.

26. Edmund Kobina Abaka, *Kola is God's Gift: Agricultural Production, Export Initiatives & The Kola Industry in Asante & the Gold Coast, 1820–1950* (Athens, OH: Ohio University Press, 2005), p. 57.

27. Ibid., 62.

28. K. Y. Daaku, "Aspects of Pre-Colonial Akan Economy," *International Journal of Historical African Studies*, Vol. 5, No. 2 (1972), pp. 420–421 in Abaka, *Kola is God's Gift*, 63.

29. Ibid.

30. Ibid., 62.

31. Royal Anthropological Society, *Rattray Field Notes*, MS 107: 5, 1 in Abaka, *Kola God's Gift*, pp. 64–65.

32. Daaku, "Aspects of Pre-Colonial Akan Economy," 244 in Abaka, *Kola is God's Gift*, 67.

33. Akosua Perbi, *A History of Indigenous Slavery in Ghana: From the 15th Century to the 19th Century* (Accra, Ghana: Sub-Saharan Publishers, 2007), p. 113.

34. Ibid. Elders of family remembered although the former captive had been adopted into the family through marriage, ultimately he or she was a captive and his or her descendants were traced to the former captive as well, but never discussed.

35. Rattray, *Ashanti Law and Constitution*, p. 40.

36. Bayo Holsey, *Routes of Remembrance: Refashioning the Slave Trade in Ghana* (Chicago, Ill: University of Chicago Press, 2008), p. 75.

37. Gareth Austin, *Labour, Land and Capital in Ghana: From Slavery to Free Labour in Asante, 1807–1956* (University of Rochester Press, 2005), p. 175.

38. Klein, 183.

39. Austin, *Labour, Land and Capital in Ghana*, 175.

40. R. S. Rattray, *Ashanti Law and Constitution* (London: Oxford University Press, 1929), p. 40 in Enid Schildkrout, "The Ideology of Regionalism in Ghana," in William A. Shack and Elliot P. Skinner, eds., *Strangers in African Societies* (Berkeley, CA: University of California Press, 1979), p. 189.

41. Perbi, 118.

42. Austin, 175.

43. Wilks, *Asante in the Nineteenth Century*, p. 178 in Gareth Austin, "'No Elders Were Present': Commoners and Private Ownership in Asante, 1807–1896," *The Journal of African History*, Vol. 37, No. 1 (1996), p. 1.

44. Bayo Holsey, *Routes of Remembrance: Refashioning the Slave Trade in Ghana* (Chicago, Ill: University of Chicago Press, 2008), p. 42.

45. Enid Schildkrout, "The Ideology of Regionalism in Ghana," in William A. Shack and Elliot P. Skinner, eds., *Strangers in African Societies* (Berkeley, CA: University of California Press, 1979), p. 190.

46. Ivor Wilks, *Asante in the Nineteenth Century: The Structure and Evolution of a Political Order* (Cambridge: Cambridge University Press, 1990) in Anatole Norman Klein, *Inequality in Asante: A Study of the forms and Meanings of Slavery and Social Servitude in Pre and Early Colonial Akan-Asante Society and Culture* (Ph.D. Diss.,: University of Michigan, 1980), pp. 95–96.

47. Raymond E. Dumett, *Imperialism, Economic Development and Social Change in West Africa* (Durham, NC: Carolina Academic Press, 2013), p. 75.

48. Perbi, 3.

49. Klein, 156.

50. Schildkrout, 189.

51. R. S. Rattray, *Ashanti Proverbs: The Primitive Ethics of Savage People* (Oxford: The Clarendon Press, 1916), p. 119.

52. Dumett, 80.

53. T. E. Bowdich, *An Essay on the Superstitions, Customs, and Arts Common to the Ancient Egyptions, Abyssinians and Ashantees* (Paris, 1821), p. 18 in Enid Schildkrout, "The Ideology of Regionalism in Ghana," in William A. Shack and Elliot P. Skinner, eds., *Strangers in African Societies* (Berkeley, CA: University of California Press, 1979), p. 189.

54. Jean Allman and Victoria Tashjian, *I Will Not Eat Stone: A Women's History of Colonial Asante* (Portsmouth, NH: Heinemann, 2000), p. 11.

55. Patrick Manning, *Slavery and African Life: Occidental, Oriental and African Slave Trades* (New York: Cambridge University Press, 1990), p. 10.

56. Ibid., 23.

57. Perbi, 78–79.

58. John D. Carolson, *Myths, State Expansion and the Birth of Globalization: A Comparative Perspective* (New York: Palgrave Macmillan, 2012), p. 76.

59. Perbi, 70.

60. Wilks, *Forests of Gold*, 55.

61. Inez Sutton, "Labour in Commercial Agriculture in Ghana in the Late Nineteenth and Early Twentieth Centuries," *The Journal of African*, Vol. 24, No. 4 (1983), p. 464.

62. Wilks, *Forests of* Gold, 55.

63. Pieter de Marees, *Description and Historical Account of the Gold Kingdom of Guinea (1602)*, trans. and ed. Albert van Dantzig and Adam Jones (Oxford: Oxford University Press, 1987), pp. 62–64 in Judith Carney and Richard Nicholas Rosomoff, *In the Shadow of Slavery: Africa Botanical Legacy in the Atlantic World* (Berkley, CA: University of California Press, 2009), pp. 55–57.

64. Carney and Rosomoff, *In the Shadow of Slavery*, pp. 55–57.

65. Patrick Manning, "Slaves, Palm Oil and Political Power on the West African Coast," *African Historical Studies*, Vol. 2, No. 2 (1969), p. 281.

66. Mikell, 24.

67. Perbi, 118.

68. Bayo Holsey, *Routes of Remembrance: Refashioning the Slave Trade in Ghana* (Chicago, Ill: University of Chicago Press, 2008), p. 42.

69. Ibid.

70. Patrick Manning, *Slavery and African Life: Occidental, Oriental and African Slave Trades* (New York: Cambridge University Press, 1990), p. 10.

71. Ibid., 23.

72. Ibid., 70.

73. Wilks, *Forests of Gold*, 55.

74. Inez Sutton, "Labour in Commercial Agriculture in Ghana in the Late Nineteenth and Early Twentieth Centuries," *The Journal of African*, Vol. 24, No. 4 (1983), p. 464.

75. Dumett, 88.

Chapter 6

The Asante–British Treaties and Conflicts, 1817–1874

By the start of the nineteenth century the market for legitimately traded goods in West Africa and within the Gold Coast began to expand. Powers of the nineteenth century, Denmark, Britain and the emerging America began their transition to capitalism by enacting a number of laws and constitutional amendments to solidify their positions in both home and developing African trade markets. As turmoil erupted in the Americas, the British were forced to relinquish control of these colonies, which affected their own economy at home and the value of its holdings in Caribbean. Moreover, in the many decades which followed, the Dutch power began to dwindle on the Gold Coast, leaving the British with the opportunity to expand its reach in the region. Thereafter, the relationship between the interior Asante state and foreign nations was forever changed due to changes in fort ownership and the desire for expansion beyond the coastline. This resulted in numerous treaties being signed, the ending of diplomatic relationships and wars over territories throughout the century.

The Asante in the years after their creation hoped to establish and maintain a diplomatic relationship with each nation along the coastline. These acts of diplomacy began with the first Asantehene, Osei Tutu, who initiated this by first creating relationships with interior states and later establishing connections with Europeans. Furthermore, these numerous acts of diplomacy undertaken by the Asante were well witnessed by the various trade treaties signed between the interior state and the Europeans awaiting along the coastline, namely those agreed upon with the Dutch and British beginning in the mid to late nineteenth century. Most important to the period of 1817 to 1874 were those signed between the Asante and British. Asantehene Osei Tutu agreed upon a series of treaties beginning in 1817 that he believed could normalize the relationship with the Asante and British as well as repair any damage done to the connections with another Akan state, the Fante, by their expansion toward with the coast during the eighteenth century.[1]

Nevertheless, with the passage of the several laws and amendments prohibiting slavery, the trade in Africans continued on for nearly another eighty years illegally. Indeed, the number of captives leaving the African coast after 1807 did not drop significantly enough to affect all areas of Africa until well into the 1860s. On the Gold Coast, these numbers suggest something very different from that of the other areas of West Africa; between 1807 and 1840, the number of captives being transported from the region dropped considerably in the first thirty years after the trade was closed. (See Table 6.1.) This was also a striking difference from the previous numbers of captives transported from the region in the years between 1700 and 1807 as discussed in Chapters 3 and 4.

Undoubtedly, the laws and amendments which officially abolished the slave trade had a wide range of effects on Europeans and coastal traders. Albeit, some nations and traders were able to adjust to the changes, in the Gold Coast in particular, others were not able to do so easily; this was the case for the Dutch. Moreover, these new laws and amendments regarding the slave trade and its closure had very different impact on the Asante in comparison with the coastal merchants. The Asante as an interior state within the Gold Coast were in the process of becoming a nation which focused on bulk goods for trade. Although this transition proved to be a long process, the decision to trade legitimate goods in the form of bulk items and agricultural goods in the years which followed the closure of the slave trade proved the Asante were able to successfully move away from the trade in captives. Although the progression to legitimate goods was carried out over a number of years, acts of diplomacy by the Asante state were needed to ensure this process was completed.

This successful transition made by the Asante from captives to legitimate goods made the interior region of the Gold Coast or Greater Asante a

Table 6.1 30 Years of Exportation from the Gold Coast Following the Passage of Abolition Laws

	Spain/ Uruguay	*Portugal/ Brazil*	*Great Britain*	*Netherlands*	*USA*	*France*	*Denmark/ Baltic*	*Totals*
1807–1810	0	0	6,375	0	3,830	0	0	10,204
1811–1820	0	0	0	0	0	0	0	0
1821–1830	2,968	0	0	0	0	1,078	0	4,045
1831–1840	2,711	0	0	0	0	0	0	2,711
Totals	5,678	0	6,375	0	3,830	1,078	0	16,960

Source: Davis Eltis et al. *The Trans-Atlantic Slave Trade Database: Slave Voyage.* *http://slavevoyages.org/tast/assessment/estimates.faces?yearFrom=1807&yearTo=1850&embarkation=4&disembarkation=205.204.201.203.202.402.403.401.404.405.702.703.701.305.304.307.100.306.309.308.311.310.705.704.501.502.600.301.302.303* (Accessed March 1, 2015).

lucrative investment for the British in the coming decades. The years between 1817 and 1874 began well on diplomatic fronts but ultimately witnessed the outbreak of armed conflict between the British and the Asante. The conflicts between the two nations resulted in the earliest stages of British take-over of the Gold Coast in the late nineteenth century. The treaties and conflicts on the Gold Coast between the British and the Dutch as well as those signed between the British and the Asante dramatically altered the political and economic course of the region and its people.

By the mid-nineteenth century, areas of the African continent, once considered off limits to European traders who feared dying, were eventually explored and opened for trading opportunities. The Gold Coast was no exception to this new opportunity for interior trading, as Europeans on diplomatic missions began to move away from the confines of the coastline. Once finally leaving the coastline and reaching the interior of the region, they soon came to realized they had reached the center of Greater Asante. Kumasi in the center of the Asante territory and Salaga to its north were visited by Europeans beginning in 1817 and likewise, traders from neighboring states converged on Kumasi and Salaga. Both cities served as centers of trade where goods arriving from as far north as Hausaland and beyond and from Europe were exchanged. Consequently, Salaga with its dense population and Kumasi with its rural economy thrived as wealthy metropolis.

Numerous European traders reached the city of Kumasi and Salaga beginning in 1817, and continuously trekked to the area through 1874. Furthermore, the first European traders to arrive in Kumasi and Salaga were T. E. Bowdich and Joseph Dupuis; Bowdich later left a valuable record of his tour of the two cities in his work *Mission from Cape Coast to Ashantee*. He discussed the distances between the two cities and there separation from the smaller towns that sat along the numerous trade routes. His information was undoubtedly of great value to European traders and importantly to the colonial minds back in Europe. He wrote "The 10 days pull from Adda to Odentee, and the 4 journies by land thence to Sallagha, agree very well with the distance and position of that place, as before calculated by the 17 days route from Commassie. . . . Seven days from Sallagha, N. E. according to the Moors. . . ."[2] These coordinates were used by later travelers and the British military to reach both cities.

Joseph Dupuis, on his part, wrote in his *Journal of a Residence in Ashantee* that "Salagha, the chief city of these districts, who station I have assigned 8° latitude 0° 25 longitude east, is reported to be twice the size of Coumassay, and the population, of whom nearly one sixth part are Moslems, to be about four hundred thousand souls. . . ."[3] The population of Kumasi during the nineteenth century is estimated to be between 30,000 and 40,000.[4] That a sizeable Muslim community was stationed in Salaga, most of whom would be traders, indicates the extensive trade that existed between the city and Muslim states to the north. On the other hand, it is estimated that, during this period, about 1,000 Muslims resided in Kumasi, all near the Asantehene palace.[5] Moreover, it is to be mentioned that Christianity, on the other hand, found its way into Greater Asante following the Asante expansion to the south and their direct contact with the European missionaries.[6]

Highly developed network of trade routes connected Kumasi and Salaga to smaller markets that surrounded them and to distant Hausaland and Mossi territory.[7] Albeit, the major centers reached by these highways included Gaya, Jenne, Niger, Daboya, Tamale, Ouagadougou stretching into Hausaland and the Mossi territory.[8] Importantly these routes were used to transport captives from Kumasi and Greater Asante to slave ports near Dahomey well before agricultural products became the chief commodities of choice for traders.[9]

Salaga was, to all intents and purposes, the biggest slave market in the Asante territory and throughout the Gold Coast for that matter. Captives sold at the Salaga slave market were collected from as far inland as Mossi and Hausa land before being transported through Kumasi and ultimately to the coastal markets. (See Figures 6.1 and 6.2.) Benedict Der highlights the travels of several missionaries including David Asante, Theophilus Opuku who reached the city in 1877 and Philip Bus in 1878. Each traveler commented on the extensive numbers of captives reaching Salaga daily, estimating nearly 1600 reached the city each day of their stay and could be purchased for twenty to eighty shillings. But, upon reaching the city one year later, noted the trade in captives continued as these individuals were being used as farm laborers and domestic servants.[10]

In addition to being an important supplier of captives, Salaga, at the time of the visits by Thomas E. Bowdich and Joseph Dupuis was the largest kola market in West Africa.[11] Benedict Der writes, "Asante traders transported large amount of kola nuts to Salaga for sale in exchange for slaves. . . ."[12] Other items traded in the city included yams, rice meat, vegetables, sheabutter, salt, European goods, African fabrics, woolens, leather ware, ivory, ostrich, copper, brass, iron and gold dust.[13]

Furthermore, Salaga's sister city of Kumasi was surrounded by a prosperous and thriving rural economy. Thomas E. Bowdich described the planting technique around Kumasi saying ". . . the yams and groundnuts were planted with much regularity in triangular beds, with small drains around each. . . ."[14] In fact, Kumasi's economy depended to a large extent on the production of food stuffs. [15] Citizens around the city developed sizeable farming units for that purpose, incorporating captive labor into the economy.[16] This thriving agricultural economy which surrounded Kumasi again makes the territory more valuable to the growing British interests of the late nineteenth century.

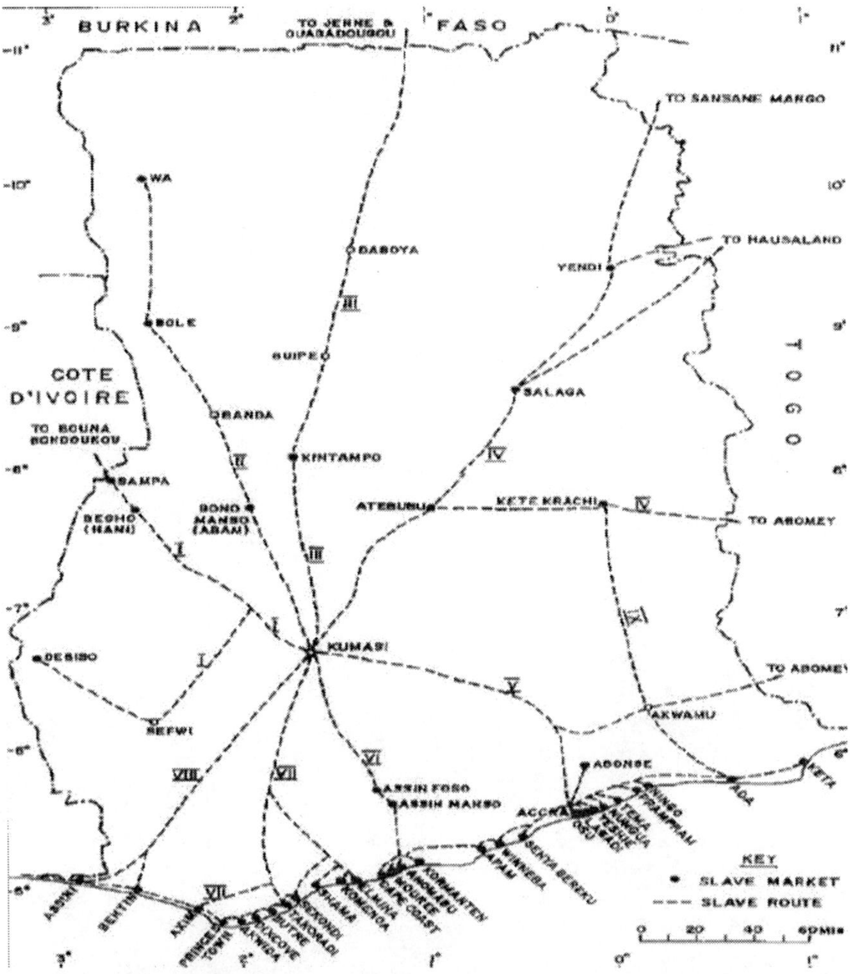

Figure 6.1 Gold Coast Markets and Trade Routes. *Source*: Akosua Perbi, *A History of Indigenous Slavery in Ghana: From the 15th Century to the 19th Century* (Accra, Ghana: Sub-Saharan Publishers, 2007), p. xx. Reproduced, with permission from Sub-Saharan Publishers, P.O. Box 358, Accra Ghana.

Private ownership of agricultural land brought wealth with it, as witnessed by the growing number merchant families in and around the region of Greater Asante. Indeed, wealthy elites also emerged in and around Kumasi and began to make use of captive labor in a number of capacities.[17] Albeit, captive labor on farming units owned by wealthy elites in the mid-nineteenth century worked in an early system of sharecropping, making the captives traded in Salaga an essential unit of Asante economy.[18]

Figure 6.2 Slave Sites and Centers. *Source*: Akosua Perbi, *A History of Indigenous Slavery in Ghana: From the 15th Century to the 19th Century* (Accra, Ghana: Sub-Saharan Publishers, 2007), p. xxiii. Reproduced with permission from Sub-Saharan Publishers, P.O. Box 358, Accra Ghana.

Thus, the abolition of the Trans-Atlantic Slave Trade did very little to slow down the internal trade in captives in the interior of the Gold Coast. In fact, the development and expansion of the rural economy in Asante land sped up the acquisition of captives by Asante families and individuals. As the rural economy around Kumasi expanded, the need for captive labor grew commensurately as did the wealth of individuals. In other words, landownership led to the emergence of wealthy elites in Greater Asante.

The first two decades of the nineteenth century witnessed a series of military confrontations between the Asante and British forces culminating in the establishment of colonial rule over the Gold Coast in 1874. During this period, the Asante made frequent attempts to extend their domain to as far south as the coastal areas. They were however denied access by British forces stationed in the territory, which also hoped to expand their territory as well.

As previously discussed, as the Asante began their expansion toward the coast, a number of conflicts occurred as a result of this movement from Greater Asante. Wars were fought in 1807, 1811, 1814–1816, 1823–1824, 1826–1831, 1863 and again 1874, which included the Aasnte, Fante and British forces. Nevertheless, conflicts between the British and Asante were narrowly avoided in 1820 and again in 1824, which resulted in several trade treaties being signed. Consequently, each of these previously mentioned conflicts had a significant impact on the Gold Coast, parties involved and those not involved, as well as the relationship between the Asante and British just prior to the start of colonial rule.

In the meanwhile, a number of peace and trade treaties were signed by the two nations that eased the tenuous relationship. The first treaty was signed in 1817 by Asantehene Osei Tutu and the British agent/trader Thomas E. Bowdich. Bowdich, as previously mentioned became one of the earliest European traders to reach the interior of the Gold Coast and to come into contact with Asante in there kingdom. Moreover, controversial after its final passage, Article one of the first Peace and Commerce Treaty called for peace between the two nations while article five of the treaty permitted a British officer to permanently reside in Greater Asante, namely Kumasi.[19] Joseph Dupuis later commented on this treaty and the controversial versions writing:

> The treaty, as published in Mr. Bowdich's work, compared with what was actually written, and deposited with the king, is a garbled statement. I cannot say less. In the original document, which is now in my keeping, the pompous name of Boitene Quama, king of Dwabin, is nowhere to be found. It would seem that this association of the two sovereigns was calculated to awaken a more lively interest, and thus only can I account for an attempt to deceive government and the public, by means, I can believe, unprecedented in the annals of the British diplomacy. The article, No. 9, showing the king's dispositition to send his own children to Cape Coast for education is falsely inserted, and every other article is disfigured or misinterpreted more or less.[20]

A second treaty of Peace and Commerce was signed in 1820 by Asantehene Bonsu and the British agent, Joseph Dupuis. The second treaty stipulated that the Asante relinquish to the British all territories surrounding Cape Coast Castle.[21] As late as the 1860s the territory became one which was highly disputed involving not only the British but also the Dutch and Asante as well. Moreover, later correspondence from the eventual leader of the British forces, Sir Garnet Wolseley and the then Asantehene KariKari, point to the disagreements between the two over the coastal territories, which both believed they held claims over.

In late months of 1823, the British government assigned the command of their forces in the Gold Coast to Sir Charles McCarthy, a veteran general who had served for several years in Sierra Leone. He wasted no time in engaging the Asante fighters who were advancing steadily toward the Fante territory stretching along the coast. Although peace treaties had been signed, forces were already heading toward an armed conflict with one another. Furthermore, it is believed that the Asante assembled an army of 20,000 men strong.[22] British Parliamentary records, however, report that the Asante forces numbered 15,000 men while Sir Charles McCarthy had an army of 1,000 soldiers.[23]

Even after the signing of treaties of Peace and Commerce notwithstanding, the two nations, Britain and the Asante, entered into serious military confrontation as early as 1824 and several more thereafter. Albeit, during these early conflicts, the British realized the Asante was indeed a formidable force. The power of this Asante army was evident with their defeat of the British in 1824 who were led by Sir Charles McCarthy. With the introduction of new weaponry in the coming years this altered the inland trading and maritime trading as well.[24] Sir Charles McCarthy died in the ensuing battle and was replaced by London Committee with Commander George MacLean, who was named Governor of the Gold Coast.

New commander George MacLean continued, for several years, to defend the Fante territory in the face of numerous Asante attacks. On his arrival MacLean quickly realized the peace negotiations with the Asante and British were not very encouraging.[25] However, in 1831, MacLean signed an agreement with Asantehene Osei Akoto, one of the most important treaties ever signed in the Gold Coast. For many years to come, this Treaty of Peace and Free Trade stabilized relations between Britain and the Asante.[26] Immediately, the British and other European nations increased their trading activities with the Gold Coast. Thereafter, it is reported that between 1833 and 1841, some 864 trading vessels arrived on the Gold Coast.[27] In other words, larger and larger amounts of goods were exported from the Gold Coast and, at the same time, British imports, particularly cotton, arrived in the area in huge quantities.[28]

While MacLean himself believed he was carrying out the wishes of the British Crown, colonial officials themselves did not agree. Officials believed MacLean was solely concerned with the interests of business merchants and traders alike and not the British Crown. Other concerns from British officials highlighted his lack of interests in suppressing the slave trade, which they made a top priority in 1807 as well as increasing jurisdiction over territories which they believed brought along unwanted conflicts. MacLean believed increasing trading opportunities ultimately increased peace between the two nations.[29]

Asantehene Kwaku Dua Panin, who succeeded Asantehene Akoto, abided by the terms of the agreement signed in 1831 for a time. As a late as 1854, he was able to sum up his existence with the British Governor Stephen Hill, writing:

> I have not the least spark of anger in me, I am glad to be always at peace with You, as the late Governor Maclean does with me that in his time, no disturbance at all; I hope you may go on so with me the same and I shall accommodate you anything likewise you shall want from me.[30]

Furthermore, he outlawed the practice of panyarring[31] in Asante as a way of acquiring captives in hopes of maintaining some peace with the British but still, he continued to prepare the Asante for the impending military confrontations with the British forces. He also entered into several agreements with the Dutch who still resided on the Gold Coast. The Asante-Dutch agreements of 1837–1838 permitted the Dutch to station on the Gold Coast a small military unit consisting of African troops supplied by Asantehene Akoto, in exchange for weapons. By 1841 the British realized they needed to replicate the work of MacLean, and began to negotiate formal treaties to acquire more claims on the Gold Coast.[32]

Agreements made between Asante and Dutch stipulated that the Asantehene meet the Dutch demand for gold. Nevertheless, the Asante was unable to meet those demands, and ultimately the Asantehene fell into a sizable debt to the Dutch only to have much of the debt forgotten because they themselves were in debt. Consequently, the Dutch could not maintain their presence on the Gold Coast. They therefore turned their attention elsewhere all but forgetting the gold owed to them by the Asantehene.[33] In the coming years, they slowly began to rid themselves of all their possessions on the Gold Coast.

In the meanwhile, the British forces were on a continuous standby in anticipation of fresh Asante attacks on the coast. Although their fears lacked concrete evidence, they nonetheless believed that the attacks were imminent. In a letter addressed to the British Military Secretary in February 1863, Major Cochrane suggested that the British should begin to prepare themselves in the face of an anticipated attack by the Asante.[34] Nevertheless, by 1863 the connections between the Asante and the British had reached a point of no return due to false rumors of attacks being transmitted back and forth and by 1866 the diplomatic relationship had rapidly declined.[35]

T. Fredrick Elliot of the Colonial Office at Cape Coast Castle, however, wrote back to the War Office arguing that such attacks were no more but false rumors. Elliot in a letter to the Colonial Office to the War Office wrote:

> The Colonial Office to the War Office Downing Street, 24 March 1863 Sir, I have the laid before the Dukes of Newcastle your letter of the 18th instant, transmitting a copy of a letter from the officer commanding the troops on the Gold Coast, in which he reports the existence of rumors to the effect that the hostilities against the British settlements are threatened by the King of Ashantee. . . . The Duke of Newcastle desires me to state that such rumors have not been infrequent, and have usually proved unfounded; that they do not appear to his Grace sufficiently weighty on this occasion to call for orders from home to . . . request that cruisers on the Coast. . . . I have, & c.T. Frederick Elliot[36]

All the same, by 1867 the British were well prepared to extend their coastal territory further northward onto the edge of Asante Kingdom. Moreover, their hopes to extend their sphere first brought them into contact with the Dutch from whom they were able to negotiate the purchase of their Gold Coast properties.

While trading on the Gold Coast flourished, the British crown began to take the necessary steps to rid themselves of the final monopolies over trading that the African Company and Company of Merchants Trading in Africa had established within the region. These companies owned and governed the British forts and castles on the Gold Coast beginning in 1823 and lasting through 1843, well before the British Crown was finally able to take possession of them.[37]

In January 24, 1850, the British Crown passed a number of ordinances setting in motion the early stages of British claim to the Gold Coast as a protectorate. Accordingly, the area was declared a dependency attached to Sierra Leone. Furthermore, the 1850 ordinance closed down all the operations of the two companies and transferred all their possessions on the Gold Coast to the British Crown. A portion of the ordinance reads, ". . . And we do hereby order, direct, and appoint, that all and every our said forts, territories, islands and possessions of the Gold Coast do forthwith cease to be annexed to and be dependencies on the said Colony of Sierra Leone."[38]

This move by the British Crown in 1850 officially annexed control of all the British forts and possessions along the Gold Coast to the Colony of Sierra Leone. This included control of areas which surrounded Cape Coast Castle, Elmina Castle creating a distinct division between Dutch and British possessions. Immediately, the British turned their attention to acquiring Dutch possessions, a task which was planned in the months immediately following their decision to abolish the slave trade. In a letter from Zachary Macaulay to Lord Castleragh, he wrote, "The forts of the Gold Coast, if properly employed might be made very important engines. . . . In addition . . . it might be advisable to obtain possession of two or three Dutch forts . . . which . . . if this were effected, we should possess almost the entire control of that line . . . which extends from Cape Three Points to Rio Volta."[39] This division was a line which was drawn true north along Sweet River reaching the Southern border of the Asante Kingdom giving the Dutch the Western portion and the British the Eastern portions of the Gold Coast.[40] Albeit, by 1867, the Dutch were experiencing great financial strain were forced to sell their possessions on the Gold Coast to the British.

Eventually, the British seized the Dutch possessions on the Gold Coast, expanding further their commercial grip as well as their sphere of influence over the area. In fact, the Dutch sold a number of their forts to the British in 1830 and a few more in 1867.[41] By 1872, the Dutch transferred all of their final possessions on the Gold Coast to the British Crown, including Elmina, Commenda, Chama, Dixcove, Fort Dorothea and Apollonia. [42] Seven years later, the British established their overall colonial rule in the Gold Coast. (See Figures 6.3 and 6.4.) According to Sir John Charles Dalrymple Hay the British protected territory as a an area stretching from the Slave Coast near the meridian of 1° east of Greenwich to the meridian of 3° 10 W., a point 12 miles to the eastward of the mouth of the river Asssini.[43] This vast area covered the ports of Cormantin, Accra and Apam.[44]

Once in control of the entire coastline, the British declared the region a colony of the Crown.[45] Thereafter, the British turned their attention on capturing the interior portion of the Gold Coast. Namely, the British sought the most lucrative region, Greater Asante, which by this period had successfully transitioned to trading agricultural goods.

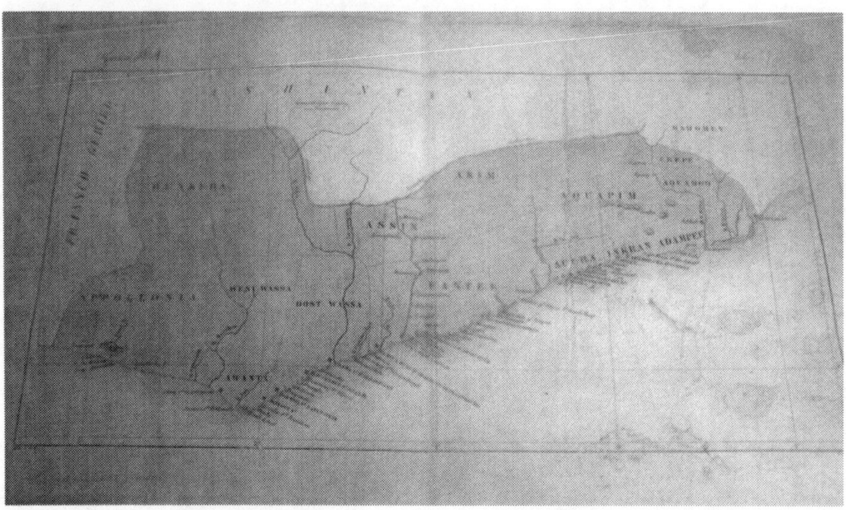

Figure 6.3 Map of Gold Coast Showing British and Dutch Possessions on the Gold Coast. *Source*: *Convention Between Her Majesty and the King of the Netherlands for an Interchange of Territory on the Gold Coast of Africa,* Signed at London, March 5, 1867, British National Archives (FO 925/ 472). Photo provided by author.

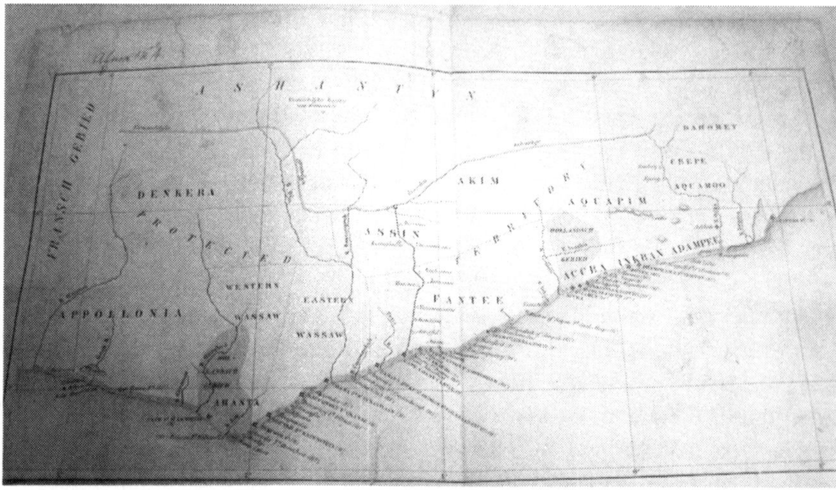

Figure 6.4 Map of British Protectorate After Gaining Dutch Possessions on the Gold Coast. *Source*: Convention Between Her Majesty and the King of the Netherlands for an Interchange of Territory on the Gold Coast of Africa, Signed at London, March 5, 1867, British National Archives (FO 925/ 472). Photo provided by author.

The seven year period between 1867 and 1874 set the stage for a final turning point in the history of the Gold Coast and Asante-British relations. During this era, much of the Gold Coast, by military force of the British, was turned into a protectorate also known as a protected territory, ending the thirty years of peace between the Asante and British. In previous decades, the region and people were merely participants in trading which crossed the Atlantic Ocean. Once the British were able to acquire the region, the Gold Coast proved to be a critical element to the British sphere of influence and its growing capitalist regime. Moreover, once turned into a protected territory, the new emerging British Empire stretched as far north as the Southern border of the Asante Kingdom.

The creation of this British protectorate dramatically affected trading to and from the region. Moreover, the British expansion and invasion of the Asante territory did very little to increase trade from the region as exports and imports declined to £76, 955 and £53, 764, respectively.[46] Rhoda Howard-Hassmann explains that the "Period of Ghana's integration into world-capitalist system in 1874 coincides with period of development and consolidation of capitalism and capitalist production in Western Europe."[47] This move to turn the Gold Coast into a British protectorate was implemented nearly eleven years prior to the Scramble for Africa and the Berlin Conference of 1884–1885.

Moreover, the Asante hoped to limit the reach of the expanding British Protectorate by raising a military consisting of its own warriors and its neighboring allies. Although there was an extended period of peace between the British and Asante the possible expansion of the British Protectorate all but ended these peaceful relations between the two nations. The peace between the two nations was also impacted by the British reluctance to give up chief Gjanin several years earlier but peace continued. This continued until the rise of Asantehene Kofi KariKari who remembered this British insult and acknowledged this could be only avenged through warfare.[48] In the early months of 1873, then Asantehene Kofi KariKari hoped to stop this British expansion, sent a force of 12,000 men across the Pra River, considered to be the divide between the two nations.[49]

These 12,000 Asante troops crossed the Pra River and first attacked the Akims who were viewed as allies to the British. Although the British hoped to remain neutral, they reinforced their stance that they could only protect their coastal territories, namely the forts. While the Akims were upset with this treatment or lack of support, they soon found the inaction on part of the British to be both disheartening and disgusting. Moreover the Asante viewed the territory of Elmina as their own, while the British insisted this region was there property. Within distance of Elmina, the Asante also hoped Cape Coast to come into their possession and quickly gained the support of local Elminans. In response, the British were able to raise an army of nearly 20,000 troops and post them only miles away from the town. This became the first signs the British were willing to both defend and extend their power beyond the coastline and their forts.[50]

Missionaries who were among the Asante at the time of this trek across the Pra River also reported their accounts about the army moving toward the coastline. The British Governor was informed of the Asante arrival along with the white men who were traveling alongside them. These men were described as having shaved heads, with portions of nose and ears cut off and carrying the kings drum.[51]

This military campaign to extend their power was left to Sir Garret Joseph Wolseley a thirty-seven-year old, described as having clean-cut features, exceedingly sharp with blue eyes, possessing both courage and brain power at the time of the appointment to Gold Coast. Prior to accepting this appointment, Wosley was ensured he was not to stay in the Gold Coast longer than the Ashanti Expedition expected and he was allowed to pick his own officers.[52] The British within the year of the arrival of Sir Major General Garret Joseph Wolseley crossed the Pra River making their way into the Kumasi. Furthermore, the British also made the decision to take the region of Greater Asante and further extend its established protectorate from the coastline.

Sir Garret Joseph Wolseley, prior to appointment as the leader of the Ashanti Expedition, fought in the Burma War (1852–1853), the Crimean War (1854–1856) where he lost sight in left eye, Indian Mutiny (1857–1858) and the Third China War (1860–1861). Working his way through the military ranks during these campaigns, by 1873 Wolseley was well prepared to take the lead of the British military forces in the Gold Coast.[53]

Several European soldiers soon followed the arrival of Wolseley on the Gold Coast who took the lead of commanding these troops. Those soldiers which arrived were given a ration which included bread, salt, fresh meat, rice or peas, potatoes, salt, pepper, tea and sugar, all of which were key staples of any European diet.[54] This increase in British troops along the Gold Coast caused a great stir among the Asante leadership and troops.

The increase in British troops along with their possible attack on Kumasi caused Asantehene to call on his army to assemble and to be prepared for an impending attack on the region. Once his troops were collected Asantehene Kofi KariKari ordered them to move forward to their outposts and secure any captives remaining. The remaining captives were, M. Bonnet a French missionary, along with Mr. and Mrs. Ramseyer and their children. Although the Asantehene was able to collect some troops and secure his captives, General Woseley and his troops were quickly advancing toward center of Greater Asante. In the weeks and months which followed, Asantehene Kofi KariKari hoped to slow the advancement of these troops.[55]

Although the Asantehene Kofi KariKari hoped to slow the advancement of British troops, by the end of 1873, the British claimed the Gold Coast coastline to be their possession. In doing so they also limited any foreign vessels from entering or leaving the territory thereafter. This was done to once again reiterate the intention of moving further inland after capturing the Dutch possessions and removing any other threats. Thereafter, official notice was issued on December 15, 1873, which read:

> I hereby declare that from the date. . .that portion of the Gold Coast stretching from Elmina Westward as bar as Bushan—to wit the districts occupied by the enemy or his allies which lie adjacent to ST. GEORGE D' ELMINA, COMMENDA, CHAMA, SECONDEE, TACORADY and BUSHAN . . . which is embraced between a in Latitude 4. 26. N, and Longitude 1. 58. W . . . such like districts in the occupation of the enemy or his allies which lie adjacent to AQUIDAH, BRANDENBERG, AXIM, and APOLLONIA—are placed in a state of Blackade. . . . Al measures therefore which are authorized by the Law of Nations and the respective treaties between Her Majesty and the different Neutral Powers, will be enforced . . . against all vessels which may attempt to violate the Blockade.
>
> W. N. W. Hewett[56]

Moreover, just prior to the final decision made by the British to invade the region of Greater Asante and its center city Kumasi there were several letters sent between Sir Garret Joseph Wolseley, commander of the British troops on the Gold Coast, and then Asantehene Kofi KariKari. Nonetheless, the Asantehene was well aware of the detrimental political and economic effects war had on the interior state, hoping he could settle any disputes between the two nations through confidentially and peacefully.[57] The correspondence between the two carried on for several weeks and months and was ultimately responsible for stopping the British advancement on several different occasions. Nevertheless, the British forces continued to encroach upon the area of Greater Asante and Kumasi. In this series of letters between the Commander Wolseley and Asantehene KariKari, the Asante King hoped for a peaceful resolution to the issues between the two nations before war ensued.

Moreover, in the first of many letters between the two Wolseley quickly made his intentions to the king known. He stated his purposes were for the Asantehene to withdraw all his forces from territories occupied by their allies, they should deliver anyone captured from an ally of Her Majesty and they guarantee ample compensation to all those injured. Wolseley also ensured a new peace treaty between the two nations to include freedom of wrongfully detained persons and payments of gold to the Queen.[58]

In a letter sent to the Queen Victoria of England through Commander Wolseley, Asantehene KariKari hoping to keep the peace between the two thriving nations wrote:

Coomassi, January 21, 1874

My Good Friend,

I beg at the same time to acquaint your Excellency my grief respecting the rapid advancement your Excellency's force are making in my territory since I have written your Excellency of my having coincided with the terms you offered in your letter, I thought, as friend who wishes not any disorder in the country, would have stopped their progress and patiently allowed matters to be amicably settled between us. I beg also to say that, since I have no quarrel of any kind with your Excellency, you would stop the progress of the forces and let us go on with peaceful negotiation. I will make Ammankwatia, who has acted contrary to my instructions, pay the amount your Excellency as if you only keep patience and stop the advancement of the forces

We are, & c.
(For His Majesty Kofi Kalkaree)
(Signed) Yan Nankwi
Kueku Poku

Kofi Buake
His Excellency Major-General Sir G. Wolseley,
C.B. K.C.M.G[59]

Although the Asantehene refers to the Queen as a friend, and asks for her to slow the progression of her troops across the Pra River, this does little to stop the movement of forces toward the center of Greater Asante. In a reaction to the letter from Asantehene to the Queen, Commander Wolseley responds with his own letter in a matter of days to his request to slow the troop progression toward his capital city. In his letter dated for January 29, 1874, Commander Wolseley writes:

Delchiam, January 29, 1874,

King,

I HAVE received your Majesty's two letters. . . . I find that, instead of using the time I gave you in making peaceable arrangements, you have taken advantage of it to collect your armed men. . . . If you want peace, withdraw all your armed men at once behind Coomasse. . . . As I have already told your Majesty, I wish to visit you peaceably . . . with an escort of white men . . . as soon as peace is signed I shall order all my troops . . . back . . . across the River Prah. . . . I halted four days at Fommanah to please your Majesty. I cannot halt again until you have complied with my terms.

I am, King, your true Friend,

G. J. Wolseley,
Major-General and Administrator, Gold Coast[60]

Just days after correspondence between Wolseley and Asantehene Kari-Kari, Wolseley wrote in a journal, "Unless I have to fight a very heavy battle I hope to sleep in Koomassie to-morrow night. If the resistance is as serious as the day before & I have to lose another 100 men I do not expect to be there until the 4th instant."[61] General Wolseley in his strategy to attack and capture Kumasi believed he had weakened the Asante and he could easily march his force into the city with little to no resistance from the state.

In the days which followed the Asantehene hoped to stop the pending attack from Wolseley and his men, but the general and his forces did not slow. Correspondence continued to flow between the two men, with one of last letters just before the attack on Kumsai coming from Wolsely. In his effort to stop his attack on Kumasi and to gain the trust of the Asantehene, Wolseley asked for several high-ranking officials to be turned over to him immediately along with any prisoners they acquired through warfare. General Wolseley wrote to the Asantehene:

February 3, 1874,

King,

You have deceived me so before, that I cannot halt until hostages are in my possession. As time presses, I will consent to accept for to-day your mother and Prince Mensah. Both shall be well treated by me. You can trust my word. If you send them to me this evening, I will halt my army this side of the river Ordah. Unless you send them at once, my army shall march upon Coomassie.

General Wolseley.[62]

The next day Wolseley wrote the King again, questioning why he has deceived on him. While previous letters were addressed to the Asantehene from outside Kumasi, the next letter was addressed to the Asantehene from inside the capital, proving his previous threats to be true. Albeit, he promised the Asantehene again the dignity and respect accorded with the position of his mother and Prince.

Coomassie February 4, 1874,

King,

You have deceived me, but I have kept my promise to you. I am in Coomassie and my only wish is to make a lasting peace. . . . I have shown you the power of England, and now I will be merciful. As you do not wish to give up your mother and Prince Mensa. . . . I will make peace with you to-morrow. . . . If either your Majesty, or your royal mother, or Prince Mensa, will come to see me to-morrow. . . . I will treat you with all the honour due to your royal dignity, and allow you to return in safety. You can trust my word.

General Wolseley[63]

The correspondence which passed between the two men suggests the Asantehene was more than willing to negotiate with Wolseley to avoid conflict. Prior to the Asantehene KariKari ultimately pulled his troops and remaining people from Kumasi. Furthermore, although the Asantehene hoped to slow the advancement of British troops, the intent of Wolseley was to take Kumasi from the Asante. The route taken by the General Wolseley his troops took directly through the Fante territory and across the Pra River before finally reaching Greater Asante and its capital Kumasi. (See Figures 6.5–6.7)

Within a matter of days Major-General Wolseley pushed his troops across the River Pra, ultimately burning Kumasi to the ground and forcing the Asante into a peace treaty. The treaty signed between the Asante and the British, after the Asante Expedition and the burning of Kumasi, contained clauses that impelled the Asante to renounce the rights to territories within the British Protectorate as well as clauses defining trade between nations. The treaty reads:

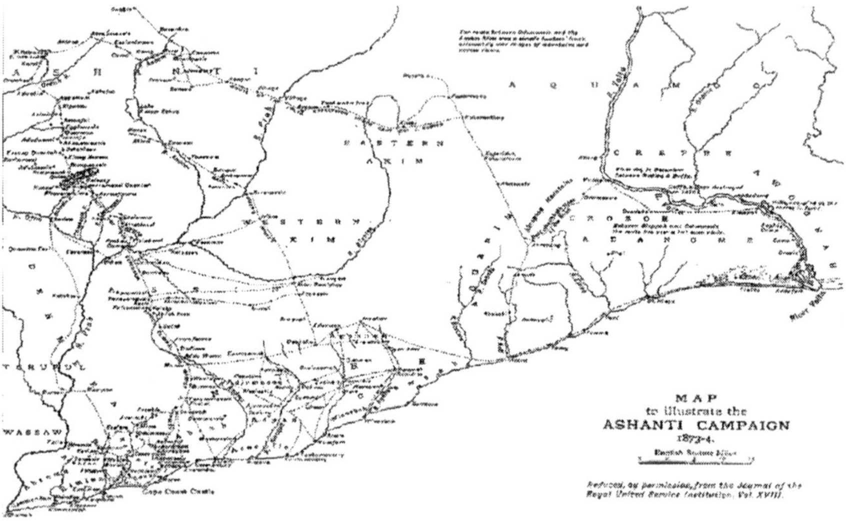

Figure 6.5 Ashanti Campaign Map, 1873–1874. *Source*: Ian F.W. Beckett, ed., Wolseley and Ashanti: The Asante War Journal and Correspondence of Major General Sir Garnet Wolseley, 1873–1874 (England: The Army Records Society, 2009), p. xii. Reproduced with permission from the *Journal of the Royal United Services Institute* (Vol. 28, 1884/85), now the RUSI Journal (www.rusi.org).

Ashantee Treaty of Peace and Fommanah, 13 February 1874, Cape Coast, 14 March 1874

Treaty of peace between Major General Sir Garret Joseph Wolseley acting on behalf of Her Majesty Victoria Queen of Great Britain and Ireland. . .acting on behalf of His Majesty Koffee Kalkalli, King of Ashantee-

1. There shall be hereafter perpetual peace between the Queen of England and Her allies on the Coast . . . and the king King of Ashanti and all his people on the other part-
2. The King of Ashanti promises to pay the sum of fifty thousand ounces of approved gold . . . to Her Majesty the Queen of England by the late war; and undertaken to pay one thousand ounces of Gold forthwith . . .
3. The King of Ashanti on the part of himself and his successors renounces all right or title to any tribute . . . from the Kings of Denkera, Assin, Akin, Adansi and other allies of Her Majesty formerly subject to the Kingdom of Ashanti.
4. The King on the part of himself and of his heirs and successors does herby . . . renounce forever all preteusions to supremacy over Elmina, or over any of the tribes formerly connected with the Dutch government . . . as well as to any . . . the British government in respect of Elmina or any other of the British forts and possessions on the Coast.

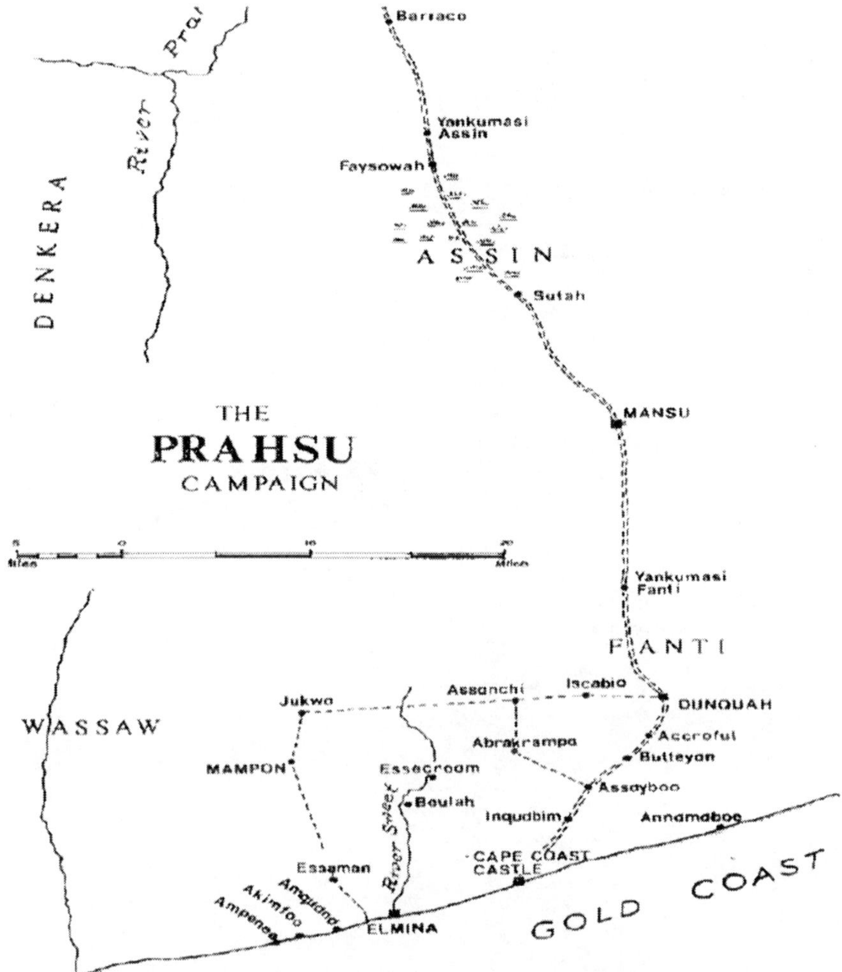

Figure 6.6 Ashanti Campaign Routes to River Pra, 1873–1874. *Source*: Leigh Maxwell, *The Ashanti Ring: Sir Garnet Wolseley's Campaigns, 1870–1882* (Great Britain: Leo Cooper Publishing, 1985), p. 7.

5. The king will at once withdraw all his troops from Appolonia and its vicinity . . .
6. There shall be freedom of trade between Ashanti and the Her Majesty's Forts on the coast, all person being at liberty to carry their merchandise from the Coast to Coomassie, or from that place to any of Her Majesty's possessions on the Coast.
7. The King of Ashanti guarantees that the road from Coomassie to the River Prah shall always be kept open and free from bush to a width of fifteen feet.

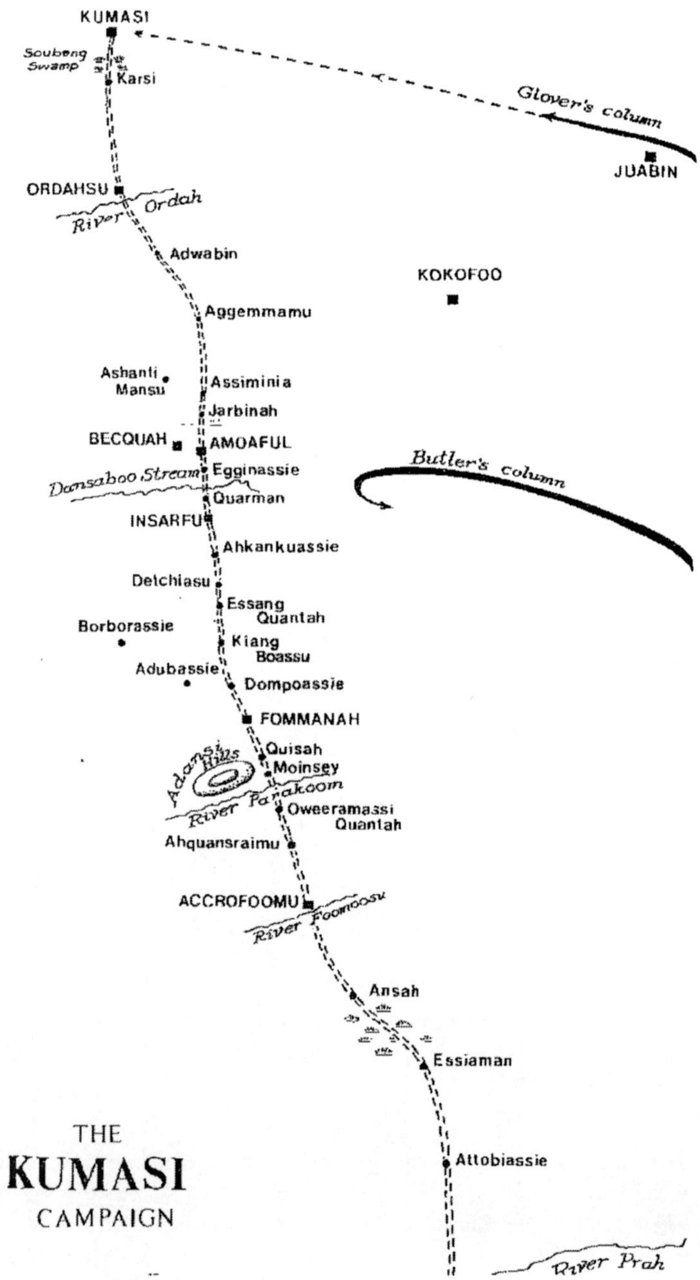

Figure 6.7 Ashanti Campaign to Kumasi, 1873–1874. *Source*: Leigh Maxwell, *The Ashanti Ring: Sir Garnet Wolseley's Campaigns, 1870–1882* (Great Britain: Leo Cooper Publishing, 1985), p. 56.

8. As Her Majesty's subjects and the people of Ashantee are henceforth to be friends for ever, the king, in order to prove the sincerity of his friendship for Queen Victoria, promises to use his best endeavours to check the practice of human sacrifice . . . as the practice is repugnant to the feelings of all Christian nations.
9. One copy of this treaty shall be signed by the King of Ashantee and sent to the Administration of Her Majesty's government at Cape Coast.
10. The Treaty shall be known as the Treaty of Fommanah.[64]

Albeit, the agreement made between the two nations resulted in the Treaty of Fommanah ending the conflict and extended the British Protectorate. By the end of the conflict the total cost absorbed by Britain was £800,000, a sum within their original projected costs. The Ashanti Army had been officially defeated, Kumasi was now in the hands of the British, Asantehene Kofi KariKari was dethroned, only to be replaced by Asantehene Mensa Bonsu. This transition officially ended any further military actions in the region until 1896 when they attacked Prempeh I.[65] This major conflict lasting from 1873 to 1874, forever changed the relationship between the Asante and the British and introduced modern British weaponry into the Gold Coast, leaving a fear among the political elite of the interior state.[66]

One of the critical clauses in the treaty called for the final abolition of slavery within areas of the Gold Coast Colony. The Gold Coast, the British and Asante had been dependent on captives in the production of legitimately traded items. Hence, it is argued that the call to abolish slavery coupled with increased dependency on the legitimate economy of the nineteenth century in the Gold Coast threatened to eliminate its principal source of labor and the system of credit that had been established for decades.[67] Albeit, Asante trade with the Europeans flourished tremendously during the period. Writing in 1896, J. E. Casely Hayford stated:

> It was part of the State System of Ashanti to encourage trade . . . chiefs then sent down to the coast caravans of tradesmen . . . sometimes two to three hundred strong, to barter ivory for Europeans goods, or to buy such goods with gold dust. . . . Down to 1873 a constant stream of Ashanti traders might be seen daily. . . . Thus every member of the State from the King downwards, took an active interest in the promotion of trade and in keeping open of the trade routes into the interior.[68]

The abolition of slavery and encouragement of legitimate trade were key reasons for British colonial encroachment into Asante homeland. In the first place, the British administration saw Asante territory as a way to further increase trading, investment and commercial enterprises. In order to achieve this goal the administration set out to break down the traditional rules that severely restrained British commercial enterprise in the region.[69]

The picture of a prosperous Kumasi economy in the center of the Asante Kingdom that J. E. Casely Hayford gave in 1896 was in direct contrast to the one given by F. Boyle in his 1874 work, *Through Fanteeland to Coomassie: A Diary of the Ashantee Expedition* in a chapter titled "The Metropolis of Murder." He describes the Kumasi, the center of Greater Asante, as:

> A town where blood is plastered, like a pitch coating, over trees and floors and stools—blood of a thousand victims; yearly renewed, where headless bodies make common sport, where murder pure and simple, monotonous massacre of bound men, is the one employment of the king, and the one spectacle of the populace.[70]

Such comments ultimately set the stage for the British justification of their Asante Expedition into the interior of the Gold Coast in 1874. Two years after the burning of Kumasi, the British Special Commissioner, Sir Gouldsbury, gave a detailed account of the current state of the Asante nation. He wrote:

> I am convince that were it not for the recent prompt action taken by Your Excellency with reference to the Ashantee, and the state of anxiety and uncertainty into which my sudden and unannounced march to Sahara threw them, they would have made . . . this an attempt, and I believe a successful one, to re-establish their ascendancy over Saharah.[71]

Traders returning from Salaga described the condition of captives in the city and in the Kingdom generally as horrific. The British manipulated these reports to justify their 1874 conquest of Asante state arguing that their main and only reason to conquer and colonize the Kingdom was to abolish slavery in the area.

The Asante Expedition of 1873–1874 resulted in several milestones for British imperial rule. The expedition accomplished the following:

1. Change in British attitude to a pro-imperialist stance.
2. Put an end to Ashanti state building.
3. The use of African military force.
4. The use of white military in Africa.[72]

The fall of Kumasi in British hands in 1874 enabled the colonial administration to establish uninterrupted link between all regions of the Gold Coast from north to south. Each of the regions, the coast, Greater Asante and Northern Territory, was now under the control of the British Crown.[73]

This acquisition extended the British protectorate further into the interior of the Gold Coast. Moreover, Edward Reynolds argues this began a new era of economic development for the Gold Coast as region was now being operated by the British government ultimately leading a decline of the Asante state.[74]

The final cost of the Asante Expedition was substantial to the British Parliament and European business interests along the Gold Coast. Final costs of the Asante Expedition were divided among three sources: War Office, Colonial Office and Admiralty. Medicine, surgical instruments, allowances, clothing and daily pay were all covered by the War Office at an estimated total cost of £260,000. An estimated expense for the Colonial Office was £150,000 and the Admiralty expenditures were £760,000. Estimates of the total cost of the Asante Expedition lasting from 1873 to 1875 were totaled at £815,000.[75]

The passage of abolition laws did not deter the Asante of the Gold Coast from continuing the practice forms of slavery in the interior. In fact, between 1807 and 1874, the illegal slave trade within the Gold Coast was in full swing. The Asante continued to pour captives into the illegal slave trading network and at the same time they engaged themselves fully in the trade of bulk export goods, that is, items considered legitimately traded products. Like the plantations of South America, the Caribbean Islands and North America, the Gold Coast and its African states became dependent on slave labor to perform the day-to-day agricultural and mining tasks. The British administration considered the exploitation of forced labor an unacceptable hindrance to their economic ambitions in the changing world economy.

With the expansion of the British Protectorate into the Asante territory in the late nineteenth century, the push against slavery within the state intensified. Previous to any push to end slavery in Greater Asante by the British, runaway captives were routinely returned to their owners. In a letter dated December 10, 1862, Governor R. Pine in a letter to the Duke of Newcastle wrote, "Gladly would I try an experiment, and send back these subjects to Ashantee, for if confidence were once created between this Government and Ashantee, the greatest obstacle in the way of amicable relations between us would be removed. . . . I feel that I am estranging, if no exasperating the most powerful King on this coast, and upon whom, according to his ideas, I am committing a gross injustice."[76]

Returning these captives to their owners reinforced the idea servitude, but as the British began to see the increased value in the state this idea soon loosened.[77] Although several Asante chiefs opposed ending slavery within their state, then British Governor Strahan called a meeting informing them, their pawns and captives were to be set free. Chiefs opposed this ruling and by November 1874, Strahan agreed to only set captives free if cruelty could be proved by anyone.

> it was decided that no slave could leave his or her master or mistress unless proof of cruelty or maltreatment when such slave would be entitled to his or her freedom . . . the question of pawns was settled by the debtor being held liable for the amount that the pawn had been given as security . . . the amount should be recovered on the pawn leaving.[78]

This ruling was altered again by a December giving captives manumission papers and declaring any form of slavery permanently abolished.

Thereafter, the British swiftly passed the Gold Coast Slave Dealing Abolition Act of 1874 and the Gold Coast Emancipation Ordinance of 1874. The first ordinance made it illegal to import any captive into the Gold Coast; the second implied that no rights over captives by a master could be legally enforced. Nevertheless, this was opposed by chiefs who continued to hold captives through the 1880s only to be freed during later Asante–British wars. This push to end slavery coincided with the attempts by the British to consolidate power on the Gold Coast in the latter stages of the century.[79]

The highly developed trading system with routes connecting all regions of the Gold Coast from north to south allowed the Asante to transition away from exporting captives to bulk export commodities. In this changing economy, the Asante developed a rural economy that brought about capitalism among them through the growth of private ownership and the accumulation of personal wealth. Eventually, the accumulation of wealth altered the structure of Asante families, creating a middle class in the Kingdom, able to challenge the authority of the ruling elite. Although the Asante had transitioned away from trading captives, the use of these individuals still proved useful to the economy. Nevertheless, trading between the two nations continued to flourish and by the latter stages of the nineteenth, there was a sharp decline in the use of captives by the Asante. In the years after the burning of Kumasi, the trade in gold, palm oil and palm kernels grew in value making the need for captive labor invaluable, although their use was abolished (see Table 6.2).

Table 6.2 Export Trade of the Gold Coast (Values in pound Sterling)

	Gold Dust		*Palm Oil*		*Palm Kernels*	
Year	*Ounces*	*Value*	*Gallons*	*Value*	*Tons*	*Value*
1875	11,801	42,484	2,686,528	224,594	4,677	47,253
1876	17,280	62,308	3,865,007	306,000	7,655	67,645
1877	10,611	38,199	3,458,700	260,087	7,828	62,624
1878	11,147	40,129	3,889,917	295,246	5,251	48,707
1879	15,479	55,724	3,746,981	280,725	6,217	53,114
1880	9,125	32,865	3,420,279	307,114	9,511	101,606

Gold Coast Blue Books for the years shown. £1.00 = US $4.86.

Source: Raymond E. Dumett, *Imperialism, Economic Development and Social Change in West Africa* (Durham, NC: Carolina Academic Press, 2013), p. 175.

Nevertheless, although these trades began to flourish, by the start of the 1870s, the Asante experienced several conflicts with the British and signed a host of treaties to promote trading between the two nations. While peace between the two nations seemed imminent with the signing of trade treaties, the British forces surged ahead in 1874 to burn Kumasi and establish the Colony of the Gold Coast. Thus, the British assumed full control over of Asante economy, trade and destiny, several years prior to the "Scramble for Africa." That development signaled the demise of the exploitation of captive labor. As early as 1881, the British had direct access to the area of Greater Asante and the City of Kumasi (see Figure 6.8). Similar to previous hopes of the political and economic elite, the Asante in the 1880s hoped to limit the impact of wars on the state as evidenced by Basel missionaries Buck and Huppenbauer entering the forest zone, and writing:

> The people do not like war at all, but it is said the Englishmen are coming against them. They expect war, as they have heard something of soldiers stationed at Prahsue, but they will certainly not begin. Perhaps, if they are attacked, they will defend themselves, but they are also quite displeased with their government and some speak of running away.[80]

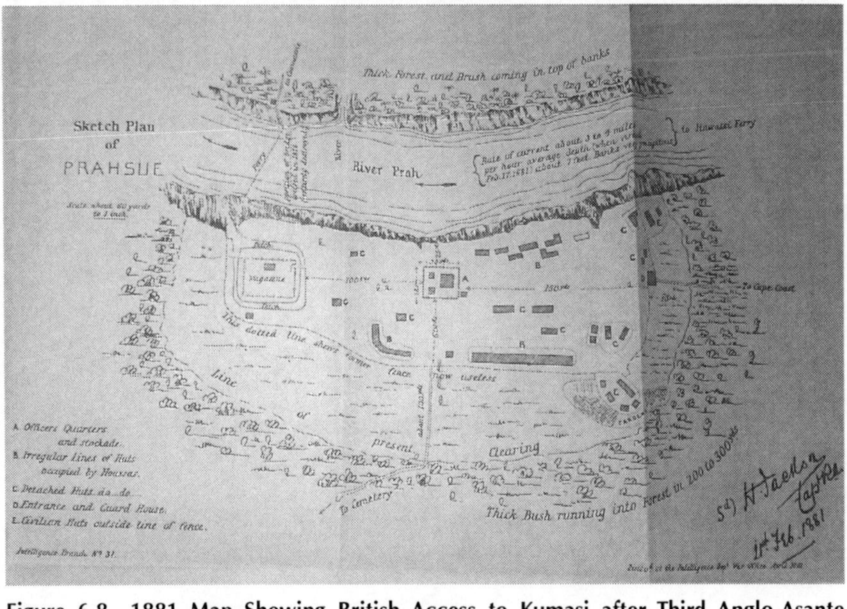

Figure 6.8 1881 Map Showing British Access to Kumasi after Third Anglo-Asante War. *Source*: Sketch Plan of Prahsue, British Parliamentary Papers, *Correspondence On Ashanti and Gold Coast Affairs, 1874–83, Volume 60, Colonies in Africa* (Ireland: Irish University Press, 1971).

Although, the use of captives had been declared illegal and a trading system was developed, this did very little to limit the impending attack on the state which came in 1896. During this attack, which became known as the Anglo-Asante War of 1896, the British crossed the Pra River. This final conflict ultimately led to the final capture of the area known as Greater Asante by the British.

NOTES

1. Joseph K. Adjyae, *Diplomacy and Diplomats in Nineteenth Century Asante* (University Press of America: Lanham, MD, 1984), p. 3.

2 T. E. Bowdich, *Mission from Cape Coast to Ashantee* (London: 1819), p. 177 In Marion Johnson, ed., Salaga Papers, Vol. 1 (Legon, Ghana: Institute of African Studies, 1965), p. acc. no. SAL/71.

3. Joseph Dupuis, *Journal of a Residence in Ashantee* (London: 1820), p. xxxix in Marion Johnson, ed., Salaga Papers, Vol. 1 (Legon, Ghana: Institute of African Studies, 1965), p. acc. no. SAL/84/1.

4. Ivor Wilks, "Aspects of Bureaucratization in Ashanti in the Nineteenth Century," *The Journal of African History*, Vol. 7, No. 2 (1966), p. 215.

5. Donna J. E. Maier, "Islam and the Idea of Asylum in Asante." In *The Cloth of Many Colored Silks: Papers on History and Society in Honor of Ivor Wilks*, eds. John Hunwick and Nancy Lawler (Evanston, Ill: Northwestern University Press, 1996), pp. 323–324.

6. Margaret Priestley, *West African Trade and Coast Society: A Family Study* (London: Oxford University Press, 1969), p. 19.

7. Edward Reynolds, *Trade and Economic Change on the Gold Coast, 1807–1874* (New York: Longman Group, 1974), p. 35.

8. Benedict Der, *The Slave Trade in Northern Ghana* (Accra, Ghana: Centre for Savanna Art and Civilization, 1998), p. 14.

9. Gwedolyn Mikell, *Cocoa and Chaos in Ghana* (New York: Paragon House, 1989), p. 29.

10. Der, 17–19.

11. Ibid., 17.

12. Ibid., 15.

13. Ibid.

14. T. E. Bowdich, *Mission from Cape Coast to Ashantee* (London: 1819), 323–325 in Ivor Wilks, *Forests of Gold: Essays on the Akan and the Kingdom of Asante* (Athens, OH: Ohio University Press, 1993), p. 49.

15. Ivor Wilks, *Forests of Gold: Essays on the Akan and the Kingdom of Asante* (Athens: OH, Ohio University Press, 1993), p. 50.

16. Ibid.

17. Ibid.

18. Gareth A. Austin, *Land, Labour and Captial in Ghana: From Slavery to Free Labour in Asante, 1807–1956* (Rochester, NY: University of Rochester Press, 2005), p. 104.

19. Peace and Commerce Treaty with Ashanti, September 7, 1817 in C. W. Newbury, *British Policy Towards West Africa, Select Documents, 1786–1874* (Oxford: Clarendon Press, 1965), pp. 284–285.

20. Joseph Dupuis, *Journal of a Residence in Ashantee, Comprising Notes and Researches Relative to the Gold Coast, and the Interior of Western Africa* (London: Henry Colburn, 1824), pp. 162–164 in William H. Worger, Nancy L. Clark and Edward A. Alpers, eds. *Africa and the West: From the Slave Trade to Conquest, 1441–1905*, Vol. 1 (New York: Oxford University Press, 2010), p. 144.

21. Treaty of Peace and Commerce with Ashanti, March 23, 1820 in C. W. Newbury, *British Policy Towards West Africa, Select Documents, 1786–1874* (Oxford: Clarendon Press, 1965), pp. 288–289.

22. Carl Christian Reindorf, *History of the Gold Coast and Asante, Based on Traditions and Historical Facts, Comprising a Period of More Than Three Centuries From About 1500 to 1860* (Cape Coast: Gold Coast Book Depot, 1895), pp. 191–196.

23. *Report from the Select Committee on West Coast of Africa: Together With the Minutes of Evidence Appendix and Index August 5, 1842*, Public Records and Archives Administration Department, Accra, Ghana ADM 5/3/3.

24. James Anquandah, *Rediscovering Ghana's Past* (Accra, Ghana: Sedeco Enterprise, 1982), pp. 128–129.

25. John Donnelly, *An Introduction to the History of West Africa*, 3rd ed. (London: Cambridge University Press, 1962), p. 126.

26. Treaty of Peace and of Free Commerce, April 27, 1831 in C. W. Newbury, *British Policy Towards West Africa, Select Documents, 1786–1874* (Oxford: Clarendon Press, 1965), pp. 293–294.

27. *Proceedings of the Select Committee on West Coast of Africa, March 1842*, Public Records and Archives Administration Department, Accra, Ghana ADM 5/3/2.

28. Wilks, *Forests of Gold*, 153.

29. Donnelly, *A History of West Africa*, 129.

30. *Further Papers Relating to the Warfare Between the Fantis and the Ashantis*, C. 456, 1855, p. 13 in Joseph K. Adjyae, *Diplomacy and Diplomats in Nineteenth Century Asante* (University Press of America: Lanham, MD, 1984), p. 5.

31. Payarring, which had been practiced in Asante prior to 1838, is generally used a way of acquiring a captive when an individual could not pay off a debt to a creditor. The creditor then took on the individual as a captive until the debt was paid off. This system was similar to that of pawning.

32. Donnelly, 130.

33. Larry Yarak, *Asante and the Dutch, 1744–1873* (Oxford: Clarendon Press, 1990), p. 232.

34. Letter Commodore Wilmot to Sir B. W. Walter, April 14, 1863, *British Parliamentary Papers, Papers Concerning the Gold Coast and Surrounding Districts, 1850–1873, Colonial Africa, Ghana*, Vol. 57 (Ireland: Irish University Press, 1971), p. 9.

35. Thomas J. Lewin, *Asante Before the British: The Prempean Years, 1875–1900* (Lawrence, KS: The Regents Press of Kansas, 1978), p. 44.

36. Letter T. Frederick Elliot to War Office, Downing Street, March 24, 1863, *British Parliamentary Papers, Papers Concerning the Gold Coast and Surrounding*

Districts, 1850–1873, Colonial Africa, Ghana, Vol. 57 (Ireland: Irish University Press, 1971), p. 10.

37. Raymond Dumett and Marion Johnson, "Britain and the Suppression of Slavery in the Gold Coast Colony, Ashanti and the Northern Territories." In *The End of Slavery in Africa*, eds. Suzanne Miers and Richard Roberts (Madison, WI: University of Wisconsin Press, 1988), p. 73.

38. Charter under the Great Seal of the United Kingdom to provide for the Government of Her Majesty's Forts and Settlements on the Gold Coast, January 24, 1850. *Ordinances Relating to Her Majesty's Forts and Settlements on the Gold Coast, 1843–1859,* Public Records and Archives Administration Department, Accra, Ghana ADM 4/1/1

39. Zachary Macaulay to Lord Castlereagh, May 8, 1807, in William H. Worger, Nancy L. Clark and Edward A. Alpers, eds. *Africa and the West: From the Slave Trade to Conquest, 1441–1905*, Vol. 1 (New York: Oxford University Press, 2010), pp. 137–138.

40. Sir Edward Hertslet, *The Map of Africa by Treaty Great Britain &France to Zanzibar*, 2nd ed. (London: Harrison and Sons, 1896), p. 678.

41. Edward Reynolds, "Economic Imperialism: The Case of the Gold Coast," *The Journal of Economic History*, Vol. 35, No. 1 (March, 1975), pp. 96–97.

42. *Convention Between Her Majesty and the King of the Netherlands for an Interchange of Territory on the Gold Coast of Africa*, Signed at London, March 5, 1867, British National Archives (FO 925/ 472).

43. Sir John Charles Dalrymple Hay, *Ashanti and The Gold Coast: And What We Know of It, A Sketch* (London: Edward Sanford, 1874), p. 7.

44. Ibid, 9–10.

45. Reynolds, 97.

46. Edward Reynolds, *Trade and Economic Charge on the Gold Coast, 1807–1874* (New York: Longman Press, 1974), p. 139.

47. Rhoda Howard-Hassmann, *Colonialism and Underdevelopment in Ghana* (London: Croom Helm, Ltd, 1978), p. 17.

48. Friedrich August Ramseyer and Johannes Kuhne, *Four Years in Ashantee: By the Missionaries Ramseyer and Kuhne* (London: James Nisbet & Co., 1875) pp. 201–202.

49. Leigh Maxwell, *The Ashanti Ring: Sir Garnet Wolseley's Campaigns, 1870–1882* (Great Britain: Leo Cooper Publishing, 1985), p. 8.

50. George Alfred Henty, *The March to Coomassie*, 2nd ed. (London: Tinsley Brothers, 1874), pp. 9–11.

51. Ramseyer and Kuhne, 216.

52. Ibid, 14–15.

53. Ian F.W. Beckett, ed., *Wolseley and Ashanti: The Asante War Journal and Correspondence of Major General Sir Garnet Wolseley, 1873–1874* (England: The Army Records Society, 2009), p. 17.

54. Sir Henry Brackenbury, *The Ashanti War, A Narrative Prepared from Official Documents by Permission of Major-General Sir Garnet Wolseley, Vol. 1* (London: William Blackwood and Sons, 1876), p. 321.

55. Maxwell, 58–59.

56. "Official Notice," *Gold Coast Gazette*, No. XXX (Cape Coast), January 31, 1874.

57. Lewin, *Asante Before the British*, 46.

58. Letter from Sir Garnet Wolseley to King Kofi Kakari, January, 1874, in Ian F. W. Beckett, ed., *Wolseley and Ashanti: The Asante War Journal and Correspondence of Major General Sir Garnet Wolseley, 1873–1874* (England: The Army Records Society, 2009), pp. 314–318.

59. Letter from Asantehene Kofi Kalkaree to Her Excellency, Queen of England, January 21, 1874. *British Parliamentary Papers, Correspondence On Ashanti and Gold Coast Affairs, 1874–83, Volume 60, Colonies in Africa* (Ireland: Irish University Press, 1971), p. 18.

60. Letter from Major-General Garrett Joseph Wolseley to Asantehene Kalkaree, January 29, 1874. *British Parliamentary Papers, Correspondence On Ashanti and Gold Coast Affairs, 1874–83, Volume 60, Colonies in Africa* (Ireland: Irish University Press, 1971), p. 23.

61. Sir Garnet Wolseley Journal February 1–2, 1874, in Ian F.W. Beckett, ed., *Wolseley and Ashanti: The Asante War Journal and Correspondence of Major General Sir Garnet Wolseley, 1873–1874* (England: The Army Records Society, 2009), p. 380.

62. Letter from Sir Garnet Wolseley to King Kofi Kakari, February 3, 1874, in Ian F. W. Beckett, ed., *Wolseley and Ashanti: The Asante War Journal and Correspondence of Major General Sir Garnet Wolseley, 1873–1874* (England: The Army Records Society, 2009), p. 386.

63. Letter from Sir Garnet Wolseley to King Kofi Karikari, February 4, 1874, in Ian F. W. Beckett, ed., *Wolseley and Ashanti: The Asante War Journal and Correspondence of Major General Sir Garnet Wolseley, 1873–1874* (England: The Army Records Society, 2009), p. 388.

64. Ashantee Treaty of Peace and Fommanah, February 13, 1874, Cape Coast, March 14, 1874, British National Archives (FO 93/6/4).

65. Maxwell, *The Ashanti Ring*, 87.

66. Lewin, *Asante Before the British*, 47.

67. Gerald M. McSheffrey, "Slavery, Indentured Servitude, Legitimate Trade and the Impact of Abolition in the Gold Coast, 1874–1901: A Reappraisl," p. 355.

68. J. E. Casely Hayford, *Gold Coast Native Institutions* (London, 1903), pp. 95–96. In Ivor Wilks, *Forests of Gold: Essays on the Akan and the Kingdom of Asante* (Athens: OH, Ohio University Press, 1993), p. 153.

69. Arhin, 372.

70. F. Boyle, *Through Fanteeland to Coomassie: A Diary of the Ashantee Expedition* (London, 1874), p. 343. In Clifford Williams, "Asante: Human Sacrifice or Capital Punishment? An Assessment of the Period 1807–1874," *The International Journal of African Historical Studies*, Vol. 21, No. 3 (1988), p. 436.

71. Gouldsbury Report of his Journey into the Interior of the Gold Coast, dated Accra, March 27, 1876, PRO Co 96/ 119 Nos. 515–6 in Marion Johnson, ed., Salaga Papers, Vol. 1 (Legon, Ghana: Institute of African Studies, 1965), p. acc. no. SAL/76/1.

72. Thomas J. Maholchic, "The Anglo-Ashanti War of 1873–1874" (MA Thesis, Howard University, December, 1972), pp. iii–iv.

73. W. E. F. Ward, *A History of Ghana* (London: 1958), p. 24.

74. Edward Reynolds, *Trade and Economic Change on the Gold Coast, 1807–1874* (New York: Longman Press, 1974), pp. 174–175.

75. War Office: Precis, Cost of the Ashanti Expedition, April 13, 1874, W. O. 33/26 (1874) in C. W. Newbury, *British Policy Towards West Africa: Select Documents, 1786–1874*, Revised Edition (Brookfield, VT: Ashgate Publishing, 1992), p. 644.

76. British Parliamentary Papers, Vol. 61, *Governor R. Pine to the Duke of Newcastle: Ashanti Fugitives,* December 10, 1862 in C. W. Newbury, *British Policy Towards West Africa: Select Documents, 1786–1874*, Revised Edition (Brookfield, VT: Ashgate Publishing, 1992), pp. 310–311.

77. Beverly Grier, "Pawns, Porters, and Petty Traders: Women in the Transition to Cash-Crop Agriculture in Colonial Ghana," in Paul Lovejoy and Toyin Falola, ed. *Pawnship, Slavery and Colonialism in Africa* (Trenton, NJ: Africa World Press, 2003), p. 311.

78. W. W. Claridge, *A History of the Gold Coast and Ashanti*, Revised Edition (London: Frank Cass Publishing, 1964), p. 176. In Francis Agbodeka, *African Politics and British Policy in the Gold Coast: A Study in the Forms and Force of Protest, 1868–1900* (Evanston, Ill: Northwestern University Press, 1971), pp. 56–57.

79. Francis Agbodeka, *African Politics and British Policy in the Gold Coast: A Study in the Forms and Force of Protest, 1868–1900* (Evanston, Ill: Northwestern University Press, 1971), pp. 57–60.

80. *Further Papers Regarding the Affairs of the Gold Coast*, C. 3386 (August, 1882), in Thomas J. Lewin, *Asante Before the British: The Prempean Years, 1875–1900* (Lawrence, KS: The Regents Press of Kansas, 1978), p. 49.

Chapter 7

Conclusion

The Akan Diaspora and the Memory of Trans-Atlantic Slave Trade in Ghana Today

During the era of the Trans-Atlantic Slave Trade, the Gold Coast began as an importer of captives in exchange for gold deposits in its massive gold fields. As the demand for captives increased at the height of the Trans-Atlantic Slave Trade and as the New World economy developed a greater need for labor, the Gold Coast region transitioned into a major exporter of captives during the seventeenth century. The Gold Coast region remained an exporter of captives well into the mid-nineteenth century during the trade's illegal era. Captives leaving the Gold Coast were taken to a number of locations in the United States (Virginia, Maryland, Georgia and South Carolina), South America (Colombia) and the Caribbean (Jamaica). In these various locations, captives from the Gold Coast became well known throughout, largely for being a rambunctious group responsible for and leading several insurrections. Although well known for their insurrections, many also worked as skilled labor, as blacksmiths, weavers and traders as well as cultivators of land.[1]

Focusing on the impact of the Akan and Asante, particular emphasis is placed on the economies and the various locations within the Caribbean and North America where captives from the Gold Coast were taken. Captives from the Gold Coast who were taken to these locations were often referred to as Koromantin. During the Trans-Atlantic Slave Trade, these captives made impact on the areas they arrived. Captives from the Gold Coast were often preferred in specific areas to work in agriculture and in the mining of specific items, in particular gold.

The impact of captives from the Gold Coast, making up the Akan Diaspora referred to as Kormantin, also spelled Cormantin and Kromantyn, greatly impacted the areas they were taken, having lingering effects economically and culturally. Although the Gold Coast provided fewer captives than areas such the Senegambia to the west, the Slave Coast to the east and Angola further south, the emergence of a Akan Diaspora shows the impact of Trans-Atlantic Slave Trade not only on this region of Africa but on the areas to which these captives were ultimately taken as well.

While captives were being taken from the Gold Coast prior to the formation of the Akan state, after the formation of the Asante their impact on the trade in captives increased. Akosua Perbi in discussing the volume of captives leaving the Gold Coast and where they were taken writes:

> The extent of Ghana's involvement in the Atlantic trade, the duration of the traffic (about 200 years) and the sheer number of victims had significant effects on the country. It has been estimated that between 1620 and 1807 Ghana alone provided about 16% of the total slave output required from Africa by the U.S.A. Between 1733 and 1807 Ghana supplied 13.3% of slaves needed by South Carolina. Between 1710 and 1769 Ghana provided 16% of slaves required by Virginia. In the total English trade, Ghana supplied 18.4% between 1690 and 1807 and 12.1% of the total Atlantic trade for the period 1701–1807.[2]

Although the output of captives leaving the Gold Coast varied throughout the period, the impact of these captives on the local economy undoubtedly had an effect on the area to which they were taken. Although the time frame which the Gold Coast participated in the slave trade is shorter, the percentage Kormantin captives reaching specific areas of the Americas remained at a steady rate.

The independence of the United States in 1776 brought about monumental changes, which affected the economy of the Caribbean, Britain as well as the emerging interests of America which varied between the Northern and Southern states. Wealthy Northern ship owners from the United States beginning in 1776 began finance voyages by hiring independent slave traders as well as make voyages to the coast of Africa themselves. Ship owners acquired captives to be sold in areas of the Southern United States, the Caribbean and South America. Well into the nineteenth century the Northern owners largely financed voyages to Africa, while Southern land owners bought captives to work on agricultural plantations. Akan captives were taken to several areas of the United States, especially the areas of modern day Georgia, Virginia and South Carolina.

Of the many slave traders and financiers in the United States, one of the most well-known owners to trade on the Gold Coast was Rhode Islander and ship owner, James De Wolf. However, there were many De Wolfs to be involved in the slave trade, including James, George, John, Levi, William who were all related to Mark Anthony De Wolf who himself became involved in the slave trade working with his father-in-law, Simeon Potter. James De Wolf himself financed a number of voyages to the West African coastline and in particular to the Gold Coast in the early years of the nineteenth century prior to the United States abolishing the trade in captives. Prior to this, the De Wolfs became involved in the trade after the American Revolution. James De Wolf a Revolutionary War veteran became a hero fighting against the British Army, becoming wealthy slave trader prior to turning 25.[3] The impact of the Akan Diaspora in the United States varied greatly from the impact on the island of Jamaica and the South American territory of Colombia. Two reasons for the varying impact in the United States were largely based upon the numbers of captives brought from the Gold Coast and the agricultural areas in which they worked.

Although James De Wolf did not transport any captives to the state of Rhode Island, he was just one of the many citizens of the state to be directly involved in the slave trade. De Wolf financed voyages and traded from the castles Elmina and Cape Coast, two of the most well-known and recognized castles along the Gold Coast. The state of Rhode Island abolished the importation of captives into the state in 1787. Passed in October 1787, the Rhode Island law read:

> An act to prevent the slave trade and to encourage the slow abolition of slavery. This act prohibited and censured trade under penalty of 100 pounds for each person 1,000 pounds for each vessel.[4]

This law did little to affect the trade in captives De Wolf had established, as the family slowly built a fortune using African labor on their plantations in the Caribbean, in particular the territory of Cuba.

Between 1787 and the War of 1812, the De Wolf's became one of the richest families in the state of Rhode Island and were actively involved in the state government and its day-to-day operations. With the United States Navy still in its infancy, the De Wolf also owned more ships than the navy, which they used to trade in captives. Recently, the remaining members of De Wolf family in Rhode Island traced the legacy of James and his brother George De Wolf and the fortune which the two amassed, both of whom were Rhode Island financiers of slave voyages. In his work on the De Wolf family, Thomas De Wolf writes:

> The man who had the most money in New England in the War of 1812 was James De Wolf. During the war De Wolf was a privateer, essentially a legalized pirate authorized by the government to seize enemy ships and share the booty with the government. . . . The De Wolf family actually owned more ships in 1812 than the United States Navy. Though many people in Bristol believed . . . that the slave trade . . . federally outlawed. . . . There were still activities with Cuba and the South, but in terms of direct voyages between

African Bristol, James De Wolf was cautious. . . . Slave trading had been illegal in Rhode Island since 1787, but many in the trade, including the De Wolfs, ignored the law . . . the De Wolfs . . . continued ownership of Cuban plantation and the shipping of trading of slave-produced goods.[5]

The De Wolf's and their large fleet of ships and ship captains whom they could call on were both successful and unsuccessful in their slave trading from the coast of Africa during the late eighteenth and early nineteenth centuries. Even after the trade in African captives was officially abolished by the United States in 1808, the De Wolf's, without fear of persecution by the United States judicial system, continued to finance voyages for captives.

On a typical voyage, financed by James De Wolf, captained by Jonathan Dennison, the ship contained several items including alcohol such as rum, brandy, gin and wine, which they used to purchase captives.[6] In a letter to one of his ship captains, Captain Jonathan Dennison, only two years before the United States, officially abolished the slave trade to its citizens, James DeWolf writes:

Bristol, R. I. 18th July 1806

Capt. Jonathan Dennison

Sir,

Your having engaged to go a Voyage to Africa in my ship *Ann*, my Instructions are that you proceed with all possible Dispatch direct to Cape Coast, and make Trade at that Place and its Vicinity, and purchase as many good, healthy young Slaves as may be in your power to purchase, by bartering away your present Cargo with the Natives; and after compleating your Business in Africa, you will proceed to Monte Video in South America, and there dispose of your Slave, and purchase in Return Cargo of Ox Hides and dried Beef, and some Tallow and other Produce of that Country, such as you may judge will pay a handsome Profit, and after compleating your Business there, you will return home to this Port with all possible Dispatch.

I am, Sir,

Your Friend and Owner,
Jas. De Wolf[7]

On this voyage, Captain Jonathan Dennison was able to procure a substantial number of captives from both Elmina and Cape Coast Castle as instructed by the ship owner James De Wolf, before setting sail for Monte Video. Although little information remains on what happened to the *Ann* on its voyage back across the Atlantic, there is evidence suggesting the ship was first ordered by the British sloop of war *Medusa*, a British anti-slave trading vessel, to proceed directly to Maldeno.

Captain Dennison, once refusing to do so, continued on with the *Ann* and was later fired on and captured by the British sloop of war *Leda*, another British anti-slave trading vessel. Ultimately captured, the *Ann* was ordered to the Cape of Good Hope before being condemned in London as a lawful prize. It is believed the captives ultimately went to the use of the British crown.[8] Moreover, the seizure of the ship and others carrying legally traded items in open waters served as a component to the start of the War of 1812. This also became an issue again in 1842, leading the passage of the Webster-Ashburton Treaty also known as the Washington Treaty. Although this is one instance of being thwarted by the British anti-slave trading squadron there were other attempts made by Jonathan Dennison that proved successful. (See Table 7.1.)

Similar to other voyages made on behalf of owner James De Wolf, the mainland of the United States was not the principal slave landing ground.

Many United States slave traders who traveled to the Gold Coast for Akan captives ultimately transported there cargo to several of today's modern day states of the Southern and Mid-Atlantic areas of the country. James De Wolf and his fleet of ships became the most recognized Americans to reach the area. Kwasi Konadu states, "In North America, the Carolinas (primarily South Carolina) received the most Gold Coast shipments, with 102 direct voyages, followed by Virginia (32), Georgia (12), and Maryland (7). . . ."[9] Similar evidence from Michael Gomez suggests more Gold Coast captives found their way to Virginia and Maryland, than South Carolina and Georgia.[10] In South Carolina, the Gullah retained several different African languages, one of which was found among the Ga of the Gold Coast.[11] Of those captives who did arrive from the Gold Coast, this also began to bring about several stereotypes of Akan captives. Akan captives or Cormantin as they are referred, in the Caribbean, upon arrival were regarded as ferocious people

Table 7.1 Outcome of Voyages Made by Capt. Jonathan Dennison on Behalf of James De Wolf

Voyage Identification Number	*Vessel Name*	*Captain's Name*	*Year Arrived with Slaves*	*Principal Region of Slave Purchase*	*Principal Region of Slave Landing**
36856	Ann	Dennison, Jonathan	1805	Gold Coast	Rio de la Plata
36884	Ann	Dennison, Jonathan	1807	Gold Coast	Southeast Africa and Indian Ocean islands

Source: David Eltis et al., *The Trans-Atlantic Slave Trade Database*, http://slavevoyages.org/tast/database/search.faces?yearFrom=1514&yearTo=1866&anycaptain=Jonathan+Dennison&fate4=1.2.3.4&anyowner=&natinimp=. (Accessed January 25, 2011).

on the other hand in the United States they were seen as unskilled yet hard workers with an endowed physical ability.[12]

During the final years of British control and dominance over the mainland colonies of the North America, the trade of captives arriving from the Gold Coast grew from 0 to nearly 5,000 to the areas of the Chesapeake, the Carolinas and Georgia. By the end of the legal era of slave trading in 1808, over 42,000 captives had been brought from the Gold Coast to the United States with the largest numbers reaching the areas of the Carolinas and Georgia. Presented below, the chart shows the growth of trading to the Chesapeake and the areas of the Carolina and Georgia over twenty-five year periods beginning in 1717. (See Table 7.2.)

While the numbers of captives reaching the Chesapeake region along with those arriving in the Carolinas and Georgia remained a relatively small number prior to 1750, afterward there is a spike in the number of captives arriving. This spike in captives is especially noticeable in those reaching the Carolinas and Georgia beginning in 1751. Between 1776 and 1807 the number of captives again grew by 3,000 captives to nearly 8,500 between 1776 and 1800 and over 9,000 between 1801 and 1807.

In 1655, the British Caribbean expanded with Oliver Cromwell's capture of the then Spanish region, Jamaica, making it the largest island owned by the nation in the Caribbean and eventually surpassing Barbados, then the most valuable British territory in the Caribbean, in value.[13] The capture of Jamaica expanded the British Atlantic Empire, stretching it from the Northern fringes of North America to several areas in the South Caribbean.

In the vast chain of Caribbean islands, specifically the British Caribbean, many of the Akan captives leaving the Gold Coast were taken directly to the areas of first Barbados and Guiana, with the largest of the population landing in the island of Jamaica after its capture. Just as the British began

Table 7.2 Gold Coast Captives Arriving in the United States from 1717–1807

	Mainland North America					
	Chesapeake		*Carolinas / Georgia*		*Totals*	
	Embarked	*Disembarked*	*Embarked*	*Disembarked*	*Embarked*	*Disembarked*
1717–1725	3,148	2,722	2,033	1,627	5,180	4,349
1726–1750	5,214	4,345	786	666	5,999	5,012
1751–1775	5,166	4,381	12,894	10,900	18,059	15,281
1776–1800	0	0	10,190	8,587	10,190	8,587
1801–1807	78	68	10,570	9,243	10,648	9,311
Totals	13,605	11,517	36,472	31,023	50,077	42,540

Source: David Eltis et al., *The Trans-Atlantic Slave Trade Voyages Database*, http://slavevoyages.org/tast/assessment/estimates.faces?yearFrom=1717&yearTo=1807&embarkation=4&disembarkation=203.202 (Accessed December 28, 2010).

to expand their territories in the Western world, they also began to establish trading relationships on the Gold Coast. This influence on the Gold Coast increased with their direct contact with Akan coastal states, especially the Fante state, and the construction of forts and castles. Once gaining control of Jamaica and expanding its influence on the Gold Coast, the region became one of the largest suppliers of British captives. According to Anne C. Bailey:

> In fact, there is a particularly strong link between Ghana and Jamaica in terms of slave origins. Slaves sold on the then Gold Coast came to be known as "Cormantin" Negroes—a name from the coastal port Coramantin, where the English built their first port in 1631, said to be the "first slave prison on the coast." In almost two hundred years, nearly seven million slaves were exported through this port.[14]

In the 1700s as the British involvement in the Trans-Atlantic Slave Trade grew, the island of Jamaica became the main disembarkation point for British captives with those from the Gold Coast being the most sought after.[15]

As shown below (see Table 7.3), between 1700 and 1807, the preference for Akan captives on the island of Jamaica was so prevalent the island received over 200,000 more captives than the next closest recipient, Barbados.

The number of captives exported from the Gold Coast to the island of Jamaica also coincided with the number of ship board revolts and the large maroon population of Jamaica. Between 1704 and 1807, there were sixty-two recorded slave revolts with one-third of those coming on voyages to Jamaica. Akan captives entering Jamaica came to shape the culture, plantation economy and maroon communities there.[16]

Table 7.3 Gold Coast Captives taken to the British Caribbean Between 1700 and 1807

	British Caribbean					
	Jamaica	*Barbados*	*Antigua*	*St. Kitts*	*Grenada*	*Dominica*
Gold Coast	329623	88376	35941	23483	27943	3843
Totals	329623	88376	35941	23483	27943	3843

	British Caribbean					
	British Guiana	*St. Vincent*	*Montserrat / Nevis*	*Trinidad / Tobago*	*Other British Caribbean*	*Totals*
Gold Coast	28896	14153	13940	6256	9632	582087
Totals	28896	14153	13940	6256	9632	582087

Source: David Eltis et al., *The Trans-Atlantic Slave Trade Voyages Database*, http://slavevoyages.org/tast/assessment/estimates.faces?yearFrom=1700&yearTo=1807&embarkation=4&disembarkation=305.304.307.306.309.308.311.310.301.302.303 (Accessed December 28, 2010).

The Akan influence in Jamaica is largely measured by the slave insurrections that occurred on the island, gaining them a reputation. James Anquandah in discussing those Africans referred to as Cormantin taken to Jamaica writes:

> But it is a matter of history that slaves exported from the Gold Coast as a whole "distinguished" themselves enough to be known in the New World as "Cormantin Negroes," a name derived from the coastal port called Cormantin where the English built their first trading-post in 1631 (later Fort Amsterdam). . . . It is estimated that during the 17th and 18th centuries an average of around 35,000 "Cormantins" were exported annually from the Gold Coast. . . . But the "Cormantins" built for themselves a reputation as the most daring, stubborn . . . of all the African slaves in the New World. They often spearheaded slave mutinies and the Jamaican Parliament attributed the series of the mid-18th century slave revolts to "the turbulent Cormantin Negroes" notorious both for their ferocity and their dislike of farm chores and dirty work.[17]

Many of these insurrections which occurred in Jamaica were directly linked to those captives brought from the Gold Coast. As a result of these several insurrections which occurred many were directly attributed to captives of Cormantin origin.

Many of the insurrections occurring in Jamaica between 1712 and 1831 had signs of Cormantin influences. During the first Maroon War, a fifteen year war lasting from 1725 to 1740, evidence suggests that the Jamaican maroon population was led by former captives from the Gold Coast under the command of Cudjoe.[18] Under Cudjoe, the Jamaican maroon society, men made up the warrior caste as well as the hunters, while women did the agricultural work. This society closely resembled the Akan state from which many of maroons came from.[19]

By 1760, another rebellion was on the horizon, again led by maroons of Cormantin origin as the maroon population trekked between sugar plantations gaining new followers along the way.[20] According to Joseph J. Williams, "Such I well know was the origin of the Negro rebellion which happened in Jamaica in 1760. It arose at the instigation of a Koromantyn Negro of the name Tacky. . . ."[21] The maroon insurrections continued occurring again during the 1770s at the height of the American Revolution and the early stages of decline in the value of British Caribbean sugar producing colonies.[22]

The fiercest of the Akan/Cormantin slave revolts to occur in Jamaica began in 1831, two years before the decision to end slavery in all British territories. Beginning only two days after Christmas, this revolt although not well orchestrated resulted in the death of several whites in Jamaica, ultimately dealing the final blow to the Jamaican economy already in decline.[23] Hearing the news that emancipation was coming, several slaves on sugar plantations planned a revolt, only to be subdued by owners who anticipated the attack. William Knibb a missionary in Jamaica discussed the revolt in a letter two months afterward stating:

> The first information I received of the intended revolt was on the 26th of December, when Mr. Blyth called upon me at Falmouth, and stated that the parish of St. James was in an awful state of excitement, and that he feared a rebellion among slaves would be the result, unless we took the most prompt measures to undeceive the negroes, who had imbibed the notion they were free. . . . On the evening of the 26th I started for Montego Bay, and early on the following morning rode to Salter's Hill . . . I spent the whole of the time . . . speaking to the people, assuring them that no free paper had arrived, begging them to go to their work on the morrow, and not be led away in sin and violence.[24]

Ultimately put down, this slave insurrection dealt a blow to the British Caribbean economy as they were ultimately sct free two years later.

The island of Jamaica a British territory saw an increase in the number of captives of Cormantin origin just as their reach on the Gold Coast expanded. The impact of these captives is seen during the numerous insurrections which occurred onboard ships destined for Jamaica and revolts which occurred. Both Monica Schuler and Orlando Patterson believe that the Akan rebellions that occurred in Jamaica were carried out by Cormantins, who were linked to the Asante, learning to fight in guerilla warfare tactics.[25]

The Haitian Revolution combined with the Maroon Wars and the Industrial Revolution ensured the final days of slavery in the British Empire. The early debates regarding the value of slavery in the British colonies began as early as 1790, and by the time the slave trade was abolished in 1807, a quarter of the Jamaican plantation estates had already been sold to pay off debts.[26] In 1833 the British, Parliament officially abolished slavery in all its colonial territories, which stretched from the Caribbean to the coast of Africa. Moreover this had an impact on trade treaties signed between the British and the Fante and Asante States on the Gold Coast.

The Trans-Atlantic Slave Trade from the Gold Coast went through several different phases of growth and expansion before its ultimate decline. During the 1700s, the British, the largest of the slave dealing nations, began to expand both its reach on the Gold Coast and in areas of the Caribbean and North America. As the Asante began its push from the interior toward the coastline, the numbers of captives leaving the Gold Coast also increased. Due in part to the growing warfare between states, the British, one of many nations trading along the Gold Coast, saw an increase in the numbers of captives they received.

Over nearly two hundred years of British exportation of captives from the Gold Coast, several areas of North America and the Caribbean received people from the region, which expanded its slave trading during the 1700s. Through the 1700s into the 1800s, British vessels continually arrived with cargoes of Cormantin captives from the Gold Coast. Outside the British Empire many of these Cormatin captives were taken to areas of North America (i.e. Virginia and South Carolina), the Caribbean (i.e. Jamaica) and South America (i.e. Colombia). The impact of the Akan or Cormantin captives varied in each location, but wherever they were taken, they were known for their warlike attitudes and the impact they made on the local economy. While this influence on the African Diaspora has been well documented, as the 200th Anniversary of the Abolition of the Trans-Atlantic Slave Trade approached an in depth analysis of interior states remained a lacking study during the era. Nevertheless, the Gold Coast has been a central region to the start of the slave trade and eventually the closing in the nineteenth century.

In recent years, following the many celebrations by countries and organizations around the world, to commemorate the 200th Anniversary of the Abolition of the Trans-Atlantic Slave Trade, new evidence has been presented which sheds new light on its final years. Much of this new evidence has shed light onto the roles of key individuals, organizations and governments from the continents of Europe, Africa, the Caribbean, South America and North America. Of the several celebrations which occurred around the world, each nation involved focused on specific themes. In Britain the focus was on their humanitarian efforts and in America celebrations highlighted the idea of reparations for the descendants of trade victims, African Americans. In the Caribbean Islands, discussions focused on the dehumanization of people as well the role of humanitarians in closing the trade.

Although these commemorative events occurring on both sides of the Atlantic Ocean garnered worldwide attention, each overlooked the changing economy of the era which altered the trade itself. Moreover, the changing economy of the nineteenth century led to the closure of the trade in captive Africans. Ultimately, these worldwide events also overlooked the impact of large African states, which lined the West African coastline and eventually those interior nations. These interior nations during the Trans-Atlantic Slave Trade played a critical role in supplying captives and later the transition to legitimately traded goods.

During the early years of European contact with Africa, the Gold Coast served as one of the first landing grounds, thus beginning the search for gold. Furthermore, it was this search for gold which resulted in European nations staking out claims to its coastline beginning in the fifteenth century. Ultimately, this search for gold put the Gold Coast region in the center of the economic ambitions of the Portuguese and later several European nations who followed. During the height of the slave trade from the region, through the eighteenth century, the Gold Coast provided captives to the United States, the Caribbean, and South America, making the region a crucial component to the European economy well into the period of colonialism.

Between 1776 and 1874, a number of changes occurred throughout the world, impacting the economies of the Caribbean, the United States, Europe and areas of Africa as well. On a regional level this period had an especially large scale impression on the Gold Coast. During this time period, people witnessed the emergence of several new nations through revolutions, the closure of the Trans-Atlantic Slave Trade and a change in the world economy. Nevertheless, along the Gold Coast several nations also emerged and became involved in the Atlantic commercial economy. On the other hand, in the years preceding the closure of the Trans-Atlantic Slave Trade, from 1776 to 1808, the export of African captives to areas of North America, the Caribbean and South America more than doubled as more traders took to the seas.

This increase in the trade of captives leaving the Gold Coast also coincides with the Asante to push to expand its empire to encompass areas of the regions coastline. By expanding their state, the Asante could remove the Fante another Akan nation, as a regional power. Moreover, this expansion process had an ability to turn the Asante an interior Gold Coast state into a West African power. While this possibility proved to be viable in the early years of the eighteenth century, by the start of the nineteenth century the British along the coastline believed otherwise as they hoped to expand their own influence. Even as the trade in Africans entered its illegal era, slave traders continually took risks to acquire Africans. Moreover, this trade in African captives continued on for over eighty years, until it ultimately slowed to its eventual close.

Although, the export trade in Africans slowly came to an end on the coast, within the interior regions of Africa there was an expansion of slavery due in part to changes in desired commodities. While the changes resulted in an expansion of slavery within specific areas, the interior nation of the Asante was able to manage the transition from captive labor to legitimate commerce without doing any damage to the state economy and treasury. Albeit, on the Gold Coast, in particular within the Asante, changes resulted in the transition from exporting captive Africans to the trade of agricultural and bulk goods to meet the needs of Muslims from the North and Europeans from the South. Later visitors entering the interior of the region witnessed these changes to the trade in Africans also highlighting the transition made by this powerful state. A transition such as this occurred over several decades as witnessed by the period between the close of the Trans-Atlantic Slave Trade and the eventual push for the start of colonization in the region.

This change from a trade in captives to one of legitimate commerce and its relevance to individual states was overlooked in the numerous celebrations around the world. Nevertheless, in Ghana, the focus of these commemorative events highlighted their independence, believing the slave trade's closure is only for those that benefitted from the trade, namely those in Europe and America. Unlike other events around the world, celebrations in Ghana, concentrated on the independence of the nation, proving a country could indeed overcome the obstacles which this trade in Africans left behind. An analysis of the years between 1807 and 1874 shows the successful transformation the region experienced in the nineteenth century and its lingering impact on the country well after independence. This period is just as critical to the history of the nation as those between 1900 and 1957, as the push to remain free and independent begins much earlier than the start of the twentieth century.

Today in the country formerly known as the Gold Coast, now Ghana, the former castles of the Trans-Atlantic Slave Trade, which housed over 1 million captives stand as reminders of both the past and the ability to overcome any obstacle. Captives leaving this region were boarded on ships bound for areas of North and South America and the Caribbean. Today, Elmina and Cape Coast, two of the many remaining castles are some of the most visited locations in West Africa by tourists from all over the African Diaspora.

While these castles can be reminders of a horrific experience for people who still reside in Africa and those residing in the African Diaspora, they are also important reminders of the economic exploitation of people as well as the struggle of individuals and families to survive. Sandra Richards writes, "But on the site of Elmina and/or Cape Coast Castle, where the slave dungeons seem to emit their own odor and presence, such self-fashioning is much harder to achieve; the fractured quality of 'family' and 'home' is much more apparent to travelers from the African Diaspora."[27] This presence is felt by individuals as they reach the castle doors prior to entering.

Further strengthening this connection, visitors from the African Diaspora who make this trek to these castles often leave behind wreaths to commemorate the lives lost (see Figures 7.1 and 7.2).

Of those wreaths left behind by individuals and groups who make the trek to these castles, many of them show exactly where visitors have come from. Most recently, United States President Barack Obama and First Lady Michelle Obama left behind a wreath to commemorate the lives lost to the Trans-Atlantic Slave Trade. While not the first United States President and First Lady to visit Africa or the one of its many remaining castles, the visit by persons of African descent from the African Diaspora is of great significance. This visit, like the many others before it and those afterward, only reiterate the bond between Africa and its descendants.

In 1994, the United Nations Scientific Educational Organization established the Slave Route Project. Launched during the General Conference at its 26th Session established the criteria to preserve castles and forts around

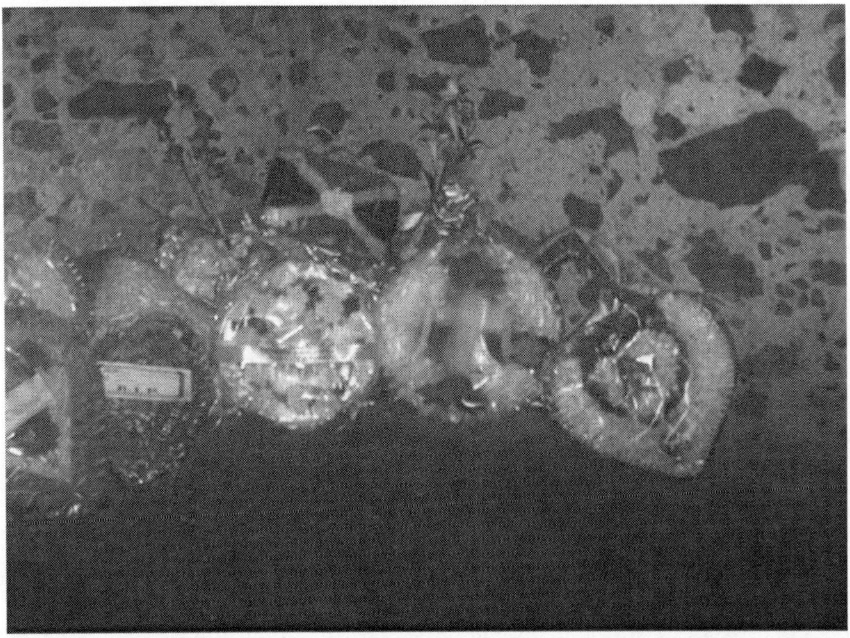

Figure 7.1 Wreaths Left Behind by Visitors to Cape Coast Castle. Photo provided by author.

Figure 7.2 Wreaths Left Behind by Visitors to Cape Coast Castle. Photo provided by author.

the world. By 2009 this project was expanded once again and was now referred to as The Slave Route Project: Resistance, Liberty and Heritage. Ultimately, this project hoped to raise awareness about slavery and crimes that were committed against humanity.[28]

As two of the most important locations to the United Nations Scientific Educational Organization, UNESCO, Slave Route Project, these castles are being preserved to boost tourism in Ghana and freeze this period of history. They are two of the many castles UNESCO has included as a part of this project located throughout West Africa. The Slave Route Project now in its twentieth year continues to preserve the memory of those who once passed through its doors. Moreover, when established the goals were to both break the silence of the slave trade and promote the global transformations and shared heritage born from this tragedy. These goals which continue to be achieved through the numerous proclamations passed each year and visitors who return to these castles to share in a common experience.[29]

While UNESCO and the Slave Route Project have developed its own plan, the country of Ghana is also hoping to widen its involvement with these locations by promoting tourism and the growth of local business interest which surround the castles.[30] Not only do these castles boost the tourism of the country, but also the economic development of surrounding merchants. Today, tourism is Ghana's fourth largest foreign exchange earner with nearly 500,000 foreigners visit the country yearly from all over the world.[31]

The Gold Coast of West Africa, in the 1470s became the central location of European contact in Africa. First the Portuguese, who were later followed by the Dutch, Danish, British, Swedish and French, all made a substantial impact on trading from Africa and in particular the Gold Coast during this early European contact with West Africa. Originally, the Gold Coast began as an importer of captives and exporter of gold and during the 1600s began the transition to an exporter of captives and importer of European manufactured goods. As an exporter of captives, the Gold Coast victims ultimately ended up in a number of locations throughout the United States, the Caribbean and eventually several locations in South America.

Beginning in the 1600s and lasting through 1800s the Gold Coast produced captives in mass numbers. Although the production of these captives was not on the scale of the Bight of Benin, the Senegambia region or Angola, the numbers of captives were substantial enough that several European nations built and maintained forts along the coastline of the region during the period. Forts built by the British, Dutch, French, Danish and Swedes lined the coastline and contributed the European economy in Africa, the New World and in their home countries as well. Central to this early contact was the trade first in gold and later in captives. Ultimately, in over two hundred years of captive exportation, the Gold Coast produced more than one million captives (see

Table 7.4 200 Years of Exportation from the Gold Coast

	Gold Coast		Totals	
	Embarked	Disembarked	Embarked	Disembarked
1619–1650	2,497	2,088	2,497	2,088
1651–1700	105,485	84,379	105,485	84,379
1701–1750	460,132	386,903	460,132	386,903
1751–1800	553,872	479,973	553,872	479,973
1801–1840	84,617	75,410	84,617	75,410
Total	1,206,603	1,028,753	1,206,603	1,028,753

Source: Davis Eltis et al., *The Trans-Atlantic Slave Trade Database: Slave Voyages*, http://slavevoyages.org/tast/assessment/estimates.faces?yearFrom=1618&yearTo=1840&embarkation=4 (Accessed February 15, 2011).

Table 7.4), who found their way across the Atlantic Ocean into the growing European economy.

Captives leaving the Gold Coast contributed to the economies of the nations where they were taken, as they worked in several different capacities, particularly in mining and agriculture. The rate of captives leaving the Gold Coast in over two hundred years of trading steadily increased over the years before the numbers finally declined.

The largest numbers of these captives were captured and transported from the Gold Coast first during the Asante formation and second, during their expansion from the interior toward the coastline. This period included several wars and creation of a highly advanced system of trade routes linking the region of Greater Asante with the coastal region and Northern territories. Captives were initially the main commodity transported along these routes.

As the external market altered their needs, the Asante people and the region of Greater Asante met the demands of a changing market, developing its own cash crop economy. Albeit, as wars continued to occur and many of the European nations who resided along the coast for more than two hundred years began to leave, the Asante nation did not decline, instead finding new partners with whom to trade. In this era, the Asante state continued to push for expansion, for trading purposes well after the Trans-Atlantic Slave Trade had been officially abolished and well after American and British cruisers patrolling for slave traders ceased. However, this expansion process was met with opposition from the British and its decision to create a permanent sphere of influence in the Gold Coast, destroying the growing Asante economy in the process.

Ultimately, this work has provided an overview of the early European contact with the Gold Coast of West Africa, the start of the Trans-Atlantic Slave Trade from the region, the role of British and American abolition efforts. This work has also proved that as demand for commodities changed, the region of Greater Asante and the Asante people met the external market demands.

Moreover, the work should be analyzed from the view point which argues there were key economic factors which lead to the closure of the slave trade. In the Gold Coast, these economic factors eventually shaped the direction of both the country and the Asante economy. Ultimately the Asante were able to impact trading both to its North and South in throughout the nineteenth century and along the way and dramatically alter the value of the illegal Trans-Atlantic Slave Trade from the Gold Coast during the era.

NOTES

1. Elizabeth M. Halcrow, *Canes and Chains: A Study of Sugar and Slavery* (Oxford: Heinemann Publishers, 1982), pp. 43–44.
2. Akosua Perbi, *A History of Indigenous Slavery in Ghana: From the 15th to 19th Century* (Accra, Ghana: Sub-Saharan Publishers, 2004), p. 68.
3. Hugh Thomas, *The Slave Trade: The Story of the Atlantic Slave Trade, 1440–1870* (New York: Simon and Schuster Books, 1997), pp. 534–535.
4. W. E. B. DuBois, *The Suppression of the African Slave Trade to the United States of America, 1638–1870* (New York: Longmans, Green and Co., 1896), p. 229.
5. Thomas Norman DeWolf, *Inheriting the Trade: A Northern Family Confronts Its Legacy as the Largest Slave-Trading Dynasty in U.S. History* (Boston, MA: Beacon Press, 2008), pp. 44–45.
6. George Fancis Dow, *Slave Ships and Slaving* (Salem, Massachusetts: Marine Research Society, 1927), p. 260.
7. James DeWolf to Captain Jonathan Dennison, Bristol, RI, July 1806 In George Francis Dow, *Slave Ships and Slaving* (Salem, Massachusetts: Marine Research Society, 1927), p. 261.
8. Ibid, 265.
9. Kwasi Konadu, *The Akan Diaspora in the Americas* (New York: Oxford University Press, 2010), p. 164.
10. Michael Gomez, *Exchanging Our Country Marks: The Transformation of African Identities in the Colonial and Antebellum South* (Chapel Hill, NC: University of North Carolina Press, 1998), p. 107.
11. Wilbur Cross, *Gullah Culture in America* (Westport, Conn: Praeger Books, 2008), p. 139.
12. Gomez, 107.
13. Kenneth Morgan, *Slavery and the British Empire: From Africa to America* (New York: Oxford University Press, 2007), p. 8.
14. Anne C. Bailey, *African Voices of the Atlantic Slave Trade, Beyond the Silence and the Shame* (Boston, MA: Becaon Press, 2005), p. 6.
15. Ibid, 14–15.
16. Kwasi Konadu, *The Akan Diaspora in the Americas* (New York: Oxford University Press, 2010), p. 149.
17. James Kwesi Anquandah, *Castles & Forts of Ghana* (Atalante, Paris: Ghana Museums & Monuments Board, 1999), p. 14.

18. Richard B. Sheridan, "The Jamaican Slave Insurrection Scare of 1776 and the American Revolution," *The Journal of Negro History*, Vol. 61, No. 3 (July, 1976), p. 292.

19. Michael Craton, *Testing the Chains: Resistance to Slavery in the British West Indies* (New York: Cornell University Press, 1982), p. 78.

20. Sheridan, 292.

21. Joseph J. Williams, *Hebrewisms of West Africa from the Nile to the Niger with the Jews*, 2nd ed. (New York: Biblo and Tannen, 1967), p. 3.

22. Sheridan, 293.

23. Gelien Matthews, *Caribbean Slave Revolts and the British Abolitionist Movement* (Baton Rouge, LA: Louisiana State University Press, 2006), p. 22.

24. John Howard Hinton and William Knibb, *Memoir of William Knibb: Missionary in Jamaica* (London: Houlston and Stoneman, 1847), p. 117.

25. Both Monica Schuler and Orlando Patterson have done extensive research on slavery and revolts. See: Monica Schuler, "Ethnic Slave Rebellions in the Caribbean and the Guianas," *Journal of Social History*, Vol. 3, No. 4 (Summer, 1970), p. 381. and Orlando Patterson, *Sociology of Slavery: An Analysis of the Origins, Development of Structure of Negro Slave Society in Jamaica* (London: MacGibbon and Kee, 1967), p. 381 In Richard B. Sheridan, "The Jamaican Slave Insurrection Scare of 1776 and the American Revolution," *The Journal of Negro History*, Vol. 61, No. 3 (July, 1976), pp. 292, 299.

26. Carrington, *The Sugar Industry and the Abolition of the Slave Trade, 1775–1810*, p. 219.

27. Sandra L. Richards, "What is to Be Remembered?: Tourism to Ghana's Slave Castle Dungeons," *Theatre Journal*, No. 57 (2005), p. 622.

28. United Nations Educational, Scientific and Cultural Oranization, 37th General Conference Draft Resolution: Consideration and Adoption of the Draft Medium Term Strategy for 2014–2021, 37 C/4/DR.5 (November 12, 2013). http://unesdoc.unesco.org/images/0022/002246/224603e.pdf (Accessed, June 20, 2014).

29. "20th Anniversary of the Slave Route Project," http://www.unesco.org/new/index.php?id=121196 (Accessed June 23, 2014).

30. L. A. Dei and Kwaku Boakye, "Developing the Slave Route for Tourism-Community Dynamic, Policy Implications and Strategies for the Root Tourism Project." In *The Trans-Atlantic Slave Trade: Landmarks, Legacies Expectations*, ed. James Kwesi Anquandah (Legon, Accra, Ghana: Sub-Saharan Publishers, 2007), pp. 347–349.

31. J. J. Mason and Martina Odonkor, "Historic Slave Routes Tourism: Potential for Tourism Development in Ghana and West Africa Sub-Region." In *The Trans-Atlantic Slave Trade: Landmarks, Legacies Expectations*, ed. James Kwesi Anquandah (Legon, Accra, Ghana: Sub-Saharan Publishers, 2007), pp. 358–359.

Bibliography

TREATIES

Ashantee Treaty of Peace and Fommanah, 13 February 1874, Cape Coast, 14 March 1874, British National Archives, (FO 93/6/4).

Charter under the Great Seal of the United Kingdom to provide for the Government of Her Majesty's Forts and Settlements on the Gold Coast, January 24, 1850. *Ordinances Relating to Her Majesty's Forts and Settlements on the Gold Coast,* 1843–1859, Public Records and Archives Administration Department, Accra, Ghana ADM 4/1/1.

Convention Between Her Majesty and the King of the Netherlands for an Interchange of Territory on the Gold Coast of Africa, Signed at London, March 5, 1867, British National Archives, (FO 925/ 472).

Peace and Commerce Treaty with Ashanti, September 7, 1817 in C. W. Newbury, *British Policy Towards West Africa, Select Documents,* 1786–1874. Oxford: Clarendon Press, 1965.

Proceedings of the Select Committee on West Coast of Africa, March 1842, Public Records and Archives Administration Department, Accra, Ghana ADM 5/3/2.

Treaty of Peace and Commerce with Ashanti, March 23, 1820 in C. W. Newbury, *British Policy Towards West Africa, Select Documents,* 1786–1874. Oxford: Clarendon Press, 1965.

Treaty of Peace and of Free Commerce, April 27, 1831 in C. W. Newbury, *British Policy Towards West Africa, Select Documents,* 1786–1874. Oxford: Clarendon Press, 1965.

United Nations Educational, Scientific and Cultural Organization, 37th General Conference Draft Resolution: Consideration and Adoption of the Draft Medium Term Strategy for 2014–2021, 37 C/4/DR.5.

BRITISH AND UNITES STATES

Slave Trade Acts

An Act for the Abolition of the Slave Trade, 47 Geo 3, Session 1, c. 36.

British Foreign Slave Trade Act, An Act to Regulate, for a Limited Time, the Shipping and Carrying Slaves in British Vessels from the Coast of Africa 28, Geo 3 c. 54.

British Foreign Slave Trade Act, An Act to Regulate, for a Limited Time, the Shipping and Carrying Slaves in British Vessels from the Coast of Africa 31 Geo 3 c 54.

British Foreign Slave Trade Act, An Act for Better Regulating the Manner of Carrying Slaves, in British Vessels from the Coast of Africa. 39 Geo 3 c. 80.

Slave Trade Act of 1794, Sections 1–4.

Slave Trade Act of 1800, Sections 1–7.

Slave Trade Act of 1803, Sections 1–3.

The Webster-Ashburton Treaty.

United States Constitution Article 1, Section 9.

PRIMARY DOCUMENTS

American Colonization Society, *The African Repository and Colonial Journal*. Washington, DC: C. Alexander, Printer, 1850.

An Accurate Account of that Horrible and Inhuman Traffic: The Slave Trade, Shewing the Treatment which the Slaves Experience, The Mode of Procuring Them, With a Description of the Iron Instruments Used in this Abominable Traffic. London: J. Fairburn, Jr., 1794.

Barbot, John. *A Description of the Coasts of North and South Guinea*. London: Henry Lintot and John Osborn, 1746.

Beecham, J. *Asantee and the Gold Coast*. London: 1841.

Benezet, Anthony. *Some Historical Account of Guinea: Its Situation, Produce, and the General Disposition of its Inhabitants, With an Inquiry Into the Rise and Progress of the Slave Trade, Its Nature and Lamentable Effects*. London: J. Phillips, George Yard and Lombard Street, 1788.

Bowdich, T. E. *Mission From Cape Coast Castle to Ashantee, with a Descriptive Account of that Kingdom*. London: Griffith & Farran, 1817.

Bosman, William. *A New and Accurate Description of the Coast of Guinea, Divided into the Gold, the Slave, and the Ivory Coasts*, 4th ed. With Introduction by John Ralph Willis and Notes by J. D. Fage and R. E. Bradbury. London: Frank Cass, 1967.

Boyle, F. *Through Fanteeland to Coomassie: A Diary of the Ashantee Expedition*. London, 1874.

Brackenbury, Sir Henry. *The Ashanti War, A Narrative Prepared from Official Documents by Permission of Major-General Sir Garnet Wolseley*, Vol. 1. London: William Blackwood and Sons, 1876.

British Parliamentary Papers, Papers Concerning the Gold Coast and Surrounding Districts, 1850–1873, *Colonial Africa, Ghana,* Vol. 57. Ireland: Irish University Press, 1971.

Bryson, Alexander. *Report on the Climate and Principal Diseases of the African Station.* London: 1847.

Canot, Theodore. *Adventures of an African Slaver: An Account of the life of Captain Theodore Canot, Trader in Gold, Ivory, and Slaves on the Coast of Guinea, Written out and Edited from the Captain's Journals, Memoranda and Conversations.* Brandtz Mayer, ed. Mineola, NY: Dover Press, 2002.

Clarkson, Thomas. *The History of the Rise, Progress, and Accomplishment of the Abolition of the African Slave-Trade.* New York: John S. Taylor, 1836.

Crow, Hugh. *Adventures of an African Slaver.* London: George Routledge & Sons Ltd., 1854.

Cruickshank, Brodie. *The Gold Coast of Africa: Including an Account of the Native Tribes, and Their Intercourse with Europeans.* London: Hurst and Blackett, Publishers, 1853.

Dalrymple Hay, Sir John Charles. *Ashanti and The Gold Coast: And What We Know of It, A Sketch.* London: Edward Sanford, 1874.

Dalzel, Archibald. *The History of Dahomey: An Inland Kingdom of Africa.* London: Author, 1793.

DeWolf, Thomas Norman. *Inheriting the Trade: A Northern Family Confronts Its Legacy as the Largest Slave-Trading Dynasty in United States History.* Boston, MA: Beacon Press, 2008.

"Documents Relating to the United States and Liberia," *The American Journal of International Law*, Vol. 4, No. 3, Supplement: Official Documents, (July, 1910), *Act* of March 3, 1819 Relative to the Slave Trade.

Dupuis, Joseph. *Journal of a Residence in Ashantee.* London: 1820.

Ellis, A. B. *A History of the Gold Coast of West Africa.* London: Chapman and Hall, 1893.

Equiano, Olaudah. *Interesting Narrative of the Life of Olaudah Equiano.* London: Heinemann Publishers, 1996.

Falconridge, Alexander. *An Account of the Slave Trade on the Coast of Africa.* London: J. Phillips, 1788.

Foote, A. H. *The Africa Squadron: Ashburton Treaty and Consular Sea Letters Reviewed in an Address.* Philadelphia: William F. Geddes, 1847.

Further Papers Relating to the Warfare Between the Fantis and the Ashantis, C. 456, 1855.

Goodell, William. *Slavery and Anti-Slavery: A History of the Great Struggle in Both Hemispheres, With a View of the Slavery Question in the United States*, 3rd ed. New York: William Goodell, 1855.

Johnson, Marion. ed., Salaga Papers, Vol. 1. Legon, Ghana: Institute of African Studies, 1965.

Knibb, William. *Memoir of William Knibb: Missionary in Jamaica.* London: Houlston and Stoneman, 1847.

Mansfield, J. S. *Remarks on the African Squadron.* London: James Ridgway Press, 1851.

Marees, Pieter de. *Description and Account of the Gold Kingdom of Guinea* (1602). New York: Oxford University Press, 1987.

Matson, James Henry. *Remarks on the Slave Trade and African Squadron*, Knowsley Pamphlet Collection. 1848.

Mayer, Brantz. *Captain Canot; Twenty Years of an African Slaver Being an Account of His Career and Adventures on the Coast, in the Interior, on Shipboard, and in The West Indies*. New York: D. Appleton and Company, 1854.

Meredith, Henry. *An Account of the Gold Coast of Africa: With a Brief History of the African Company*. London: Longman, Hurst, Rees, Orme, and Brown, Paternoster Row, 1812.

Newbury, C. W. *British Policy Towards West Africa: Select Documents,* 1786–1874. Oxford: Clarendon Press, 1965.

"Official Notice," *Gold Coast Gazette*, No. XXX, (Cape Coast), January 31, 1874.

Proceedings of the Select Committee on West Coast of Africa, March 1842, Public Records and Archives Administration Department, Accra, Ghana ADM 5/3/2.

Rattray, Captain R. S. *Ashanti*, 2nd ed. NY: Negro Universities Press,1969.

Reindorf, C. C. *History of the Gold Coast and Asante: Based on Traditions and Historical Facts, Comprising A Period of More Than Three Centuries from about 1500 to 1860*. Christianborg, Gold Coast: Basel Mission Book Depot, 1895.

Remarks on the Colonization of the Western Coast of Africa, by the Free Negroes of the United States, and the Consequent Civilization of Africa and Suppression of the Slave Trade. New York: W. L. Burroughs' Steam Power Press, 1850.

Report from the Select Committee on West Coast of Africa: Together With the Minutes of Evidence Appendix and Index August 5, 1842, Public Records and Archives Administration Department, Accra, Ghana ADM 5/3/3.

The Foreign Slave Trade, A Brief Account of its State, of the Treaties Which Have Been Entered Into, and of The Laws Enacted for its Suppression, From the Date of The English Abolition Act to the Present Time. London: John Hatchard and Son, 1837.

Ward, William Ernest Frank. *A Short History of the Gold Coast*, 2nd ed. Berkley, CA: University of California Press, 1939.

———. *A History of Ghana*, 3rd ed. London: Allen & Unwin, 1966.

———. *The Royal Navy and Slavers*. New York: Pantheon Books, 1969.

Snelgrave, William. *A New Account of Some Pats of Guinea and the Slave Trade*. London: James, John and Paul Knapton, 1734.

Stanley, Henry M. *Coomassie and Magdala: The Story of Two British Campaigns in Africa*. London: Sampson Low, Marston & Company, 1891.

Wilberforce, William. *A Letter on the Abolition of the Slave Trade*. London: Luke Hansard and Sons, 1807.

Yule, Lieutenant Henry. *The African Squadron Vindicated*. London: James Ridgway, Piccadilly, 1850.

CORRESPONDENCE

Letter from the Acting Governor of Mina to the Queen, April 18, 1557, and Anonymous Report on Mina, September 29, 1557.

Letter Commodore Wilmot to Sir B. W. Walter, 14 April 1863, *British Parliamentary Papers, Papers Concerning the Gold Coast and Surrounding Districts,* 1850–1873, *Colonial Africa, Ghana*, Vol. 57. Ireland: Irish University Press, 1971.

Letter from Sir Nicholls of the Gold Coast to the Lords of the Treasury, British Parliament, Received July 5, 1836. Letter Book, Sierra Leone and African Forts, Vol. 5, 1836, PRO British National Archives. CO 267/136.

George Washington Papers at Library of Congress, 1741–1799: Series 4. General Correspondence, 1697–1799. Treasury Department, April 2, 1793, Officers of the Revenue Cutters.

George Washington to Oliver Wolcott, Jr., September 6, 1796. The Writings of George Washington from the Original Manuscript Sources, 1745–1799. John C. Fitzpatrick, Editor.

General Ayres to the Secretary of the Navy, February 24, 1823.

Mr. Slidell, The Committee on Foreign Relations, *Journal of the Senate of the United States of America,* 1789–1873, Tuesday, June 13, 1854.

United States President John Tyler to Senate, *Journal of Executive Proceedings of the Senate of the United States of America* 1841–1845, August 11, 1842.

Letters, Perry to Goldsborough, March 28, 1843; to Kennon, April 7, 1843; to Upshur, April 13, 1843, in Perry Letter Books, National Archives, M206.

Letters, Perry to Upshur, May 16, 1843; to Tatnall, May 20, 1843; to Upshur, in Perry Letter Books, National Archives, M206.

Mr. Slidell, The Committee on Foreign Relations, *Journal of the Senate of the United States of America,* 1789–1873, Tuesday, June 13, 1854.

Journal of Executive Proceedings of the Senate of the United States of America 1841–1845, May 16, 1842.

Letter Commodore Wilmot to Sir B. W. Walter, 14 April 1863, *British Parliamentary Papers, Papers Concerning the Gold Coast and Surrounding Districts,* 1850–1873, *Colonial Africa, Ghana*, Vol. 57. Ireland: Irish University Press, 1971.

Letter T. Frederick Elliot to War Office, Downing Street, 24 March 1863, *British Parliamentary Papers, Papers Concerning the Gold Coast and Surrounding Districts,* 1850–1873, *Colonial Africa, Ghana*, Vol. 57. Ireland: Irish University Press, 1971.

Letter from Sir Garnet Wolseley to King Kofi Kakari, January, 1874 in Ian F. W. Beckett, ed., *Wolseley and Ashanti: The Asante War Journal and Correspondence of Major General Sir Garnet Wolseley,* 1873–1874. England: The Army Records Society, 2009.

Letter from Asantehene Kofi Kalkaree to Her Excellency, Queen of England, January 21, 1874. *British Parliamentary Papers, Correspondence On Ashanti and Gold Coast Affairs,* 1874–83, *Volume 60, Colonies in Africa.* Ireland: Irish University Press, 1971.

Letter from Major-General Garrett Joseph Wolseley to Asantehene Kalkaree, January 29, 1874. *British Parliamentary Papers, Correspondence On Ashanti and Gold Coast Affairs,* 1874–83, *Volume 60, Colonies in Africa.* Ireland: Irish University Press, 1971.

Letter from Sir Garnet Wolseley to King Kofi Kakari, February 3, 1874 in Ian F. W. Beckett, ed., *Wolseley and Ashanti: The Asante War Journal and Correspondence of Major General Sir Garnet Wolseley,* 1873–1874. England: The Army Records Society, 2009.

Letter from Sir Garnet Wolseley to King Kofi Karikari, February 4, 1874 in Ian F. W. Beckett, ed., *Wolseley and Ashanti: The Asante War Journal and Correspondence of Major General Sir Garnet Wolseley,* 1873–1874. England: The Army Records Society, 2009.

Governor R. Pine to the Duke of Newcastle: Ashanti Fugitives, 10 December 1862.

ARITCLES

Akinjogbin, I. A. "Archibald Dalzel: Slave Trader and Historian of Dahomey." *The Journal of African History*, Vol. 7, No. 1, (1966), pp. 67–78.

Akpan, M. B. "Black Imperialism: Americo-Liberian Rule Over the African Peoples of Liberia, 1841–1964." *Canadian Journal of African Studies*, Vol. 7, No. 2 (1973), pp. 217–236.

Arhin, Kwame. "Aspects of the Ashanti Northern Trade in the Nineteenth Century." *Journal of the International African Institute*. Vol. 40, No. 4 (October, 1970), pp. 363–373.

———. "Rank and Class Among the Asante and Fante in the Nineteenth Century." *Africa: Journal of the International African Institute*, Vol. 53, No. 1 (1983), pp. 2–22.

———. "The Financing of Ashanti Expansion, 1700–1820." *Africa: Journal of the International African Institute*, Vol. 37, No. 3 (July, 1967), pp. 283–291.

———. "The Structure of Greater Ashanti, 1700–1824." *The Journal of African History*, Vol. 8, No. 1, (1967), pp. 65–85.

Austen, Ralph A. Review of *From Slave Trade to 'Legitimate' Commerce: The Commercial Transition in Nineteenth-Century West Africa*, by Robin Law. *The Journal of African History*, Vol. 38, No. 1 (1997), pp. 133–135.

Austin, Gareth. "No Elders Were Present: Commoners and Private Ownership in Asante, 1807–96." *Journal of African History*, Vol. 37, No. 1 (1996), pp. 1–30.

Bethell, Leslie. "The Mixed Commissions for the Suppression of the Trans-Atlantic Slave Trade in the Nineteenth Century." *The Journal of African History*, Vol. 7, No. 1 (1966), pp. 79–93.

Adu Boahen, "The Origins of the Akan," *Ghana Notes and Queries*, No. 9 (November, 1966), pp. 3–10.

Breitborde, L. B. "City, Countryside and Kru Ethnicity," *Africa: Journal of the International African Institute*, Vol. 61, No. 2 (1991), p. 191.

Carrington, Selwynn H. H. "The American Revolution and the British West Indies' Economy." *Journal of Interdisciplinary History*, Vol. 17, No. 4, Caribbean Slavery and British Capitalism (Spring, 1987), pp. 823–850.

Caulker, Patrick S. "Legitimate Commerce and Statecraft: A Study of the Hinterland Adjacent to Nineteenth-Century Sierra Leone." *Journal of Black Studies*, Vol. 11, No. 4 (June, 1981), pp. 397–419.

Chamberlin, Christopher. "Bulk Exports, Trade Tiers, Regulation, and Development: An Economic Approach to the Study of West Africa's 'Legitimate Trade'." *The Journal of Economic History*, Vol. 39, No. 2 (June 1979), pp. 419–438.

Gérard Chouin, "The 'Big Bang' Theory Reconsidered: Framing Early Ghanaian History," *Transactions of the Historical Society of Ghana New Series*, No. 14 (2012), pp. 13–40.

Clark, Garcia. "Class Alliance and Class Formation in Ghanaian Trading and State Formation." *Review of African Political Economy*. No. 49, Democracy and Development (Winter, 1990), pp. 73–82.

Curtin, Philip D. "The Lure of Bambuk Gold." *The Journal of African History*, Vol. 14, No. 4 (1973), pp. 623–631.

———. The End of the White man's Grave? Nineteenth Century Mortality in West Africa, *Journal of Interdisciplinary History*, Vol. 21, No. 1 (Summer, 1990), pp. 63–88.

Davis, Arthur. "Columbus Divides the World." *The Geographical Journal*, Vol. 133, No. 3 (September, 1967), pp. 337–344.

Davis, Ronald W. "The Liberian Struggle for Authority on the Kru Coast." *The International Journal of African Historical Studies*. Vol. 8, No. 2 (1975), pp. 222–265.

Dickson, K. B. "Trade Patterns in Ghana at the Beginning of the Eighteenth Century." *Geographical Review*. Vol. 56, No. 3 (July, 1966), pp. 417–431.

Dodoo, Jr., Robert. "Ashanti Cultural Resource Elements and Their Relevance to the Perception and Utilization of Resources." *African Studies Review*, Vol. 14, No. 1 (April, 1971), pp. 55–81.

Dumett, Raymond E. "African Merchants of the Gold Coast, 1860–1905—Dynamics of Indigenous Entrepreneurship." *Comparative Studies in Society and History*, Vol. 25, No. 4 (October, 1983), pp. 661–693.

———. "John Sarbah, the Elder, and African Mercantile Entrepreneurship in the Gold Coast in the Late Nineteenth Century." *The Journal of African History*, Vol. 14, No. 4 (1973), pp. 653–679.

Henige, David. "John Kabes of Komenda: An Early African Entrepreneur and State Builder." *The Journal of African History*, Vol. 18, No. 1 (1977), pp. 1–17.

Ibo, Jonas. "Le Phénomène Krouman a Sassandra: la marque d'une institution séculaire," *Canadian Journal of African Studies*, Vol. 32, No. 1 (1998), pp. 65–94.

Inikori, Joseph E. "Slavery and the Development of Industrial Capitalism in England." *Journal of Interdisciplinary History*, Vol. 17, No. 4, Caribbean Slavery and British Capitalism, (Spring, 1987), pp. 771–793.

———. "The Import of Firearms into West Africa, 1750–1807: A Quantitative Analysis." *The Journal of African History*. Vol. 18, No. 3 (1977), pp. 339–368.

Johnson, Marion. "The Slaves of Salaga." *The Journal of African History*. Vol. 27, No. 2, Special Issue in Honour of J.D. Fage (1986), pp. 341–362.

Jones, Wilbur Devereux. "The Influence of Slavery on the Webster-Ashburton Negotiations." *Journal of Southern History*. Vol. 22, No. 1 (February 1956), pp. 48–58.

Kaufmann, Chaim D. and Robert A. Pape, "Explaining Costly International Moral Action: Britain's Sixty-Year Campaign Against the Atlantic Slave Trade," *International Organization*, Vol. 53, No. 4 (Autumn, 1999), pp. 631–668.

Kea, R. A. "Firearms and Warfare on the Gold Coast and Slave Coast from the Sixteenth to the Nineteenth Centuries." *The Journal of African History*, Vol. 12, No. 2 (1971), pp. 185–213.

Law, Robin. "The Original Manuscript Version of William Snelgrave's New Account of Some Parts of Guinea," *History in Africa*, Vol. 17 (1990), pp. 367.

Lever, J. T. "Mulatto Influence on the Gold Coast in the Early Nineteenth Century: Jan Nieser of Elmina." *African Historical Studies*, Vol. 3, No. 2 (1970), pp. 253–261.

Lovejoy, Paul E. "Commercial Sectors in the Economy of the Nineteenth-Century Sudan: The Trans-Saharan Trade and the Desert-Salt Trade." *African Economic History*. Vol. 13 (1984), pp. 85–116.

———. "Polanyi's "Ports of Trade": Salaga and Kano in the Nineteenth Century." *Canadian Journal of African Studies*. Vol. 16, No. 2 (1982), pp. 245–277.

Lovejoy, Paul E. and David Richardson. "British Abolition and its Impact on the Slave Prices Along the Atlantic Coast of Africa, 1783–1850," *The Journal of Economic History*, Vol. 55, No. 1 (March 1995), pp. 98–119.

———. "The Business of Slaving: Pawnship in West Africa, 1600–1810." *The Journal of African History*, Vol. 42, No. 1 (2001), pp. 67–89.

Manning, Patrick. "Slaves, Palm Oil, and Political Power on the West African Coast." *African Historical Studies*, Vol. 2, No. 2 (1969), pp. 279–288.

Mazwell, John. "Ashanti: Kumasi—The Garden City of West Africa." *Journal of the Royal African Society*, Vol. 27, No. 107 (April, 1928), pp. 219–233.

McCaskie, T. C. "Innovational Eclecticism: The Asante Empire and Europe in the Nineteenth Century." *Comparative Studies in Society and History*, Vol. 14, No. 1, (January, 1972) pp. 30–45.

McSheffrey, Gerald M. "Slavery, Indentured Servitude, Legitimate Trade and the Impact of Abolition in the Gold Coast, 1874–1901." *The Journal of African History*, Vol. 24, No. 3 (1983), pp. 349–368.

Porter, R. "The Crispe Family and the African Trade in the Seventeenth Century." *The Journal of African History*, Vol. 9, No. 1 (1968), pp. 57–77.

Postma, Johannes. "The Dimension of the Dutch Slave Trade from Western Africa." *The Journal of African History*, Vol. 13, No. 2 (1972), pp. 237–248.

Priestley, Magaret. "The Ashanti Question and the British: Eighteenth-Century Origins." *The Journal of African History*, Vol. 2, No. 1 (1961), pp. 35–59.

Priestley, Magaret and Ivor Wilks. "The Ashanti Kinds in the Eighteenth Century: A Revised Chronology." *The Journal of African History*, Vol. 2, No. 1 (1960), pp. 83–96.

Reynolds, Edward. "Economic Imperialism: The Case of the Gold Coast." *The Journal of Economic History*, Vol. 35, No. 1 (March, 1975), pp. 94–116.

Richards, Sandra L. "What is to Be Remembered?: Tourism to Ghana's Slave Castle Dungeons." *Theatre Journal*, No. 57 (2005), pp. 617–637.

Rodney, Walter. "African Slavery and Other Forms of Social Oppression on the Upper Guinea Coast in the Context of the Atlantic Slave Trade." *The Journal of African History*, Vol. 7, No. 3 (1966), pp. 431–443.

———. "Portuguese Attempts at Monopoly on the Upper Guinea Coast." *The Journal of African History*, Vol. 6, No. 3 (1965), pp. 307–322.

———. "Gold and Slaves on the Gold Coast." *Transactions of the Historical Society of Ghana*, Vol. 10 (1969), pp. 13–28.

Sanders, James. "The Expansion of the Fante and the Emergence of Asante in the Eighteenth Century." *The Journal of African History*, Vol. 20, No. 3 (1979), pp. 349–364.

———. "Palm Oil Production on the Gold Coast in the Aftermath of the Slave Trade: A Case Study of the Fante." *The International Journal of African Historical Studies*, Vol. 15, No. 1 (1982), pp. 49–63.

Smith, Robert. "The Canoe in West African History." *The Journal of African History*, Vol. 11, No. 4 (1970), pp. 515–533.

Sutton, Inez. "Labour in Commercial Agriculture in Ghana in the Late Nineteenth and Early Twentieth Centuries." *The Journal of African History*, Vol. 24, No. 4 (1983), pp. 461–483.

Vinson, Robert Trent. "The Law as Lawbreaker: The Promotion and Encouragement of the Atlantic Slave Trade by the New York Judiciary System, 1857–1862." *Afro-American Historical Association of the Niagara Frontier*. Vol. 20, No. 2 (July, 1996), pp. 35–58.

Waldman, Loren K. "An Unnoticed Aspect of Archibald Dalzel's the History of Dahomey." *The Journal of African History*, Vol. 6, No. 2 (1965), pp. 185–192.

Wilks, Ivor. Review of *A New and Accurate Description of the Coast of Guinea* by William Bosman. *The Journal of African History*. Vol. 9, No. 1 (1968), pp. 164–166.

———. "Aspects of Bureaucratization in Ashanti in the Nineteenth Century." *The Journal of African History*, Vol. 7, No. 2 (1966), pp. 215–232.

———. "On Mentally Mapping Greater Asante: A Study of Time and Motion." *The Journal of African History*, Vol. 33, No. 2 (1992), pp. 175–190.

Williams, Clifford. "Asante: Human Sacrifice or Capital Punishment? An Assessment of the Period 1807–1874." *The International Journal of African Historical Studies*, Vol. 21, No. 3 (1988), pp. 433–441.

Yarak, Larry W. "Elmina Note: Myth and Reality in Asante-Dutch Relations." *History in Africa*. Vol. 13 (1986), pp. 363–382.

———. "West African Coastal Slavery in the Nineteenth Century: The Case of the Afro-European Slave-owners of Elmina." *Ethnohistory*. Vol. 36, No. 1, Ethnohistory and Africa (Winter, 1989), pp. 44–60.

BOOKS

Abaka, Edmund Kobina. *Kola is God's Gift: Agricultural Production, Export Initiatives & The Kola Industry in Asante & the Gold Coast,* 1820–1950. Athens, OH: Ohio University Press, 2005.

Adams, John *Sketches Taken During Ten Voyages to Africa, Between the Years 1786 and 1800*, Reprint. New York, Johnson Reprint Corporation, 1970.

Adderley, Rossane Marion. *New Negroes: Slave Trade Abolition and Free African Settlement in the Nineteenth-Century Caribbean*. Bloomington, IN: Indiana University Press, 2006.

Adi,Hakim and Marika Sherwood. *Pan-African History: Political Figures from Africa and the Diaspora Since 1787*. New York: Routledge Press, 2003.

Adjaye, Joseph. K. *Diplomacy and Diplomats in Nineteenth Century Asante*. New York: Lanham Books, 1984.

Allman, Jean and Victoria Tashjian. *I Will Not Eat Stone: A Women's History of Colonial Asante*. Portsmouth, NH: Heinemann, 2000.

Agbodeka, Francis. *African Politics and British Policy in the Gold Coast: A Study in the Forms and Force of Protest,* 1868–1900. Longman Press: New York, 1971.

Anquandah, James Kwesi. *Castles and Forts of Ghana*. Ghana Museums and Monuments Board: Atalante, Paris, 1999.

———. "Researching the Historic Slave Trade in Ghana-An Overview" in *The Trans-Atlantic Slave Trade: Landmarks, Legacies, Expectations, Proceedings of the International Conference on Historic Slave Route Held at Accra, Ghana on 30 August–2 September, 2004*, ed. James K. Anquandah. Legon, Accra, Ghana: Sub-Saharan Publishers, 2007.

——— ed. *The Trans-Atlantic Slave Trade: Landmarks, Legacies, Expectations, Proceedings of the International Conference on Historic Slave Route Held at Accra, Ghana on 30 August–2 September, 2004*. Legon, Accra, Ghana: Sub-Saharan Publishers, 2007.

Arhin, Kwame. *West African Traders in Ghana in the Nineteenth and Twentieth Centuries*. London: Longman, Inc., 1979.

Ashun, Ato. *Elmina, The Castle and the Slave Trade*. Cape Coast, Ghana: Nyakod Printing Works, 2004.

Austin, Gareth. *Labour, Land and Capital in Ghana: From Slavery to Free Labour in Asante,* 1807–1896. Rochester, NY: University of Rochester Press, 2005.

Bailey, Anne C. *African Voices of the Atlantic Slave Trade, Beyond the Silence and the Shame*. Boston, MA: Beacon Press, 2005.

Bakewell, Peter. *A History of Latin America to 1825*, 3rd ed. United Kingdom: Wiley-Blackwell, 2010.

Beckett, Ian F. W., ed. *Wolseley and Ashanti: The Asante War Journal and Correspondence of Major General Sir Garnet Wolseley,* 1873–1874, (England: The Army Records Society, 2009), p. xii.

Belmessous, Saliha, ed. *Empire By Treaty: Negotiating European Expansion,* 1600–1900. New York: Oxford University Press, 2015.

Bevans, Charles I. ed. *Treaties and Other International Agreements of the United States of America,* 1776–1949, Vol. 12. Washington, DC: Department of State Publication, 1974.

Blackburn, Robin. *The Making of New World Slavery*: From the Baroque to the Modern, 1492–1800. London: Verso Books, 1998.

Boahen, A. Adu. *Ghana: Evolution and Change in the Nineteenth and Twentieth Centuries*. London: Longmans, 1975.

———. *Britain, the Sahara, and the Western Sudan,* 1788–1861. Oxford: Clarendon Press, 1964.

Boahen, A. Adu and James B. Webster. *The Revolutionary Years: West Africa Since 1800*. London: Longmans, 1967.

Bovill, E. W. *The Golden Trade of the Moors*, 2nd ed. Princeton, NJ: Markus Weiner Publishers, 1999.

Brooks Jr., Gerorge E. *The Kru Mariner in the 19th Century: An Historical Compendium*. Newark, DE: Liberian Studies Association in America, Inc., 1972.

———. *Yankee Traders, Old Coasters and African Middlemen: A History of American Legitimate Trade With West Africa in the Nineteenth Century*. Boston: Boston University Press, 1970.

Busia, K. A. *The Position of the Chief in the Modern Political System of Ashanti*. Oxford: Frank Cass and Company, Ltd., 1968.

Caporaso, James A. and David P Levine. *Theories of Political Economy*. New York: Cambridge University Press, 1992.

Carrington, Selwyn H. H. *The Sugar Industry and the Abolition of Slave Trade,* 1775–1810. Gainesville, FL: University Press of Florida, 2002.

Carolson, John D. *Myths, State Expansion and the Birth of Globalization: A Comparative Perspective*. New York: Palgrave Macmillan, 2012.

Carney, Judith and Richard Nicholas Rosomoff. *In the Shadow of Slavery: Africa's Botanical Legacy in the Atlantic World.* Berkley, CA: University of California Press, 2009.

Clarke, John Henrik. *Christopher Columbus and the Afrikan Holocaust: Slavery and the Rise of European Capitalism*, 3rd ed. Brooklyn, NY: A & B Publishers Group, 1998.

Cross, Wilbur. *Gullah Culture in America*. Westport, Conn: Praeger Books, 2008.

Cutin, Phillip. *The Atlantic Slave Trade: A Census*. Madison, WI: University of Wisconsin Press, 1969.

Daaku, K. Y. *Osei Tutu of Asante*. London: Heinemann Publishers, 1976.

Davidson, Basil. *Black Mother: The Years of the African Slave Trade*. Boston, MA: Little Publishers, 1961.

Davis, David Brion. *In the Image of God: Religion, Moral Values, and Our Heritage of Slavery*. New Haven, CT: Yale University Press, 2001.

———. *The Problem of Slavery in Western Culture*. Oxford: Oxford University Press, 1967.

Dei, L. A. and Kwaku Boakye. "Developing the Slave Route for Tourism-Community.

Dynamic, Policy Implications and Strategies for the Root Tourism Project." in *The Trans-Atlantic Slave Trade: Landmarks, Legacies Expectations*, ed. James Kwesi Anquandah. Legon, Accra, Ghana: Sub-Saharan Publishers, 2007.

Der, Benedict G. *The Slave Trade in Northern Ghana*. Accra, Ghana: Woeli Publishing Services, 1998.

Diouf, Sylviane A. ed. *Fighting the Slave Trade: West African Strategies*. Athens, OH: Ohio University Press, 2003.

Dow, George Francis. *Slave Ships and Slaving*. Salem, Massachusetts: Marine Research Society, 1927.

DuBois, W. E. B. *The Suppression of the African Slave Trade to the United States of America,* 1638–1870. New York: Longmans, Green and Co., 1896.

Dumett, Raymond E. *Imperialism, Economic Development and Social Change in West Africa*. Durham, NC: Carolina Academic Press, 2013.

Edwards, Bernard. *Royal Navy Versus the Slave Traders: Enforcing Abolition at Sea, 1808–1898*. Great Britain: Pen & Sword Books, 2007.

Eisenstadt, S. N., Michel Abitbol and Naomi Chazan, eds. *Early State in African Perspective, Culture, Power and Division of Labor*, Vol. 3, Netherlands: EJ Brill Publishers, 1988.

Fage, J. D. *Ghana: A Historical Interpretation*. Madison, WI: University of Wisconsin Press, 1959.

———. *An Introduction to the History of West Africa*. London: Cambridge University Press, 1955.

———. *Africa Discovers Her Past*. London: Oxford University Press, 1970.

Fage, J. D. and William Tordoff. *A History of Africa*. London: Hutchinson and Company, 1978.

Farrar, Tarikhu. *Building Technology and Settlement Planning in West African Civilization: Pre-Colonial Akan Cities and Towns*. Lewiston, NY: Mellen University Press, 1996.

Falola, Toyin, ed. *Ghana in Africa and the World: Essays in Honor of Adu Boahen*. Trenton, NJ: Africa World Press, Inc., 2003.

———. *Pawnship, Slavery and Colonialism in Africa*. Trenton, NJ: Africa World Press, 2003.

Fehrenbacher, Don E. *The Slaveholding Republic: An Account of the United States Government's Relations to Slavery*. New York: Oxford University Press, 2001.

Feinberg, Harvey M. *Africans and Europeans in West Africa: Elminans and Dutchmen on the Gold Coast During the Eighteenth Century*. Philadelphia, PA: The American Philosophical Society, 1989.

Franklin, John Hope. *From Slavery to Freedom: A History of African Americans*, 8th ed., New York: Alfred A. Knopf, 2004.

Frost, Diane. *Work and Community Among West African Migrant Workers Since the 19th Century*. Liverpool: Liverpool University Press, 1999.

Fynn, J. K. *Asante and Its Neighbors*, 1700–1807. Evanston, Ill: Northwestern University Press, 1971.

Gallagher, Aileen. *Prince Henry the Navigator: Pioneer of Modern Exploration*. New York: The Rosen Publishing Group, 2003.

Garrard, Timothy F. *Akan Weights and the Gold Trade*. New York: Longman Group, 1980.

Getz, Trevor. *Slavery and Reform in West Africa: Toward Emancipation in 19th Century Senegal and Gold Coast*. Athens, OH: Ohio University Press, 2004.

Gilliland, C. Herbert. *Voyage to a Thousand Cares: Master's Mate Lawrence with the Africa Squadron*, 1844–1846. Annapolis, MD: Naval Institute Press, 2004.

Gomez, Michael. *Exchanging Our Country Marks: The Transformation of African Identities in the Colonial and Antebellum South*. Chapel Hill, NC: University of North Carolina 1998.

Greene, Sandra E. *Gender, Ethnicity, and Social Change on the Upper Slave Coast: A History of the Anlo-Ewe*. Portsmouth, NH: Heinemann Publishers, 1996.

Gutkind, Peter C. W. and Immanuel Wallerstein, eds. *The Political Economy of Contemporary Africa*. Beverly Hills, CA: Sage Publications, 1976.

Halcrow, Elizabeth M. *Canes and Chains: A Study of Sugar and Slavery*. Oxford: Heinemann Publishers, 1982.

Harms, Robert. *The Diligent: A Voyage Through the Worlds of the Slave Trade*. New York: Basic Books, 2002.

Harris, Joseph E. *Africans and their History*, Revised ed. New York: Mentor Books, 1987.

Hartman, Saidiya. *Lose Your Mother: A Journey Along the Atlantic Slave Route*. New York: Farrar, Straus and Giroux, 2007.

Hayford. J. E. Casely. *Gold Coast Native Institutions*. London, 1903.

Henty, George Alfred. *The March to Coomassie*, 2nd ed. London: Tinsley Brothers, 1874.

Hertslet, Sir Edward. *The Map of Africa by Treaty Great Britain & France to Zanzibar*, 2nd ed. London: Harrison and Sons, 1896.

Hill, Poly. *Migrant Cocoa Farmers of Southern Ghana: A Study of Rural Capitalism*. London: Cambridge University Press, 1970.

Hogg, Peter C. *The African Slave Trade and its Suppression: A Classified and Annotated Bibliography of Books, Pamphlets and Periodical Articles*. London: Frank Cass, 1973.

Holsey, Bayo. *Routes of Remembrance: Refashioning the Slave Trade in Ghana*. Chicago, Ill: University of Chicago Press, 2008.

Howard-Hassmann, Rhoda. *Colonialism and Underdevelopment in Ghana*. London: Croom Helm, Ltd, 1978.

Howell, Raymond. *The Royal Navy and the Slave Trade*. London: Croom Helm Publishers, 1987.

Huber, Magnus. *Ghanaian Pidgin English in its West African Context: A Sociohistorical and Structural Analysis*. Philadelphia, PA: John Benjamins Publishing, 1999.

Inikori, Joseph. *Forced Migration: The Impact of the Export Slave Trade on African Societies*. New York: Africana Publishing Co., 1972.

———. *Africans and the Industrial Revolution in England: A Study in International Trade and Economic Development*. New York: Cambridge University Press, 2002.

Jenkins, Paul, ed. *West African Past: African Pastors and African History in the Nineteenth Century*, 2nd ed. Basel, Switzerland: Basel Mission Archive, 2000.

July, Robert William. *Origins of Modern African Thought: Its Development in West Africa During the Nineteenth and Twentieth Centuries*. Trenton, NJ: Africa World Press, Inc., 2004.

Kea, Ray A. *Settlements, Trade, and Polities in the Seventeenth-Century Gold Coast*. Baltimore, MD: John Hopkins University Press, 1982.

Kern, Florence. *John Foster Williams' U.S. Revenue Cutter Massachusetts*. Washington, DC: Alised Enterprises, 1976.

Keynes, John Neville. *The Scope and Method of Political Economy*, 3rd ed. London: Macmillan and Co., 1904.

Kimble, David. *A Political History of Ghana: The Rise of Gold Coast Nationalism, 1850–1928*. Oxford: Clarendon Press, 1963.

King, Irving H. *The Coast Guard Under Sail: The US Revenue Cutter Service, 1789–1865*. Annapolis, MD: Naval Institute Press, 1989.

———. *George Washington's Coast Guard: Origins of the US Revenue Cutter Service,* 1789–1801. Annapolis, MD: Naval Institute Press, 1978.

Konadu, Kwasi. *The Akan Diaspora in the Americas*. New York: Oxford University Press, 2010.

Kwadwo, Osei. *An Outline of Asante History*. Kumasi, Ghana: O. Kwadwo Enterprise, 1994.

Law, Robin ed. *From Slave Trade to 'Legitimate' Commerce: The Commercial Transition in Nineteenth-Century West Africa*. New York: Cambridge University Press, 2002.

Law, Robin. *Ouidah: The Social History of a West African Slaving Port,* 1727–1892. Athens, OH: Ohio University Press, 2004.

Levtzion, Nehemia and Randall L. Pouwels, eds. *The History of Islam in Africa*. Athens, OH: Ohio University Press, 2000.

Lewin, Thomas J. *The Asante Before the British: The Prempean Years,* 1875–1900. Lawrence, KS: The Regents Press of Kansas, 1978.

Lovejoy, Paul E. *Transformations in Slavery: A History of Slavery in Africa*, 2nd ed. New York: Cambridge University Press, 2000.

Lynn, Martin. *Commerce and Economic Change in West Africa: The Palm Oil Trade in the 19th Century*. United Kingdom: Cambridge University Press, 1997.

Malowist, M. "The Struggle for International Trade and its Implications for Africa"

Bethwell A. Ogot, ed. *General History of Africa: Africa from the Sixteenth to the Eighteenth Century*, Vol. V. Berkley, CA: United Nations Educational, Scientific and Cultural Organization, 1992.

Manning, Patrick. *Slavery and African Life: Occidental, Oriental, and African Slave Trades*. New York: Cambridge University Press, 1990.

———. "Slavery & Slave Trade in West Africa, 1450–1650" *Themes in West Africa's History*, ed. Emmanuel Kwaku Akyeampong. Athens, OH: Ohio University Press, 2006. pp. 99–117.

Mannix, Daniel P. and Michael Cowley. *A History of the Atlantic Slave Trade: Black Cargoes*. New York: Viking Compass Book, 1962.

Mason, J. J. and Martina Odonkor. "Historic Slave Routes Tourism: Potential for Tourism Development in Ghana and West Africa Sub-Region." in *The Trans-Atlantic Slave Trade: Landmarks, Legacies Expectations*, ed. James Kwesi Anquandah. Legon, Accra, Ghana: Sub-Saharan Publishers, 2007.

Martin, Jane. "Krumen Down the Coast: Liberian Migrants on the West African Coast in the Nineteenth Century." *Working Papers*, No. 64, Boston, MA: Boston University Press, 1982.

Matthews, Gelien. *Caribbean Slave Revolts and the British Abolitionist Movement*. Baton Rouge, LA: Louisiana State University Press, 2006.

Leigh Maxwell, *The Ashanti Ring: Sir Garnet Wolseley's Campaigns,* 1870–1882, (Great Britain: Leo Cooper Publishing, 1985), p. 56.

McCarthy, Mary. *Social Change and the Growth of British Power in the Gold Coast: The Fante State,* 1807–1874. New York: Lanham Books, 1983.

McCaskie, T. C. *State and Society in Pre-Colonial Asante*. Great Britain: Cambridge University Press, 1995.

McCaskie, T. C. and Ivor Wilks, eds. *The History of Ashanti Kings and The Whole Country Itself and Other Writings by Otumfuo, Nana Agyeman Prempeh I*. London: Oxford University Press, 2003.

Meillassoux, Clause. *The Anthropology of Slavery: The Womb of Iron and Gold*. Chicago, Ill: University of Chicago Press, 1991.

Miers, Suzanne and Richard Roberts, eds. *The End of Slavery in Africa*, Madison, WI: University of Wisconsin Press, 1988.

Mikell, Gwendolyn. *Cocoa and Chaos in Ghana*. New York: Paragon House, 1989.

Morgan, Kenneth. *Slavery and the British Empire: From Africa to America*. New York: Oxford University Press, 2007.

Murray, David R. *Odious Commerce: Britain, Spain and the Abolition of the Cuban Slave Trade*. New York: Cambridge University Press, 1980.

Newbury, C. W. *British Policy Towards West Africa: Select Documents,* 1786–1874. Oxford: Clarendon Press, 1965.

Newson, Linda A. and Susie Minchin. *From Capture to Sale: The Portuguese Slave Trade to Spanish South America in the Early Seventeenth Century*. Netherlands: Hotei Publishing, 2007.

Nkrumah, Kwame. *Consciencism: Philosophy and Ideology for De-Colonization*, Revised Edition. New York: Monthly Review Press, 1970.

Norregard, Georg. *Danish Settlements in West Africa,*1658–1850, Translated by Sigurd Mammen. Boston, MA: Boston University Press, 1966.

Obadele-Starks, Ernest. *Freebooters and Smugglers: The Foreign Slave Trade in the United States after 1808*. Fayetteville, AR: University of Arkansas Press, 2007.

Obeng, J. Pashington. *Asante Catholocism: Religious and Cultural Reproduction Among the Akan of Ghana*. Netherlands: EJ Brill Publishers, 1996.

Okoth, Assa. *A History of Africa, Volume One: African Societies and the Establishment of Colonial Rule,* 1800–1915. Nairobi, Kenya: East African Educational Publishers, 2006.

Oppong, Christine. *Marriage Among a Matrilineal Elite: A Family Study of Ghanaian Senior Civil Servants*. London: Cambridge University Press, 1974.

Perbi, Akosua. *A History of Indigenous Slavery in Ghana: From the 15th to the 19th Century*. Legon, Accra Ghana: Sub-Saharan Publishers, 2004.

Postma, Johannes M. *The Dutch in the Atlantic Slave Trade,* 1600–1815. New York: Cambridge University Press, 1990.

Priestley, Margaret. *West African Trade and Coast Society: A Family Study*. London: Oxford University Press, 1969.

Ragatz, Lowell J. *The Fall of the Planter Class in the British Caribbean,* 1763–1833. New York: Century Company, 1928.

———. *A Guide for the Study of British Caribbean History, Including the Abolition and Emancipation Movements* 1763–1834. Washington, DC: U.S. Government Printing Office, 1932.

Rawley, James A. and Stephen D. Behrendt. *The Trans-Atlantic Slave Trade: A History*, Revised Edition. Lincoln, NE: University of Nebraska, 2005.

Rawley, James. A. *The Trans-Atlantic Slave Trade: A History*, Revised Ed. Lincoln, NE: University of Nebraska Press, 2005.

Reynolds, Edward. *Trade and Economic Change on the Gold Coast,* 1807–1874. New York: Longman Group, 1974.

Robinson, David. *Muslim Societies in African History*. New York: Cambridge University Press, 2004.

Rodney, Walter. *How Europe Underdeveloped Africa*. Washington, DC: Howard University Press, 1982.

———. *West Africa and the Atlantic Slave Trade*. Dar-es-Salam, Tanzania: East African Publishing House, 1967.

Searing, James F. *West African Slavery and Atlantic Commerce: The Senegal River Valley,* 1700–1860. Great Britain: Cambridge University Press, 1993.

Shack, William A. and Elliot P. Skinner, eds., *Strangers in African Societies*. Berkeley, CA: University of California Press, 1979.

Sherwood, Marika. *After Abolition: Britain and the Slave Trade Since 1807*. London: I. B. Tauris, 2007.

Shumway, Rebecca. *The Fante and the Transatlantic Slave Trade*, University of Rochester Press: Rochester, NY, 2011.

Smallwood, Stephanie E. *Saltwater Slavery: A Middle Passage from Africa to American Diaspora*. Cambridge, MA: Harvard University Press, 2007.

Smith, Adam. *The Wealth of Nations*, 5th ed. New York: Bantam Books, 2003.

Soodalter, Ron. *Captain Gordon: The Life and Trial of an American Slave Trader*. New York: Atria Books, 2006.

St. Clair,William. *The Door Of No Return: The History of Cape Coast Castle and the Atlantic Slave Trade*. New York: Bluebridge Press, 2007.

Strobridge, Truman R. and Dennis L. Noble, *Alaska and the U.S. Revenue Cutter Service,* 1867–1915. Annapolis, MD: Naval Institute Press, 1999.

Thomas, Hugh. *The Slave Trade: The Story of the Atlantic Slave Trade,* 1440–1870. New York: Simon and Schuster Paperbacks, 1997.

Tyler-McGraw, Marie. *An African Republic: Black & White Virginians in the Making of Liberia*. Chapel Hill, NC: University of North Carolina Press, 2007.

Wallerstein, Immanuel. *The Capitalist World Economy*. London: Cambridge University Press, 1979.

———. *World-Systems Analysis: An Introduction*, 2nd ed. Durham, NC: Duke University press, 2005.

Wiesner-Hanks, Mary E., William Bruce Wheeler, Franklin M. Doeringer and Kenneth R. Curtis, eds. *Discovering the Global Past: A Look at the Evidence, Volume II: Since 1400*, 4th Ed. Boston, MA: Wadsworth, 2012.

Wilks, Ivor. *Forests of Gold: Essays on the Akan and the Kingdom of Asante*. Athens, OH: Ohio University Press, 1993.

———. *Asante in the Nineteenth Century: The Structure and Evolution of a Political Order*. New York: Cambridge University Press, 1975.

Williams, Eric. *Capitalism and Slavery*, Chapel Hill, NC: The University of North Carolina Press, 1944.

———. *From Columbus to Castro: The History of the Caribbean* 1492–1969, New York: Vintage Books, 1984.

Williams, Joseph J. *Psychic Phenomena of Jamaica*. New York: The Dial Press, 1934.

———. *Hebrewisms of West Africa: From Nile to Niger With Jews*, 2nd ed. Chicago, IL: Research Associates School Times Publications & Frontline Distribution International Inc., 2010.

Worger, William H., Nancy L. Clark and Edward A. Alpers, *African and the West: A Documentary History, Vol. 1 From The Slave Trade to Conquest,* 1441–1905, 2nd ed. New York: Oxford University Press, 2010.

Van Dantzig, Albert. *Forts and Castles of Ghana*. Accra, Ghana: Sedeco Enterprise, 1980.

Yarak, Larry. *Asante and the Dutch,* 1744–1873. Oxford: Clarendon Press, 1990.

NEWSPAPER

New Nation Newspaper, British Prime Minister Tony Blair's Article, (November 27, 2006) http://www.number10.gov.uk/Page10487.

UNPUBLISHED DOCUMENTS

Maholchic, Thomas J. "The Anglo-Ashanti War of 1873–1874." MA Thesis, Howard University, December, 1972.

Shumway, Rebecca. *Between the Castle and the Golden Stool: Transformation in Fante Society in the Eighteenth Century*. Unpublished Dissertation: Emory University, 2004.

SPEECHES

UNESCO International Day for the Remembrance of the Slave Trade and its Abolition see: http://www.direct.gov.uk/dr_consum_dg/groups/dg_digitalassets/@dg/@en/documents/digitalasset/dg_170814.pdf.

President Joseph A. Kufuor discusses Ghana's Independence and the 200th Anniversary of the Abolition of the Trans-Atlantic Slave Trade in Joe Okyere and Nehemiah Owusu Achiaw, "Ghana Marks 200 Years of Abolition of Slave Trade," *National Commission on Culture*, (March 27, 2007). http://www.ghanaculture.gov.gh/index1.php?linkid=65&adate=27/03/2007&archiveid=1045&page=1.

Remarks by Honorable Rufus Bousquet Minister for External Affairs, International Financial Services, Information and Broadcasting at the Ceremony in Observance of the 200th Anniversary of the Abolition of the Slave Trade at Derek Walcott Square, Sunday March 25, 2007.

http://www.stlucia.gov.lc/addresses_and_speeches/rufus_bousquet/remarks_by_hon_rufus_bousquet_at_the_ceremony_in_observance_of_the_200th_ann_of_the_abolition_of_the_slave_trade.htm.

Barack Obama, President Addresses the Ghanaian Parliament in Accra, July 11, 2009. For transcript of full speech see:

http://www.america.gov/st/texttrans-english/2009/July/20090711110050abretnuh0.1079783.html. Accessed January 10, 2009

SYMPOSIUMS

Abolition and the Road to Freedom: National Archives Symposium 200th Anniversary of the Slave Trade Act of 1808. January 10, 2008.

Kwabena Adu-Boahen, "Bondage Under the Guns of the Forts: European Presence and Slavery in Coastal West Africa, 17th Century," *Africa, Europe and the Americas* 1500–1700, Workshop in Accra, Ghana 12th–26th July 2009.

INTERVIEW

Interview with Kwame Ture. May 6, 1998, Ida Lewis, ed. "Kwame Ture on Kwame Nkrumah." *The New Crisis Magazine*, July 1998.

Index

About the Author

Jarvis L. Hargrove is assistant professor at North Carolina Central University where he teaches courses in Africa, African Diaspora and African American History. He received his PhD in History from Howard University in Washington, DC in 2011.

CPSIA information can be obtained at www.ICGtesting.com
Printed in the USA
BVOW02*1115041215

427655BV00003B/4/P

9 780739 187852